PIPELINE

Contributing Authors

ART & VICKI REYES

BECCA MARTIN

BOB BLINCOE

BRANDON BOYD

BRETT CLEMENS

BRIAN GIBSON

DAN T. HAASE

DAVE HANSEN

DAVID D. RUIZ

DAVID J. WILSON

DOUG LUCAS

STEPHEN SWEATMAN

FAWN BRENTS

GLENN & SUE ASHCRAFT

GREG CARTER

HAROLD BRITTON

HAROLD & KERRY PETERS

JAMIE FARR

JON LUESINK

JOSH MCQUAID

JURG VANDYK

KENDRA VALDEZ CERVANTES

LARRY JANZEN

LARRY W. SHARP

LORRIE LINDGREN

MARK & BECKY JENNINGS

MARK MORGENSTERN

MARK STEBBINS

MATTHEW ELLISON

MICHÈLE PHOENIX

NEAL PIROLO

RUSS

RYAN HARMON

SHERRI DODD

STAN DELACOUR

STEVE BEIRN

STEVE RICHARDSON

STEVE SHADRACH

STEVE SWEATMAN

TODD AHREND

TODD RASMUSON

PIPELINE

Engaging the Church in Missionary Mobilization

DAVID J. & LORENE WILSON

WILLIAM CAREY
PRESS

Published by William Carey Press, an imprint of William Carey Publishing
10 W. Dry Creek Cir | Littleton, CO 80120 | www.missionbooks.org

William Carey Publishing is a ministry of Frontier Ventures
1605 E. Elizabeth St | Pasadena, CA 91104 | www.frontierventures.org

Andrew Sloan and Melissa Hicks, copyeditors
Mike Riester, cover and interior design

Printed in Canada
22 21 20 19 18   5 4 3 2 1   MQ 3000

Library of Congress Cataloging-in-Publication Data

Names: Wilson, David J. (David James), 1967- author.
Title: Pipeline : engaging the church in missionary mobilization / David and
    Lorene Wilson.
Description: Littleton : William Carey Press, 2018. | Includes
    bibliographical references. |
Identifiers: LCCN 2018011203 (print) | LCCN 2018012580 (ebook) | ISBN
    9780878085835 | ISBN 9780878085828 (print)
Subjects: LCSH: Great Commission (Bible) | Mission of the church. | Missions.
Classification: LCC BV2074 (ebook) | LCC BV2074 .W55 2018 (print) | DDC
    266--dc23
LC record available at https://lccn.loc.gov/2018011203

Contents

INSPIRATION

PART 3—THE LOCAL CHURCH: DEVELOPING A MOBILIZATION TEAM

PART 4—THE LOCAL CHURCH: PREPARING TO BECOME A SENDING CHURCH

IMPLEMENTATION

INITIATIVES

INNOVATION

*This book is dedicated to Marvin and Peggy Newell,
the "Mobilizers of Mobilizers."*

*Thank you for blessing us,
but more than that, you have blessed countless others
by your ministry of connecting God's people to kingdom opportunities.
May your work on earth provide you with heavenly rewards
and eternal benefits!*

Introduction

David J. Wilson

What would it look like if your local church decided to take the last words of Jesus seriously? What if pastors, elders, teachers, and lay leaders all began to understand that the Lord's Great Commission is *their* mandate?

When the decision is made to engage the church in missionary mobilization, and the vision is understood by the whole congregation, then what? Do they read more mission books together? Do they attend global conferences? Do they network with like-minded partners? Do they give more, pray more, serve more?

Yes to all the above, but they should also do something fundamentally different. They should expect the Lord to show up and move among them in powerful ways! They should expect people to hear God's voice calling them to do seemingly radical things in far-off distant places. They should expect to see the congregation get enthusiastic about extending the church's influence way beyond their walls, their city, and their nation. They should expect the Lord to pour out his Spirit in the form of people being called out of the church and into a pipeline that will channel the good news of Jesus to places that are spiritually barren and to people who are desperate for eternal hope.

What if God Is Just Waiting for Us to Build That Pipeline?

In the 1960s and 1970s, the two great superpowers of the world, the USSR and the US, were engaged in a cold war. An economic boom was taking

> What would it look like if your local church took this Great Commission mandate seriously and fully engaged the body of Christ in mobilizing the next generation of missionaries?

place that required massive amounts of oil to fuel the economic engines. The demand for oil in both nations was limited because the supply was separated by thousands of miles of difficult and isolated terrain. Therefore, both nations began to build pipelines to transport this precious commodity over hundreds (and thousands) of miles to places where it was needed most. The Trans-Alaska Pipeline in the US and the Druzhba Pipeline in Russia were both built to convey, route, channel, and process a precious resource by means of a reliable system with a constant flow and a steady supply.

That is what we hope to accomplish with this book: not a supply line for a natural resource but for a divine resource, for missionaries—cross-cultural global workers who are raised up and discipled by the local church; trained and equipped by Bible schools, seminaries, consultants, and training organizations; recruited and deployed by missionary sending agencies; and used by the Lord for his glory among the nations. We are building a "pipeline" to mobilize this precious resource by means of a reliable system with a constant flow and a steady supply.

Much of this pipeline already exists and is capable of processing candidates as they come to the *demand* side. However, there seems to be a missing feature on the *supply* side of the pipeline—the most critical piece of the missionary mobilization pipeline is the church!

I was awakened to this concept during a mission leadership conference. It appears that many missionary sending agencies use the same language and terminology regarding the pipeline of missionaries as it relates to the recruitment, training, and deployment of cross-cultural global workers. We were talking about how and where to find quality, well-prepared candidates. Much of the conversation centered around going to Bible schools, universities, seminaries, conferences, and various mission events. As a mission pastor in a church, I asked the question, "What about churches?"

The room fell silent, and we all looked at each other with blank faces. Finally, someone spoke up and said, "So, Dave, as a church leader, can you tell us the secret to getting our foot in the door of a church to do some recruiting?"

It was at this moment that I realized that we have a break in the supply line for mobilizing people to accomplish the Great Commission. All of the other parts and pieces of the pipeline were focused on being intentional and proactive in mobilizing the next generation of missionaries to the field, but the local church, in general, was still not connected to the supply side. There are many reasons for this: distracted by local concerns, desiring to keep gifted disciples close to accomplish in-house ministries, misunderstanding what Jesus actually said as he was leaving this world, outsourcing mission work to the agencies and expecting them to accomplish the Great Commission . . . just to name a few.

The Bible schools and seminaries are proactive and intentional about training and equipping young people for the task that the Lord is calling them to go and do. Training organizations, consultants, and conferences all have a well-defined and stated purpose for sending highly trained servants into all the world. Missionary sending agencies know that they exist to launch God's chosen vessels to live a life of sacrifice in places where there is no relevant gospel witness. But many in the local church seem to have lost the proactive mindset of intentionally mobilizing their brightest and best to serve among the least reached in the world.

Sure, we in the church celebrate when someone steps forward and says, "I think God is calling me to be a missionary." But often there is an element of *surprise* instead of *expectation*. We *react* to these moments of calling, instead of *anticipating* God to call them out because we have been praying for that to happen. Our default is to go through the motions of church-as-usual. So when someone raises their hand to join the Lord on his mission, it is almost like it was accidental rather than as a result of deliberate discipleship initiatives. In the words of Dr. Phil, "So how's that working for you?"

What would it look like if your local church took this Great Commission mandate seriously and fully engaged the body of Christ in mobilizing the next generation of missionaries?

There are billions of people on this planet who have no access to the good news of Christ, and there are thousands of evangelical churches that have little or no vision for reaching out to the nations. This book is designed to be a resource for churches that want to engage in the Great Commission and have a vision for taking the gospel to the nations, but need the tools, resources, and encouragement to get started. There are moments when church mission leaders need to take time to reflect and evaluate past performance and then dream about the future. This needs to be done in community, along with a group of highly motivated people who have a heart to see the name of the Lord worshiped among the nations.

In this book, a host of strategic thinkers and practitioners have come together to offer best practices and lessons learned so that churches can have a foundational place to start (or restart). At the end of each part, you will find group discussion starters ("Connecting to the Pipeline") to help your team interact with the content and adapt what they have learned for application in your specific local church.

You will read from a variety of perspectives and receive practical, hands-on insights from people who want to be part of your church's missionary pipeline. Some are in training organizations, others are consultants. Missionary sending agencies with decades of experience in sending people through the pipeline and into the world are represented. You will also discover churches with a well-developed system of cross-cultural discipleship and mentoring processes that they are eager to share with you so you won't have to reinvent the process. They have curriculum, documents, forms, and vision/mission statements that will help get you started in adapting Christ-honoring principles to your congregation. These resources are available at **www.missionarypipeline.org**.

One of the keys to your success will be the creation and development of a dedicated team that will prioritize the intentional and proactive mobilization of your church. Whenever churches get serious about something, they usually recruit people to organize around the vision. They carve out time to discuss what they need to do to make something important happen. After the vision is fleshed out, the leaders start making significant decisions regarding budget, people, and methods. The final stage is implementation.

For example, most churches believe that children's ministry is important for church growth and health. They will recruit a leader as well as a group of volunteers to serve the kids. This group will get together and discuss curriculum, plan a budget for resources, and decide what to do throughout the year to make the ministry attractive as well as effective. Then they begin to implement their plans and the ministry begins to grow.

That is what this book seeks to accomplish as it relates to missionary mobilization and engagement in the Great Commission in the local church. "Pipeline" is a metaphor that describes the flow of missionaries from birth to their moment of calling to serve the Lord, then all the way to the point when they are deployed to the mission field.

"If You Build It, They Will Come!"

If we adapt this famous line from the movie *Field of Dreams* to the concept of engaging the church to mobilize the next generation of missionaries,

> **"** If the pipeline is only built to handle
> a few workers, the Lord will probably
> only send a few workers. However,
> if the pipeline is built to accommodate many
> workers, he will send many workers. **"**

we also need to look in Scripture to find Jesus' philosophy of mobilization. Jesus said that "the harvest is plentiful, but the laborers are few. Therefore pray earnestly to the Lord of the harvest to send out laborers into his harvest" (Luke 10:2; see also Matt 9:37,38). Jesus' mobilization strategy is *prayer*. There is nothing elaborate or complicated about this strategy. Our job is to pray, and God's job is to send.

So if God is the one who calls people out to send, then why are we not seeing results? Perhaps we are not ready to receive and process them yet. The primary thesis and mission philosophy behind this book is that when the pipeline is built and ready, then the Lord will open up the floodgates with workers to tend his harvest.

If the pipeline is only built to handle a few workers, the Lord will probably only send a few workers. However, if the pipeline is built to accommodate many workers, he will send many workers. And the church is at the head of the supply line.

By the time someone gets to the missionary sending agency, they have already been influenced by their local church for over twenty years. The agency gets what the church has to offer, so the agencies need the church to step up to this challenge and send them quality candidates.

If things don't change, we will continue receiving the same results with varying degrees of success. However, if local churches begin taking the Great Commission seriously—and thereby become intentional and proactive in raising up the next generation of missionaries—they will be the fountainhead of a wellspring that will continually and abundantly supply highly qualified missionary candidates. Then the missionary sending agencies will deploy them to live and serve among those who have never heard the name of Jesus.

Lord Jesus, on behalf of your church, please forgive us. We are sorry for wandering away from your call to be *the salt of the earth* and *the light of the world.* We have not lived up to the beauty of being your "bride," of being what you intended us to become as you left this world. In our haste, we have taken up some "missions" that are not *your* mission. We have been distracted by things that seemed urgent to us, while ignoring things that were important to you. We have chosen the path of least resistance instead of the road that was marked with suffering. We have outsourced when we should have resourced. We have looked inside, instead of looking outside to see that *the fields are white for harvest.*

Restore within us the joy of our mandate and mission to *go,* to *make disciples,* to *baptize,* to *teach,* to *proclaim,* to *send,* to expect to *receive power,* to be your *witnesses;* to *all nations;* in *all the world* and to the *ends of the earth;* until the *end of the age.* May we, as the church, join the pipeline that channels grace, peace, hope, love, and eternal life to the billions who are living without Christ around the globe. For the glory of his name—Amen.

For more resources, go to: **www.missionarypipeline.org.**

FOUNDATION CHAPTER
Prayer

It All Starts Here

Doug Lucas

In the 1985 cult-favorite film, *The Goonies*, a band of kids attempt to save their homes in an effort to avoid moving and changing schools. In the process, they discover an old Spanish map that leads them on an adventure to find lost treasure and hope. At one point in the movie they are being chased by criminals. They discover a secret tunnel behind an old fireplace. Mikey (played by a very young Sean Astin) is the unlikely hero who, while gripped with fear, peers down the tunnel and then looks at the others and dares them, "It all starts here."

Today, more than ever before, we need modern-day Mikeys who are willing to look down scary tunnels and, in the face of their own greatest fears, repeat that dare to those around them. In the face of terrorism, nationalism, and political malaise, once again we need to repeat, "It all starts here." When churches become so liberal that they forget their first love, when seminaries forget to teach the simple doctrine that millions are headed to a Christ-less eternity, and when a world steeped in modernity hypnotizes us into believing that this is all there is, we have to hear Mikey's voice whispering in our ear—"It all starts here."

But what is "it" and where is "here"? For those of us who claim that God is Lord of the universe, "it" is the timeless adventure of reducing the population of hell by telling the good news of Christ—his death, burial, and resurrection—thereby helping others accept him as Lord of their lives. Only by taking this simple step can they hope to outrun the lostness that grips us. And part of our lostness is that we don't even appreciate how lost we are. "Here" is the precipice of history upon which we stand today. It is both a crisis and an opportunity, all at the same moment.

And what is the tunnel? What can possibly convey us from the danger of mediocrity to the treasure of multiplying disciples who make disciples? The Bible consistently sings but one chorus of hope, one path to fruitful outcomes, and one strategy for mobilizing troops to champion the Lord's chief cause. It all starts with prayer.

Pray to the Lord of the Harvest—Matthew 9:37–38

Near the end of Matthew chapter 9, we find Jesus and his closest followers walking through first-century towns and villages, sharing hope and help with all who need it. And there were plenty who needed it. The sick, the harassed, and the helpless were all like sheep without a shepherd. The Bible says that when Jesus saw them, his heart went out to them. When he looked at lost humanity, he had compassion on them—not only because of their state of lostness, but also because he knew that they could be found. He knew the way out of darkness. And he longed to help them find hope at the end of their struggle.

At one point, after surveying their lostness, his gaze turned from the crowds to the eyes of his closest followers. Every cry, every whimper, and every voice grew silent as he spoke. And this is what he said: "The harvest is plentiful but the workers are few. Ask the Lord of the harvest, therefore, to send out workers into his harvest field." (Matt 9:37,38, NIV)

His words were brief—but the message is timeless. In two sentences, he explains the chief strategy for mission mobilization, while hinting at the primary method for reaching the world. The chief strategy is a simple ask, and the primary method is ordinary people becoming bold enough to engage with the sick, the harassed, and the helpless in order for them to discover the Savior, thereby making Christ their Lord.

It's so simple, we overlook both the potential and the power. If the world truly was created by God (and we believe it was) and if he alone sustains it (and we believe he does), then only God knows its final end. (Gulp.) We "gulp" when we think about the world ending only because we fear that which we haven't seen—and no one has ever seen the end of time. It just hasn't happened before. The closest anyone has come, perhaps, is Noah—and that didn't go so well for the people outside the boat. (No wonder we gulp.)

For the sake of those outside the boat, it's time we asked the Lord of the harvest for help. But just as importantly, for the sake of the Lord of the harvest himself, it's time we obeyed. Because he is the only Lord and his cause is the only timeless truth. You see, the really cool part is—God does know the end. Duh! It's his world. And it's his time. And it will be his coming. And it is therefore his harvest, for he is Lord of it. He is Lord of all!

He has every right and every power to raise up harvesters. You see, we think it all depends on us. But that's only because we can't see beyond the fireplace. We can't see the end of the tunnel. If we could, we would know the treasure. And the thing is—the treasure doesn't consist of pirate booty, Spanish coins, or golden doubloons. The treasure all along has been right in front of us: The treasure is knowing Christ. Once we have that, we have everything (everything that matters, anyway).

So the weird part is that as we align ourselves with his will for the harvest, we also align ourselves with his plan for the ages—redeeming the humanity that stepped away from him in the garden. *That* is what he's been about all this time. *That* is his ultimate aim. *That* is a cause worth living for. And when we pray for that, we pray for his heartbeat itself. When we pray for that, we are praying for what broke his heart as he walked among those towns and villages. When we ask him for harvesters, we're asking him for the stuff that matters to him most.

Of course he will hear us, and of course he will answer! Everything else after that is just details. It's just tactics. It's like the matting inside the picture frame: Sure, it adds to the artwork, but the focus should be on the art, not the matting itself. The art is prayer, and all the other things we do to mobilize workers—sounding the call, removing the obstacles, developing the mobilization team, creating the events and exposures, preparing the candidates, meshing together the churches and agencies with schools and training—all of those things are just the matting. They are like a pipeline.

Obviously, we need to make sure the pipeline is in place. Why? Because we don't want anything to get in the way. We don't want to break anything. If we build the pipeline, the Lord will provide the people. If we build the pipeline, God will provide the flow.

When the Wall Is Broken, Pray—Nehemiah

Nehemiah had a cushy job. He was basically a wine taster for the king. Everything was going just fine until some out-of-town guests recounted the sad state of affairs back home in Jerusalem: "Those who survived the exile and are back in the province are in great trouble and disgrace. The wall of Jerusalem is broken down, and its gates have been burned with fire" (Neh 1:3, NIV). Now Jerusalem was like the capital of the nation-state of Israel—but even more than that. For Nehemiah's people, it was something like Scarlett O'Hara's Tara—her home place, the plantation, and her roots. Compare it to Wimbledon for tennis, Mecca for Muslims, or the Vatican for Catholics. Allowing the Vatican to become run down affects all Roman Catholics worldwide. It would bring about holy shame and humiliation to the max. CCSB to a lesser extent

Suddenly, Nehemiah's cushy job seemed rather hollow. I mean, who cares about the quality of the wine when one's very heritage is on the rocks? So yes, Nehemiah was bummed. In fact, the Bible says that hearing this news brought him to tears (Neh 1:4). So he did the one thing he knew would work: He prayed. And not just once for five minutes. He prayed night and day (Neh. 1:6)—and this went on for several days (Neh 1:4).

Well, we know what happened. God helped Nehemiah raise funds (Neh 2:4–9), make a vision trip (Neh 2:11–16), craft and deliver his mobilization message (Neh 2:17,18), and recruit and train a ton of teammates (Neh 3). And just as one might expect (after such a prayer start), it worked (Neh 6:15). Nehemiah's project (God's, actually) was a huge success. And in a Hollywood-like happy ending, Nehemiah built it, and they came (not only his clan, but also just about everybody else's). But maybe the greatest lesson isn't "If you build it, they will come." Maybe the greatest lesson is "If you pray, God will build it."

To Compel Others, Pray—Proverbs 21:1

In the fictional universe of *Star Trek*, Starfleet captains are supposed to follow what is known as the "Prime Directive." It calls for noninterference with other cultures and civilizations. Of course, Captain Kirk wasn't that great at following it. (It seemed like he violated it in practically every episode.) Captain Janeway was a bit better at it. Apparently, Christians need to be more like Kirk and less like Janeway. Why? Because Jesus wants us to interfere. He told us (literally) to "make disciples of all nations." (Matt 28:19, NIV)

That seems at first like a very tall order—until we factor in the power of prayer. Think about it. Proverbs 21:1 tells us, "In the Lord's hand the king's heart is a stream of water that he channels toward all who please him (NIV)." Who knew? The power of prayer can somehow channel even a proud king's heart. Ezra writes that the Lord changed the attitude of the emperor Darius by prompting him to order the temple to be rebuilt (Ezra 6:22). The power of prayer kept King Xerxes from sleeping (Esth 6:1) and preserved three young men from burning up in the fire (Dan 3).

And if you stop and think about it, every time a sick person asked Jesus for a miracle in the New Testament, they were, in effect, "praying" directly to Jesus for "interference"—and countless times, Jesus interfered in the course of human destiny by altering their realities. In fact, this is a large part of the premise of Myles Munroe's book *Understanding the*

Purpose and Power of Prayer: Earthly License for Heavenly Interference.[1] You see, if God is sovereign (i.e., king), then he's not really interfering. It's his sovereign right. "I make known the end from the beginning, from ancient times, what is still to come. I say, 'My purpose will stand, and I will do all that I please'" (Isa 46:10, NIV). And for our own part, since we have a mandate from the King to interfere, it's high time we became more like Captain Kirk and less like Janeway.

Now granted, we don't know when God might want to alter reality by healing the sick. But we can be 100-percent certain in every case that he wants us to pray for harvesters, because that is a prayer he has commanded us to pray. For that prayer, we actually have zero choice. Jesus commanded us to pray that others would be compelled toward the harvest. We can never know for sure which person God will compel. We only know that if we pray, he will.

To Enlist Others in the Harvest, Enlist Them to Pray—Matthew 18:19

I want to be forthright with you: I don't understand why God implies that it matters more to him when groups pray than when merely one person prays. But that's the implication of Matthew 18:19, in which Jesus says, "Again, truly I tell you that if two of you on earth agree about anything they ask for, it will be done for them by my Father in heaven" (NIV). Apparently, as Wesley Duewel writes in *Touch the World through Prayer,* there is some kind of "added spiritual power in united prayer."[2]

So what's the lesson here? Apparently, if we want to raise up more harvesters, it's fine if we print more pamphlets. It's OK to buy roll-up exhibits. It's fine to sponsor pizza lunches after chapel. But if we really want to get serious about raising up more harvesters, we would enlist more people to pray for them. *That* is a biblical certainty.

Praying as One so That the World Would Be Won—John 17:22,23

I'll give you a dollar if the next time somebody asks you to pray the Lord's Prayer, you begin spouting off John 17. Because this is the prayer that the Lord actually prayed to the Father: "I have given them the glory that you gave me, that they may be one as we are one—I in them and you in me—so that they may be brought to complete unity. Then the world will know that you sent me and have loved them even as you have loved me" (John 17:22,23, NIV).

If we truly want to mobilize, if we want to raise up a fighting force, if we want to prompt people to action—then let's pray that they can be united, intentional, and focused in reaching the world. Being one would help the world to be won.

Looking for Someone to "Stand in the Gap"—Ezekiel 22:30

David Bryant got it right in his 1984 book, *In the Gap*. His instructions about prayer were simple:

> Your suggestions to pray for an unfamiliar part of the world may surprise some at first. Others will find world-sized praying awkward. But as you lead the way with information and personal example, you will change attitudes toward praying for the world beyond your group and may even change their attitudes toward personally reaching the world.[3]

His point? The most effective way to mobilize others toward serving Christ cross-culturally just might be to engage them in praying cross-culturally, whether it be from their family room, or from the church basement, or on a prayer journey overseas.

Never Quit Praying—1 Thessalonians 5:17

Back to the movie *The Goonies*. You need to know that things didn't always go so well. Sometimes the way ahead looked fairly dark. At one point, in fact, pretty much everybody was ready to give up. The odds seemed so stacked against them. That's when Mikey gave his best speech. And the best quote from his best speech still lives on today. "Goonies never say die!"

If the Bible teaches us anything about reaching people, it's that someone has to be sent to go reach them. According to Jesus, to raise up the "reachers" we have to pray hard. And never, never, never quit. That's the framework for everything we do in mobilization. Everything else is just details.

Above all else, pray. And never, never quit praying.

Doug Lucas is the president of Team Expansion and founder/editor of Brigada (www.brigada.org) and founder/trainer of www.MoreDisciples.com and www.MissionsU.com.

Notes

[1] Myles Munroe, *Understanding the Purpose and Power of Prayer: Earthly License for Heavenly Interference* (New Kensington, PA: Whitaker House, 2002).

[2] Wesley Duewel, *Touch the World through Prayer* (Grand Rapids, MI: Zondervan, 1986), 212.

[3] David Bryant, *In the Gap: What It Means to Be a World Christian* (Regal Books, 1984), 175.

Part 1

Calling: Learning to Hear the Voice of God

The prophet Isaiah *overheard* the Lord speaking one day, "Whom shall I send, and who will go for us?" (Isa 6:8). The Lord was not necessarily speaking to Isaiah directly. He was just in the Lord's presence and listening in, because that's what you do when you draw close to God—you listen. And when you listen, you will hear God speak. Could it be that God is always calling out, asking whom he shall send? Maybe we are just not listening. There is too much noise and distraction around us, which drowns out this call of God.

Isaiah took steps so that he could listen in on the Lord. In the verses before this, he cried out to the Lord in repentance and he was restored—his guilt was removed and his sins were atoned for. This prepared him for entry into the presence of almighty God. Maybe the best place for us to start this section on "calling" is from Isaiah's example of "listening."

CHAPTER 1
Call Experiences from Scripture

God's People Answering the Call

David J. Wilson

One of my favorite movies is *The Blues Brothers*. Jake and Elwood are on a mission from God to help raise money for the orphanage in which they grew up. Several times throughout the movie, when they are facing opposition, obstacles, and hindrances to their mission, they say the classic phrase, "We're on a mission from God." They say this as an affirmation of why they cannot give up.

Even though this is just a movie tagline, it helps to illustrate the point that a clear and compelling call experience is necessary for missionaries to cling to when the work gets tough and they start to consider stepping away from the ministry. Their work will be difficult; they will experience opposition and hardship. But when they can remember their calling, the Lord brings rest to their hearts and minds, which gives them courage to continue.

While spending more than twenty years as a mission pastor in the local church, here are some of the most common questions I have heard from young people:
- "How can I know God's will for my life?"
- "How does God speak to his people?"
- "I think God wants me to serve him, but I don't feel called. What is it like to be called by God to be a pastor or missionary?"

ReMAP I and II (Reducing Missionary Attrition Project) found that of all the variables, a call experience is "vital to retention" of long-term missionaries. Most missionary sending agencies rate "a strong sense of calling" as a top priority area in their selection process when evaluating missionary candidates.[1] Without a strong sense of personal calling, there is little that will keep a missionary from quitting when the work gets hard. When individuals know that the Lord has called them for a purpose, has equipped them for the job ahead, and is guiding them along the way, they can endure any hardship because they know their suffering has meaning and purpose.

Both in Scripture and in modern situations, people have answered the Lord's calling to serve him in this world as ambassadors for a heavenly kingdom. While God speaks to everyone differently, according to their unique design, this chapter is an attempt to categorize the different ways people have heard from God so that a new generation of Christ-followers can hone their listening skills to hear his voice.

Just to demonstrate a stark contrast in the way God has called his people in Scripture, let's look at the callings of Moses, David, Esther, and Paul.

The Call of Moses—Exodus 3:2–10

And the angel of the Lord appeared to him in a flame of fire out of the midst of a bush. He looked, and behold, the bush was burning, yet it was not consumed. And Moses said, "I will turn aside to see this great sight, why the bush is not burned." When the Lord saw that he turned aside to see, God called to him out of the bush, "Moses, Moses!" And he said, "Here I am." Then he said, "Do not come near; take your sandals off your feet, for the place on which you are standing is holy ground." And he said, "I am the God of your father, the God of Abraham, the God of Isaac, and the God of Jacob." And Moses hid his face, for he was afraid to look at God.

Then the Lord said, "I have surely seen the affliction of my people who are in Egypt and have heard their cry because of their taskmasters. I know their sufferings, and I have come down to deliver them out of the hand of the Egyptians . . . Come, I will send you to Pharaoh that you may bring my people, the children of Israel, out of Egypt."

Later, in Exodus 33:11, Scripture says, "Thus the Lord used to speak to Moses face to face, as a man speaks to his friend."

The Call of David—1 Samuel 16:1–13

The Lord said to Samuel, " . . . Fill your horn with oil, and go. I will send you to Jesse the Bethlehemite, for I have provided for myself a king among his sons.... And you shall anoint for me him whom I declare to you.... Do not look on his appearance or on the height of his stature.... For the Lord sees not as man sees: man looks on the outward appearance, but the Lord looks on the heart." . . .

And Jesse made seven of his sons pass before Samuel. And Samuel said to Jesse, "The Lord has not chosen these." Then Samuel said to Jesse, "Are all your sons here?" And he said, "There remains yet the youngest, but behold, he is keeping the sheep." And Samuel said to Jesse, "Send and get him, for we will not sit down till he comes here." And he sent and brought him in. Now he was ruddy and had beautiful eyes and was handsome. And the Lord said, "Arise, anoint him, for this is he." Then Samuel took the horn of oil and anointed him in the midst of his brothers. And the Spirit of the Lord rushed upon David from that day forward.

The Call of Esther—Esther 4:13,14

Then Mordecai told them to reply to Esther, "Do not think to yourself that in the king's palace you will escape any more than all the other Jews. For if you keep silent at this time, relief and deliverance will rise for the Jews from another place, but you and your father's house will perish. And who knows whether you have not come to the kingdom for such a time as this?"

The Call of Paul—Acts 13:1-3

Now there were in the church at Antioch prophets and teachers . . . While they were worshiping the Lord and fasting, the Holy Spirit said, "Set apart for me Barnabas and Saul for the work to which I have called them." Then after fasting and praying they laid their hands on them and sent them off.

These four call experiences from Scripture highlight some of the many ways in which the Lord interacts with his people. Moses heard from God directly, with no intermediary. David was anointed through a prophet of the Lord. Esther was placed by God into a circumstance where only she could be his vessel to accomplish his purposes. And Paul (Saul) was set apart by his fellow church leaders, because they heard God's call to them as a body of believers to send these faithful missionaries on a journey as their representatives. In this instance, Paul was called out and sent by the church. However, he also had other interactions with God through visions (Acts 16:9; 18:9), through the person of Ananias (Acts 9), and by direct revelation from Jesus Christ (Gal 1:12).

Theologians like to put the call of God into two neat and tidy categories: general revelation and special revelation.[2] For the purposes of this exercise, I have decided to broaden these terms to understand calling in a more practical way to help a new generation of church leaders and missionaries hear the voice of God as he calls them to serve. By taking a closer look at God's ways of calling people, we can categorize the types of call experiences to help people in churches understand that God does not work in the same way for all people. Just as we are all designed differently, to accomplish different tasks, we are also designed to hear from God differently. Let's take a look at seven different call experiences.

Types of Call Experiences

1. **Invitational.** Jesus was walking by fishermen at work and invited them to "Follow me." Those men became his "disciples," meaning followers, learners, students, protégés, or mentees. Today, there are pastors, retired missionaries, and church leaders who can look around their congregations and, through the prompting of the Holy Spirit, invite people to step up and serve alongside them in some way. They could say, "I sense God moving in your life and I would like to invite you to join me in serving the Lord together." This begins a mentoring relationship that will guide and shape the future direction of the follower.

As Steve Harling, president of ReachBeyond (formerly HCJB), preached a sermon on mentoring, he described the "Three Gifts of a Mentor":

   a. **Affirmation:** "You are really good at this. You have a gift."
   b. **Inspiration:** "I saw you do this, and I want you to continue and grow in it."
   c. **Elevation:** "Here is your opportunity, and I'm getting out of your way."

2. **Scriptural.** Advocates of contemplative prayer, such as Richard Foster and Dallas Willard, emphasize that when people engage in spiritual disciplines like prayer, reading Scripture, meditation, and solitude, they open their hearts to hearing a message from God.

> Specifically, in our attempts to understand how God speaks to us and guides us we must, above all, hold on to the fact that learning how to hear God is to be sought only as a part of a certain kind of life, a life of loving fellowship with the King and his other subjects within the kingdom of the heavens.[3]

> Christian meditation, very simply, is the ability to hear God's voice and obey his word.[4]

While reading Scripture, some believers will sense God's prompting via passages like the Great Commission in Matthew 28 or Jesus' words in Luke 10:2 about praying to the Lord of the harvest to send out laborers. They will accept this as God speaking directly to them, and thereby accept his call to serve.

3. **Supernatural.** I realize that by including this category I have excluded myself from many evangelical social events, having just been labeled a Pentecostal / charismatic / "strange fire" neophyte. Personally, I have not experienced the miraculous gifting of tongues, prophecy, or healing, nor have I heard the voice of God audibly; but I believe that others have. Even though I have not witnessed a miracle, I still believe that God can (and does) work in supernatural ways that are beyond human reason.

   Though this portion of the chapter may be unacceptable for many, my hope and intent is to give a biblical perspective of how God has called people in the past, and how he may choose to call people in the future. Yes, abuses take place in every arena of Christianity (including among both cessationists and continuationists), but I implore you to leave your mind open to the possibility that God could choose to use dreams, visions, miraculous signs, and even an occasional burning bush to call his people into his harvest.

4. **Experiential.** Early in my walk with Christ, I was exposed to Henry Blackaby's work, *Experiencing God*. After fifteen weeks of in-depth study, I walked away with the summation that we should be "reading the signs" that God is giving us. When we do this, we will see where God is working and be compelled to join him.

   This has been my favorite part of the faith journey as a pastor and as a mobilizer for missionaries. In those times of confusion when I begin to wonder what the Lord is doing, this simple yet profound teaching has always taken me to a new depth of understanding God. The gift of being able to look around with my five temporal senses and discover an eternal perspective requires intentionality, determination, and willpower, but the reward is a greater connection with our Creator.

5. **Affirmational.** On occasion someone has come to me and said, "Dave, I want to serve the Lord, but I don't know what he wants me to do or where he wants me to go." At those moments, unless I have a specific

prompting from the Lord, I take a phrase from Alcoholics Anonymous and say, "Just do the next right thing." If the Lord affirms that, then keep doing it. If not, stop it, then "Just do the next right thing" again.

At some point, the Lord will make his will clear if you put your trust in him. "Trust in the Lord with all your heart, and do not lean on your own understanding. In all your ways acknowledge him, and he will make straight your paths" (Prov 3:5,6).

6. **Personal.** What is your story? Numerous occupational style assessment tools are available that will take into consideration the recurring themes in your life and your spiritual gifts, background, experiences, passions, desires, and abilities. It may be as simple as discovering that your love for accounting was prewired into your heart for the purpose of managing the books for a missionary sending agency.

Recently a psychology student mentioned to me that he was sensing God calling him to be a missionary, but he was almost finished with his graduate degree. He asked, "Why would God call me to be a missionary when I am training to be a therapist?" I shared with him that missionaries have strained relationships, unhealthy marriages, and traumatic experiences just like everyone else. There is a specialty in the mission world called "member care," and we need people with a counseling background to provide care for frontline workers.

So what is your story?

7. **Circumstantial.** The book of Esther is unique in many ways, but one difference from all the other books of the Bible is the fact that God is never mentioned. His existence is assumed, of course, but we don't see the typical appearance or interaction of a Creator with his creation. Queen Esther is the heroine, not because of her obedience to the Lord, but because she was in a certain place, at a certain time, when she was the only person who could affect the outcome. Her uncle Mordecai proclaims his faith by saying, "If you keep silent at this time, relief and deliverance will rise for the Jews from another place" (Est 4:14). By this, he is proclaiming that God's purposes will be accomplished, regardless of who makes it happen, thereby describing free will while at the same time understanding the determinism of God's will.

These categories are not meant to be exclusive or exhaustive, but they should serve as a starting place for your quest to hear God's voice as he is calling you into his harvest. The important thing to consider is whether you'll be obedient to him and surrender your will to his will.

I once heard Neal Pirolo describe his perspective on hearing God's voice like this, "Today, God speaks to our spirit, therefore our spirit must be on the same frequency as his! We would like to go to the local electronics store and purchase an app that would put us on his frequency. This appeals to our instant messenger and sound-bite culture, but it doesn't work that way. I, personally, have not heard the audible voice of God. I don't doubt it's possible, for he is the same yesterday, today, and forever. But there have been many occasions when my spirit must have been on the same frequency as God's, for as if he had spoken audibly, I hear the voice of God. He simply bypassed the working of the ear and went directly to my brain."

Generally speaking, God's calling is not always comfortable. Consider the four examples from Scripture given above:

1. **Moses** resisted God at first, and Exodus 4:14 states that "Then the anger of the Lord was kindled against Moses" because he kept coming up with excuses not to do what the Lord was calling him to do.

2. **David** was the least likely to succeed in his family. The small, ruddy shepherd boy wasn't even considered an option by his family when the brothers were lining up to be seen by the prophet of God. The Lord even prepared Samuel ahead of time by saying, "For the Lord sees not as man sees: man looks on the outward appearance, but the Lord looks on the heart" (1 Samuel 16:7).

3. We close the book of **Esther** thinking that if Esther had not accepted this responsibility the story would have been the same, though the book would have been named after Deborah, or Elizabeth, or Hannah—someone other than Esther. Praise God for Esther, but I wonder if someone else did not step up to the challenge "for such a time as this."

4. It took **Paul** seventeen years of preparation to go from being a persecutor of the church to serving as a carrier of Christ's message to the Gentiles. We aren't able to comprehend fully the significance of how a "Pharisee of Pharisees" would feel about being called by God to serve the "Gentile dogs," but it may be similar to a neo-Nazi skinhead being called to serve the multiethnic communities of Manhattan's

Lower East Side or South-Central Los Angeles. The call of God still changes people from what they once were to become what he wants them to be.

Even though someone may experience a call to full-time ministry or missionary service, there still needs to be checks and balances in affirming the call. God created us to be social beings and to be held accountable by each other. Because of this, some authority issues should be considered based on one's ecclesiology. For the sake of simplicity, here are four basic sources of authority to consider in affirming the call of an individual and the assumption of responsibility by mission/ministry leaders:

1. **Scripture.** Evangelical/Protestant traditions will raise Scripture to the position of highest authority in the matter of any issue regarding faith or practice. The call of God must fit within the parameters of "what the Bible says."

2. **Elders.** The presbyterian form of church governance places authority in the office of a representative body, or elders. These delegated officials make decisions and approve any appointment based on their corporate understanding of God's divine will (the group must agree). This would include the various Presbyterian and Reformed denominations.

3. **A person.** In the episcopal form of church governance, the bishop, priest, or pope is the authority and his decisions can override previous decisions. The Catholic Church and the Episcopal Church are examples.

4. **The Holy Spirit.** Charismatics and Pentecostals rely heavily on spiritual inspiration, intuition, emotional awareness, and supernatural stimulation. Many types of churches are in this category, and I would also include the Quakers, who emphasize the "inner light," as well as the Plymouth Brethren, who avoid any formal organization while fully trusting in the Holy Spirit as a ruling force.

As you can see, the question of authority can vary greatly from one church, denomination, or organization to another. Anyone who is sensing God's call to full-time ministry or missionary service should discuss this topic with their church leaders.

Equipped to Suffer

Another important consideration related to calling is equipping. It has been said that "God does not call the equipped, but he equips the called." Sometimes the Lord uses people in ways that are outside their comfort zones so that he can demonstrate his power. Moses had a speech impediment, so how could he speak with authority to crowds and to kings? David was a shepherd boy from a working-class family, so how could he be a king? Esther broke the rules by approaching the king without first being summoned. Paul had a thorn in the flesh, yet he understood that the Lord was ultimately in charge of the outcome when he said:

> But he [the Lord] said to me, "My grace is sufficient for you, for my power is made perfect in weakness." Therefore I will boast all the more gladly of my weaknesses, so that the power of Christ may rest upon me. For the sake of Christ, then, I am content with weaknesses, insults, hardships, persecutions, and calamities. For when I am weak, then I am strong. (2 Cor 12:9,10)

Most serious mission leaders find it difficult to separate "the call to missionary service" from "the call to suffer for the cause of Christ." Suffering is a part of the job description for missionaries on the field. Part of the missionary calling is to leave your friends, family, culture, language, and day-to-day sense of normalcy and move to a place where you don't know the people, cultural nuances, ways of thinking, and local expectations. The scenario is wrought with potential suffering before the adventure even begins. This is particularly relevant for those who choose to make their new home in a land that is hostile to their message.

Anyone who considers a call to the ministry or missionary service should know what Tertullian said in his apologetic work *Apology*, written about AD 200:

> Go zealously on, good presidents! You will stand higher with the people if you sacrifice us, kill us, torture us, condemn us and grind us to dust, as they demand. Your injustice is the proof that we are innocent. That is why God allows us to suffer . . . Your cruelty, however great, is no benefit to you, however it serves as an attraction to our sect. The more we are mown down by you, the more we grow. The blood of Christians is seed of a new life.

There is where we get our saying, "The blood of the martyrs is the seed of the church."

The speaker at a recent mission conference, a college professor from Cairo, Egypt, mentioned a credibility issue related to the Arab Spring in North Africa around the year 2014. Some missionaries and agencies decided that the political climate was too tumultuous, so they decided to pull out of the country until the situation stabilized. Other organizations and missionaries decided to dig deep and stay, even though they did so at great risk of a very real and present threat of danger. This speaker said:

> The locals were watching to see what the Westerners would do. The believers in Cairo were also watching. Those who stayed experienced fruit beyond their wildest expectations. Because they stayed and suffered alongside the locals, their roots in the community went deeper than if there had been no crisis at all. Because of the unstable climate and because of their willingness to endure, their credibility purchased their right to be heard. The business we are in requires us to develop credibility through suffering, a badge of honor that shows the world that we are serious.

Endurance through suffering is what makes a great story epic. Books are written, songs are sung, and movies are made to tell great stories about how someone went from rags to riches, underdog to top dog, and zero to hero. The suffering of God's people in Egypt is what made Moses an everlasting figure of deliverance. Daniel and the others in the fiery furnace experienced the presence of God only because they were willing to suffer the consequences of being obedient to the Lord. Paul suffered persecution as a result of his obedient response to his call to preach to the Gentiles.

According to tradition, all twelve disciples of Jesus suffered either cruel deaths or banishment, just because of a hope-filled message that had transformed their lives. Jesus himself was not immune to suffering during his earthly ministry, so why would we expect anything different? The call to minister cross-culturally is a call to suffer for the sake of a message and the glory of Jesus' name.

When we slow down and count the costs of accepting the call of the Lord to go and serve in some distant land, we realize that it is utter foolishness in the flesh. Hundreds of thousands of missionaries have accepted God's call to go to the nations and preach the gospel. They often encounter resistance and persecution just to share a message with people who initially reject them and their beliefs. But Scripture assures us that, with our faithful foolishness, those who are called will be rewarded:

> We preach Christ crucified, a stumbling block to Jews and folly to Gentiles, but to those who are called, both Jews and Greeks, Christ the power of God and the wisdom of God. For the foolishness of God is wiser than men, and the weakness of God is stronger than men.

For consider your calling, brothers: not many of you were wise according to worldly standards, not many were powerful, not many were of noble birth. But God chose what is foolish in the world to shame the wise; God chose what is weak in the world to shame the strong; God chose what is low and despised in the world, even things that are not, to bring to nothing things that are, so that no human being might boast in the presence of God. And because of him you are in Christ Jesus, who became to us wisdom from God, righteousness and sanctification and redemption. (1 Cor 1:23–30)

David J. Wilson served in the local church as mission pastor for over twenty years. In November 2016, he joined Avant Ministries in Kansas City, MO, as director of church relations.

Notes

[1] Rob Hay, *Worth Keeping: Global Perspectives on Best Practice in Missionary Retention* (Pasadena, CA: William Carey Library, 2007), 93–94.

[2] Millard J. Erickson, *Christian Theology* (Grand Rapids, MI: Baker, 1993), 175–98.

[3] Dallas Willard, *Hearing God: Developing a Conversational Relationship with God* (Downers Grove, IL: InterVarsity, 1999), 39.

[4] Richard Foster, *Celebration of Discipline: The Path to Spiritual Growth* (Harper: San Francisco, 1998), 17.

CHAPTER 2
Call Experiences from the Past

The Powerful Percent

Todd Ahrend

I never imagined I'd be at this crossroads. I never pictured myself at the ripe age of nineteen already facing the biggest question of my life. I enrolled in college with one goal: to be a third-grade teacher. My plans were simple. Not only would I teach, but I would marry a teacher. We would never work a holiday, have summers free to golf, and eventually retire in a beautiful Winnebago.

I had my life laid out and was excited about the path it was on. I was a believer, but for some reason I'd just left God out of the big decisions and relegated him to the Sunday morning department. My assumption was that I would happily join the ranks of countless Christians who aspire to the American Dream, never questioning my course but seeking only for God to bless it.

But then during my freshman year of college something happened—I met a guy who had purpose. He used a completely different grid to make decisions. He invited me to be part of a Bible study where we prayed for the world. This was weird. I'm thinking, "Why not pray more about me?" We met internationals on campus, we shared our faith, and we invited others to join us. He showed me passages in the Bible that revealed God's desire to see the nations reached; they were everywhere! My world started to turn upside down.

I realized that although I had been a believer for nearly five years, no one had challenged me to take personal responsibility for evangelizing the world. I hadn't even heard about missions! Sitting on my bed in my dorm room at the end of the year, I had a choice to make. I was at a crossroads: Was I going to allow God to interrupt my life with his purpose and push mine aside? Or was I going to cling to the life I had always wanted?

> " There is something about university-aged students that, more than any other group, has yielded an incredible harvest of laborers for the mission movement.
> They are the *powerful percent.* "

Until that point, I had never seriously pursued what the Bible had to say about missions. I had never wondered about the destiny of the lost. I couldn't even recall hearing any specific sermons about world evangelization. Why was I at this crossroads after being a Christian for so long? What would my family think of my change of direction? Wasn't I supposed to hear God "call" me? In that moment a flood of questions and convictions seemed to culminate into what many have called a crisis of belief.

Incredibly, these are the questions that Christian students have had to come face-to-face with for the past two hundred years. As you study history it becomes apparent: The definition of a missionary is *someone who allows God to interrupt their life*. I wasn't the first nor will I be the last. Come, hear the story of the "powerful percent" and see if it is worth giving up your dreams—even your Winnebago!

The Story of Students

There is something about university-aged students that, more than any other group, has yielded an incredible harvest of laborers for the mission movement. They are the *powerful percent.* This unique demographic makes up only 1 percent of the world, yet *most* missions momentum has always come from university students. If we charted the history of missions, it would look like a mountain, the peak of which would represent approximately thirty years, from 1886–1920, when an organization called the Student Volunteer Movement (SVM) was thriving. This is the story of the apex of the powerful percent![1]

I'm not sure what mental images come to your mind when you think of the YMCA (Young Men's Christian Association). For me, it was where I played eighth grade basketball and then went swimming. One hundred years ago it looked quite different. The YMCA was founded by George Williams in London in 1844. By 1858, a mere fourteen years later, it had spread so rapidly that it had made its way throughout Europe and onto American college campuses.[2] The YMCA was equipping students to lead Bible studies and do evangelism on campus, and challenging students to pray.

In 1885 a man named Luther Wishard was the collegiate minister for the entire YMCA. In his day, the YMCA was considered the spiritual nerve center of American colleges, and Wishard sought to use it as the vehicle to recruit students to missionary work. His method? He decided to host a four-week summer training project in Mount Hermon, Massachusetts, not only to disciple students in the basics of the Christian walk, but also to mobilize students to go to the world.

In preparation for this project, which began in July of 1886, Wishard invited two students from every campus to come. The result was that 251 students from eighty-nine campuses actually attended. One of these students was a senior from Princeton University, Robert Wilder. When the project's keynote speaker, D. L. Moody, took the stage, Robert Wilder took to prayer. By the end of the summer, they had successfully mobilized exactly one hundred students to be foreign missionaries. These came to be known as the Mount Hermon One Hundred. But the impact had only begun.

Realizing the massive number of Christian students *not* represented at the project, Wishard invited a few of the Mount Hermon One Hundred to travel from campus to campus and share God's purpose of reaching the nations. In one year, 162 campuses were visited, resulting in 2,106 students volunteering to be missionaries.

After that incredibly momentous first year, it was decided to give this movement a name. They called it the Student Volunteer Movement, because it seemed that day after day students were laying down their plans, allowing God to interrupt their lives, and upon graduation *volunteering* to board a boat and live in a distant land for the sake of the gospel. Over the entire course of its existence, this mobilization organization yielded approximately twenty thousand missionaries who went forth to the field and eighty thousand who stayed behind to support those who went.[3]

Just to put it in perspective, the cumulative total of Protestant missionaries sent out from America by the year 1870 was two thousand. In just the first year of the Student Volunteer Movement's existence, more students were recruited to go as missionaries than had been sent from the United States in the preceding century. Astounding! College presidents were even awed at the commitment of students. The president of Princeton University said, "Christians cannot but notice this event occurring before their eyes.... Has any such offering of living young men and women been presented in our age? In our country? In any age or in any country since the days of Pentecost?"[4]

By 1920, after thirty years of leading the ministry of the SVM, John Mott could look back in amazement and say, "The Volunteer Movement has furnished approximately 75 percent of the male missionaries of North America and 70 percent of the unmarried women missionaries."[5] University students truly are the powerful percent!

God using university students is not something limited to the past. It's definitely true for the present! I have spent the last two decades circling the United States to mobilize on college campuses, and one thing is sure— God is moving. He is bringing students to a crossroads and they are asking, *Am I going to allow God to interrupt my life?* Will they say yes to embracing God's heart for the world and whatever that means for them? Or will they allow their own ambitions to distract, hinder, and eventually keep them from a lifestyle that is aligned with God's heart?

Church—I want to encourage you that you have a pivotal role in this sending process! History is being written even now, and the years to come will tell of the awesome things God is doing in raising up and sending out this generation's army of laborers. As young Christian men and women encounter this crossroads, will you be there to support, challenge, and mobilize them for the sake of the nations? The nations are God's mission. The church is his vehicle.

Todd Ahrend is the founder and international director of The Traveling Team, (www.thetravelingteam.org), a national mission mobilization movement, and is the author of *In This Generation: Looking to the Past to Reach the Present.* You can also find more information at Mission Revolution, (www.missionrev.org), or email info@missionrev.org.

Notes

[1] Much of this chapter has been taken from Todd Ahrend, *In This Generation: Looking to the Past to Reach the Present* (Colorado Springs: Dawson Media, 2010). Permission granted.

[2] Clarence P. Shedd, *Two Centuries of Student Christian Movements: Their Origin and Intercollegiate Life* (New York: Association Press, 1934), 92–94.

[3] Michael Parker, *The Kingdom of Character: The Student Volunteer Movement for Foreign Missions 1886–1926*, 2nd ed., (Pasadena, CA: William Carey Library, 2008), 56.

[4] C. Howard Hopkins, *History of the YMCA in North America* (New York: Association Press, 1951), 299, 316.

[5] "North American Students and World Advance", Addresses delivered at the Eighth International Convention of the Student Volunteer Movement for Foreign Missions, Des Moines, Iowa, December 31, 1919–January 4, 1920, 62.

CHAPTER 3

Call Experiences from Today's Missionaries

Opening and Closing Doors

Glenn and Sue Ashcraft

We've all heard the adage that when God closes one door, he opens another. My call to serve in a Christian camping ministry in Spain evolved through years of closed and open doors.

At the age of four, I heard my mother telling my brother about Jesus and explaining the way to heaven. Listening to her, I knew I wanted to go to heaven with Jesus also, so at that time I prayed a simple prayer of salvation.

Being part of a strong, mission-minded church in Nebraska was one of many privileges I had growing up. When missionaries visited our church, my parents would invite them over for a meal. Seeing their faith and hearing their vibrant stories about living and serving in another part of the world captivated me.

Curt Lehman pastored the Lincoln Berean Church and used the Scriptures to encourage us to consider serving God full time. His heart for mission work touched my heart and helped set me on a path toward service for Christ.

Camping played an important role in my life. Every summer I went to a week of camp and loved it. When I was thirteen, a missionary speaker at Maranatha Bible Camp invited us to dedicate our lives to full-time service as missionaries. I went forward to make that decision publicly.

I took this call seriously, and my heart was moved by the passage in Scripture about Isaiah's call: "Then I heard the Lord asking, 'Whom should I send as a messenger to this people? Who will go for us?' I said, 'Here I am. Send me'" (Isa 6:8, NLT).

Looking at colleges, I wanted two things: good Bible training and a missions emphasis. I chose Grace College of the Bible (now Grace University) in Omaha, Nebraska, which required practical experience in serving in a church or other Christian organization. The experiences I gained through leading a Sunday school class, witnessing, and serving others were invaluable.

My oldest brother Dan was a missionary church planter in Spain. During my college years, I spent a summer with him and was inspired by his zeal to share the gospel with those around him. It was an unforgettable summer—making friends, doing street ministry, and handing out literature. Dan wanted to introduce Christian camping to his region of Spain. We ran a camp on a farmer's land, setting up tents and latrines. My brother aimed for forty campers, but 120 people showed up! We stopped up a river to swim and bathe in and redug the latrines twice. Many lives were given to God that week, and the commitment I made years earlier to serve full time was cemented in my mind.

As I began to pray and seek God's leading about where he would have me serve, a valuable lesson was learned. I took steps to serve in several different countries and ministries, but each time the doors were closed for different reasons. One ministry that interested me worked with children in Australia. But in order to serve with this mission, you were required to belong to a certain denomination. I didn't have peace in my heart about leaving my church, so God used this to show me that door was closed.

The door opened for me to return and serve in Spain, and I realized that God had a specific plan for my life. He was directing me toward ministry in this country, using the love I had gained for the Spanish people and not allowing me to proceed according to my will but to follow his.

For several years my wife and I served on a church planting team, but most of our missionary career has been spent serving at Springs of Life Camp. I have been the camp director since 1993.

When you feel called to serve God, it is vital that you don't get discouraged when opportunities that you think would be a great fit for you don't work out. Let the Lord guide you, and keep trying doors until you find the one that he opens up for you.

Whenever I would hear a sermon on Romans 10, I was struck by these verses:

For "Everyone who calls on the name of the Lord will be saved."

But how can they call on him to save them unless they believe in him? And how can they believe in him if they have never heard about him? And how can they hear about him unless someone tells them? And how will anyone go and tell them without being sent? That is why the Scriptures say, "How beautiful are the feet of messengers who bring good news!" (Rom 10:13–15, NLT)

I was convinced then, and am still convinced, that God was saying to me, "I want you to be one of those messengers." Listen to him. It is too easy today to get caught up in the noise, news, and fast pace of life around us and miss the small, still voice of God calling—asking "Who will go for us?"

Glenn and Sue Ashcraft serve with Avant Ministries as directors at Springs of Life Camp in Malaga, Spain.

A Call to Missions
Mark and Becky Jennings

The questions we are asked most frequently are "How did you end up here?" and "How did get involved with World Horizons?" We always begin our answer with two questions of our own: "Do you want the long or short version? How long do you have to hear our story?"

It goes something like this: Becky (my wife of twenty-eight years) and I have had God's mission on our hearts from a very young age. My first interest came when I was about twelve, sitting in a very traditional Presbyterian church listening to a missionary couple from Wycliffe Bible Translators give a demonstration on learning a completely new language. I was fascinated by the notion that there were people whose language had never been experienced before and who had no knowledge of Jesus or the Bible. I also had a wanderlust with foreign travel. My father had traveled around the world as a US Air Force pilot, and I wanted to see where he had been and experience different cultures.

When I was seventeen, I signed up for my first overseas mission trip with Teen Missions International. I got my first passport and raised the money needed, and then spent the summer training, traveling, and working in the Middle East. By then I understood there was a lost and dying world in need of Jesus. From then on I had reaching the nations on my heart.

Becky and I even fell in love on a mission trip. We met in college and were involved with the Baptist Student Union. They were planning a spring break trip to Massachusetts from our home state of Georgia to help a church plant—truly a cross-cultural mission experience. With all the time spent preparing, team building, and traveling in a van, one of the main things that drew Becky and me together was a calling into mission. We didn't know what that meant at the time, but it was a desire, a longing, and a purpose.

We got married seventeen months later and began to build our lives together. This call to be a part of God's mission was still a part of who we were. While we didn't go on any mission trips, we financially supported missionaries. As an elder, I was part of our small church's decision to tithe our offerings to international mission work. We would look for mission opportunities, bring them before our church body, and engage in the work of world mission. We were continually praying for our missionaries and supporting them in any way we could.

The next big thing drawing us into mission was my becoming uncomfortable in my career. I had a great job with a business owned and managed by a godly Christian man. I couldn't quite put my finger on it at the time, but I was desiring something different. I "pushed on several doors"—changing my occupation, considering a degree in higher education, and exploring starting my own business. But nothing seemed right.

A year into praying about this, I was invited to join a short-term mission trip to work with our church's missionary in Ukraine. She was part of a Ukrainian church plant that needed help with a camp for children and youth. I remember that she shared specifically about how many of these kids had absent, abusive, and negligent fathers, so what they needed were men who would be godly role models. I thought this might be what God was stirring me to do, so I signed up. That summer I went to help on the mission field for a couple of weeks.

After the first week of camp, one morning I was sitting alone in my dorm room having a "quiet time," reflecting on all that had happened the previous week. I was praying for the young people we had been ministering to and asking God to help the ministers and missionaries there in Ukraine to continue discipling these young believers. And then I heard a voice, as if someone was sitting right next to me, say, "Do you want to do this full time?"

That was it! This was what the last year of discomfort had been about. The Father was preparing my heart for this one question—much like

Isaiah 6:8: "And I heard the voice of the Lord saying, 'Whom shall I send, and who will go for us?' Then I said, 'Here I am! Send me.'"

I began to weep, to worship, and to see things so differently. I couldn't wait to go home and tell Becky what God was saying. When I told her my story, she said, "This all makes sense."

We continued to pray for another six months, inquiring what God had for us. God used a friend who was a mission pastor in another state. Becky was talking to him one night and shared that we were praying for an opportunity to serve but didn't know what that looked like. Our friend said he knew of a center in Europe that needed caretakers. Immediately Becky felt a leap in her spirit. When I came home that night she shared the conversation with me, and I immediately felt that this was what we had been praying about.

We learned more about this place and about the mission organization that ran it—World Horizons. We contacted World Horizons USA, and they sent information, applications, and reference forms, and then invited us to a conference a few weeks later. We shared with our church what we felt God was calling us into. They were so supportive and encouraging.

A few weeks later we attended the conference with applications and references in hand. All weekend, Becky and I continually looked at each other with astonishment and said, "It just fits." We had prayed for so long and God had brought us to a group of people with whom we knew we were called to serve.

All of this led to an eighteen-month process of spending time with our extended family and preparing ourselves to move abroad. This allowed us to raise financial support, share our vision of reaching the nations, and clarify God's call into cross-cultural mission. During this time, God was gracious with our four boys and also enabled us to celebrate our "lasts" in the US—our last birthdays, Valentine's Day, Christmas, Thanksgiving, Fourth of July—all these celebrations with our dear friends and family.

We have now served with World Horizons in Wales for eleven years. We are part of the support team that trains, equips, and cares for workers in over thirty nations. We also serve in a local Welsh church: reaching the lost, discipling young believers, and encouraging the saints. This is where the Lord has us now, but being amid so much mission activity, we are always asking, "Where will the Lord take us in the future?" and "What's next?"

Mark and Becky Jennings and their four sons serve with World Horizons USA in Wales, United Kingdom.

Like a Well-Watered Garden

Harold and Kerry Peters

During the first ten days of September 1967, Kerry and I had a big decision to make. Where in the world was God calling us to serve him with Gospel Missionary Union (GMU)?

When we were married on October 8, 1966, Kerry arranged to have some words from Isaiah 58:11 written on our wedding cake: "The Lord will guide you always." We didn't know at the time how significant that guidance would be for our entire lives.

Kerry had graduated from nurses' training just a few weeks before our wedding, and I had been teaching school in Maymont, Saskatchewan. That first year of our marriage we were extremely busy in our new professional positions and we also spent many hours and days in prayer about our future. We were seeking God's mind and heart concerning how and where we should invest our lives for the kingdom.

We had both grown up in evangelical, mission-minded churches. I grew up in a Christian home, while Kerry was the first one in her family to accept the Lord Jesus Christ as her personal Savior (by this time her entire immediate family had come to know the Lord).

The Context of Our Call in Our Early Years

Kerry had heard Dorothy Theobald, a missionary to India, speak in her church and Sunday school when she was about eleven years old. After that, Dorothy and Kerry began a letter-writing relationship that lasted for many years.

Due to my own spiritual rebellion against God as a teenager, I lost interest in school and failed the tenth grade. I quit going to school and spent two years working on my parents' farm. In 1958, the Lord began transforming my life. I was baptized and my life found new purpose. I returned to finish high school in my hometown.

Several experiences led to my sensitivity to God's calling. First, growing up in our small Evangelical Bible Church of about 150 people, I had been exposed to the vision that God is not willing that anyone should perish but that all should come to confess Jesus Christ as Lord (2 Pet 3:9). Second, our pastor, Rev. A. P. Toews, organized Saturday evening street meetings, which was a bold move in those years. Third, I watched my cousin, Dorothy Peters, become a missionary to

Japan when I was about twelve. Fourth, Rueben Friesen, who was also from our church, became a missionary to Mali. Childhood events such as commissioning services, receptions in the church, and going to the airport or train station to say goodbye were all part of my nurturing toward possible foreign service.

Solidifying the Call During Our College Years

Kerry and I met at Millar College of the Bible in Southern Saskatchewan, where we experienced mission-minded staff almost every day for three years. Every professor seemed to have a great passion to see the world come to know Christ. Mr. Schmidt often would be moved to tears when he taught Bible passages. Mr. Peeler gave witness by his personal ministry. Mr. McKnee shared about the missional purpose of all our lives. Because of godly men like these, Kerry and I graduated from Millar in 1963 with a desire to be part of God's amazing mission to take the gospel of Jesus Christ to the whole world.

While in college, especially as graduation approached, everybody was considering what to do with the rest of their lives. It was natural to be impressed by certain leaders and missions when they came through our Bible college. Missionary sending organizations would send representatives for recruitment visits. I remember Don Schidler of GMU because he had been coming to my church in Saskatchewan ever since I could remember. It was that extended relationship that made a big difference for me.

I know I am using lots of names here, and they won't mean anything to you personally, but these people had a significant impact on our lives. If you take anything away from our story, please know that you are important in the life of someone who is wrestling with a call from God. Your influence can either cultivate that call or complicate that call!

In my third year at Millar, I talked to Mr. Schidler concerning future possibilities in ministry, and he asked me several very strategic questions: 1) What do you think your gifts are? 2) Do you have a significant girlfriend? 3) What would you like to do in life?

My answers were: 1) Some friends and my home church leaders have suggested I have the potential to be a teacher. 2) No, I don't have a significant girlfriend (this was before Kerry and I started dating). 3) I would consider it a privilege to teach or preach the gospel anywhere that God led me.

Mr. Schidler's response was careful, gracious, and warm: 1) It seems wise that you finish college and then obtain a teaching certificate from the university. 2) You need to trust the Lord to provide a spouse who has the same vision and passion for the Lord and the lost that you have. Otherwise you will never get into (and last) in the ministries you have potential for now. 3) Don't get yourself into deep debt, because that can prevent you from ever getting into kingdom ministries.

As we remember our experience of listening for God's call, several incidents come to mind that have helped to solidify our calling and remain etched in our memory to this day. One Saturday morning I was playing catch with a friend when Doyle Klaassen came running up to me, grabbed both of my arms so I couldn't throw the ball, and then exclaimed, "Peters, when you get out of here, you'd better go right straight into missions or have a downright good reason for not doing so!" Wow, perhaps a little too enthusiastic, but memorable nonetheless.

Meanwhile, Kerry applied to the Royal Inland Nursing School in Kamloops, British Columbia. She was initially turned down because the class was full, but a few weeks later they invited her into the program because someone had dropped out. For Kerry, this special opportunity was a sign of God's leading. She knew that nursing school was a three-year commitment as a single nurse. Although a secular institution, this school didn't permit students to get married during their training unless they were willing to take a full year's leave of absence.

I served as a youth sponsor in my church in Langham, Saskatchewan. During that time Rueben and Millie Friesen came home from Mali because Millie had cancer. I remember them coming to speak to our youth meeting. Millie challenged us with these words: "We have come home because I have cancer and I can't go back. Who is going to take our place?"

One of the most impacting events happened on a Friday night when two of our church's elders, Bill Friesen and Jake Peters, came to my home. I invited them inside, but they wanted me to come out to their car. They told me that the elders had just met to pray for the young people of our church, and as a result they had been delegated to come tell me something significant: "If you sense the Lord's call on your life for ministry, we as elders agree with this call."

Wow! What a big word of encouragement from the elders! First of all, they were godly men who prayed for the young people in the church. Second, they were sensitive to the Holy Spirit and heard his voice regarding someone being called to serve the Lord. Third, they acted on the Spirit's calling and made a visit to my house. None of these men had ever gone to seminary, but I believed they were in the Word of God every day. They were certainly living out Acts 13:1–3 in this moment.

In 1967 we told our church at Langham that we were planning to attend the Candidate Orientation Program (COP) with GMU. Henry Schmidt, a respected missionary from the Congo who was a member of our church, spoke to me about our career. He said, "Now of course you are going to go to Mali, right?"

I answered, "No, I doubt it because my sister and brother-in-law, Phil and Ev Anderson, are already there with GMU. That wouldn't work, would it?"

Henry responded, "Of course it would work for you to be there as close relatives and friends serving together ten thousand miles away from home."

This seemed like a coincidental conversation at the time, but eventually it was confirmed as God's voice of providence.

Coming to a Final Decision—Where?

When Kerry and I arrived at COP, we were met by Ben Nickel for the official orientation teaching and tour. As he was concluding, he asked us, "So where are you going to go to serve the Lord?"

We both blurted out that we were expecting GMU to assign us the place they wanted us to serve. Ben responded, "It's usually best if you tell us where you sense the Lord is leading you, because that gives you assurance later on when things get tough and you start to question the decision."

We quickly understood his rationale and agreed with him. At that time, there was a little bit of language taught at training, so we needed to decide between French and Spanish. We needed to make a decision about where we wanted to serve within ten days. The clock was ticking.

We read, prayed, and interviewed every missionary that came through the mission headquarters, but nothing seemed to stand out. We looked at GMU's open fields and considered Ecuador, but decided that with ninety-eight GMU workers already there, they had enough. What difference would two more make? We considered the Bahamas. Practically every field could use a teacher and a nurse, but how would Canadians look at financially supporting someone who worked in the ideal "snowbird" vacation spot?

We were very aware of our time line, but we didn't feel desperate. Concerned? Yes. But we just kept searching, listening, and trusting. The Sunday night before we needed to inform GMU about our field of God's calling, we were in the mission guesthouse kitchen having coffee with a couple who worked for the mission. With our coffee cups in hand, one of them said out of the blue, "No field in GMU needs missionaries like Mali does right now."

We finished our coffee and all four of us scattered to our rooms for the night. Kerry and I walked hand in hand to the opposite end of that old Smithville guesthouse. Then, just before we got to our room, I put my arms around her and said, "Honey, what about Mali?" She answered, "That's what I think." All the questions, concerns, and wondering were over! God gave us a deep, settled peace about where we should serve. "And the peace of God, which surpasses all understanding, will guard your hearts and your minds in Christ Jesus" (Phil 4:7).

The Aftermath of Our Decision

From that day in September of 1967 until now, neither of us questioned our decision to go to Mali. I believe we both were honest in our search for the Lord's will and he was faithful to answer. The decision to go to Mali was huge, but there were also key decisions to be made in terms of how to do mission in that context. We needed a ministry method and focus, so we all agreed on two guiding principles:

1. **Multiplication.** We sought out faithful believers and trained them, so that they could train others, to train others . . . Basically, we adopted 2 Timothy 2:2 for our ministry method. We wanted to become multipliers, rather than addition-ers.

2. **Rivers of Influence.** Through studying the strategies of the Apostle Paul as well as contemporary missiological strategists (specifically, Dr. Ray Bakke), we decided our ministry focus would be on the larger cities and those who were already educated in the secular world.

On our twentieth wedding anniversary, while living in Bamako, the capital city of Mali, Kerry and I had supper at home (restaurants that we would enjoy for an anniversary dinner were nonexistent). We opened a Bible and reread the words that had been written on our wedding cake: "The Lord will guide you always; he will satisfy your needs in a sun-scorched land and will strengthen your frame. You will be like a well-watered garden, like a spring whose waters never fail" (Isa 58:11, NIV).

This was an incredible moment, because if there was ever a "sun-scorched land," Mali is the place. And we had been thriving there for nineteen years already. Furthermore, God had always provided for us. Physically, we were very healthy, even though the US embassy staff often claimed that living in Mali would take years off our life span.

I don't know what being "like a well-watered garden" means, but as the field director in those years I witnessed God drawing many people to himself. The national church was dynamic, and our missionary colleagues were thriving as they preached and showed *The Jesus Film* in unreached areas after it was translated in Bambara (the national language). As people came to Christ, many were following the Lord in public baptism. Kerry and I were just a small part of the "well-watered garden," because God was blessing everything that the missionaries and national believers were doing over the years. The church was growing in unprecedented ways.

Personally, we praise the Lord that our "well-watered garden" also included the blessing of having three daughters, as well as ten grandchildren. We pray that the Lord will "guide them always" and that they will someday serve in ministries at home and around the world.

But What if We Chose to Go Elsewhere?

In 1991, while working for GMU's home office, I traveled to Ecuador. While there, Henry Klassen, our veteran Quichua missionary, asked me, "Harold, how was it that you decided to go to Mali in 1967?"

I told him the story, mentioning that we had considered Ecuador, but with ninety-eight GMUers there already, we had wondered what difference we would be able to make.

Henry had a great response: "Perhaps if you and Kerry had come to Ecuador we wouldn't have had to close the Quichua Bible School due to lack of personnel."

Could we have served the Lord well in any another place? Yes, I am sure of it. My point here is that the geographic location of our ministry wasn't nearly as important as the degree of dedication to our Lord and our commitment to the work that he had given us.

Christ is building his church, and he invites us to join him in that work!

Harold and Kerry Peters served the Lord faithfully with Gospel Missionary Union from 1967 to 2005.

Resisting the Call

Art and Vicki Reyes

I had no intention of standing up—and even Billy Graham couldn't make me. It was the final night of Urbana 1976. Thousands of university students had gathered to hear how God was working throughout the world, drawing people to himself. As the president of our campus InterVarsity Christian Fellowship chapter, I had been pressured to attend Urbana—but I really had no interest in becoming a missionary.

We listened breathlessly as Dr. Helen Roseveare, Elisabeth Elliot, John Perkins, and others shared their experiences of suffering and joy. We were exhausted by the final midnight communion service. It was then that Billy Graham began his invitation, which went something like this: "If you are already serving the Lord in full-time ministry, please stand. If you are in the process of becoming a full-time servant of the Lord, please stand. If you are willing to consider missionary service, please stand." By the end of a very long invitation, there were probably only a handful of us who refused to stand.

I wasn't even willing to consider missions in 1976. Isn't it ironic that my husband and I have just completed twenty-five years as church planting missionaries in Mexico with The Evangelical Alliance Mission?

My first exposure to missionaries was at the Good News Club of a local evangelical church during my grade school years. My impression was that missionaries had no fashion sense and that they told long, long stories. A few years later, after reading books and hearing a representative from the Gideons speak at the mainline church my family attended, I decided to become a Christian. But I still had no interest in missions. I had my future planned. The only thing I had ever wanted to do was become a teacher at the elementary school in my little mountain town in Pennsylvania. It was my only career goal. That's what I did, too.

At first, I loved everything about teaching. It was a pure joy to help children blossom as they learned to read and write and acquire math skills. After a few years, however, I no longer experienced the satisfaction that I felt when I first started teaching school. In fact, I felt frustrated. I had been warned against "proselytizing" my young students, but I often felt that I was offering an incomplete education to my beloved children—especially if they had family problems. I was particularly frustrated when the alcoholic father of one of my little students ran the family from their home but the only thing I felt free to do was offer sympathy to my suffering student and her mother.

That spring, a friend who attended Moody Church invited me to her summer wedding in Chicago. She also mentioned that she had lost her roommate. That gave me an idea. Why not live in Chicago with my friend for the summer? If I could find a part-time job, I could explore Chicago, attend Moody Church, and do lots of fun activities with their singles group. It promised to be a win-win summer!

It wasn't. I was miserable for most of it. For one thing, I hung out socially with a group of adult MKs who attended Moody Church. Much to my dismay, they talked about missions a lot and were all preparing to be missionaries, having moved to Chicago to study or to work as part of their preparation for service. Then, to make matters worse, Pastor Erwin Lutzer highlighted missions constantly in his sermons and midweek Bible studies. It was awful—I felt more and more pressured to consider missions. Deep down, I must have known that I wasn't going to escape "the call" this time. It was a long summer.

Finally, near the end of the summer, I took a day off to spend time with the Lord. I ended up wrestling with him, telling him all the reasons that I could not, would not become a missionary. However, after several hours of this, I finally realized that if "he was not Lord of all, he was not Lord at all" of my life. I finally submitted to his Lordship and started planning how to make the transition to this "second career."

Grant Anderson, the pastor of education at Moody Church, advised me to finish the last few classes of my graduate degree in Pennsylvania and then go on a short-term mission trip to confirm my calling. That fall, I told my principal that I would be resigning at the end of the school year. He was very surprised, since I had just received tenure and he knew how much I loved teaching. Grieving deeply for the next ten months, I slowly bid farewell to my friends and family and the mountains that I loved so much.

That summer, I served as a missionary in the frontier area of Northern Kenya with the African Inland Mission. Due to an oversight, I didn't spend the summer in an educational setting as planned. The mistake wasn't recognized until I was almost ready to leave for Africa, and the only opening was to assist a nurse who lived on a mountain in Samburu Land and did medical safaris to various tribes.

Much to my surprise, it was a glorious summer! Lou Cameron, a godly Canadian nurse, counseled me as I struggled with a few remaining concerns, such as the reluctance to raise financial support after being independent so long. Accompanied by Sammy, a young Kenyan blood technician, we traveled from tribe to tribe giving vaccines and treating patients. Even though I couldn't understand the language, I could feel the bond of Christian affection and could see the need for full-time church planters to these northern tribes. My time in Kenya was a joyous and unforgettable experience that ignited within me a true heart for missions.

During the next few years, I took Bible classes at Moody Bible Institute and taught in Christian schools as I prepared for missionary service. I also fell in love with and married a young Mexican clinical dietician. He had come to the United States legally as a ten-year-old, had become a Christian in high school, and was planning to return Mexico to share the good news that he loved so much.

In 1992, we left for the mission field with our four-year-old daughter and two-year-old son. We have experienced the inexpressible joy of helping to start two local churches, evangelizing many adults and children, and training Mexican Christian leaders. At times it has been difficult, of course. All birthing processes are.

I still teach children, but I don't teach them to read and write. I teach them that God wants them to know him, that he loves them, and that he sent Jesus to receive the punishment for their sins.

I thank God for his insistence that I make him Lord of my life and for allowing me to serve him in Mexico. It is sobering to think that I could have missed the glorious adventure of watching him work in people's lives, bring his church together, and provide for our family throughout all these twenty-five years. I am very glad that I didn't "win"!

Art and Vicki Reyes have been church planters with The Evangelical Alliance Mission since 1992, starting churches in San José del Cabo and La Playa on the southern tip of the Baja peninsula of Mexico.

My Call Experience

Larry W. Sharp

The term "missionary call" should never have been coined. It is not scriptural and therefore can be harmful. Thousands of youth desiring to serve the Lord have waited and waited for some mysterious "missionary call" that never came. After a time they became weary of waiting and gave up on the idea of going to the mission field. —J. Herbert Kane, 1978

I am very grateful for three years of Bible school, after high school, where I studied the Scriptures and the works of Herbert Kane and others.

I understood early on that the "call" has already been given, so the question is "How and why should I make decisions that connect me with God at work in the world?" I understood that the call of God, then, was to love him and love others (Matt 22:37–39); the making of disciples was the natural result of loving and following Jesus. (Matt 28:18–20)

David Sitton declares, "Nowhere in Scripture is a mysterious (supernatural) call a prerequisite before we can respond to the Great Commission. The opposite is actually true."[1] With this assumption, all else is what Garry Friesen calls the "way of wisdom,"[2] or the freedom in Christ to make our own decisions. It made sense to me that God allows for our own decisions within the context of a holy life, obedience to his Word, and humble-servant living.

Aligned with this is the teaching that all spiritual gifts and abilities are equally "empowered by one and the same Spirit, who apportions to each one individually as he wills" (1 Cor 12:11). We read in Exodus 31:1–6 that Bezalel and Oholiab were filled with the Spirit of God, wisdom, knowledge, and understanding and were also skilled craftsmen (not priests or clergy). This encouraged me to understand that all skills, gifts, professions, and abilities are valued in a "call"—not just ordained ministry or missionary work.

To me there is no such thing as "full-time service," meaning missions or pastoral ministry. It is full-time obedience followed by making wise decisions. Colossians 3:23 made this clear to me: "Whatever you do, work heartily, as for the Lord and not for men."

I came to understand that the Greek Gnosticism I studied in my youth wasn't just a first-century philosophy but extended to Middle Ages Christianity and even to twentieth-century evangelicalism. The dualistic sacred-spiritual dichotomy has created an unbiblical hierarchy of "callings" in the church today. I am grateful that early on I learned that all work, skills, and gifts are from God.

The Reformers "discovered" this biblical truth. Os Guinness quotes Luther: "The works of monks and priests, however holy and arduous they be, do not differ one whit in the sight of God from the works of the rustic laborer in the field or the woman going about her household tasks, but all works are measured before God by faith alone."[3]

By my late teens I believed the key question was "How do I make a wise decision within my God-given freedom in Christ and obey both the Great Commandment and the Great Commission?"

When I was at a Christian university in my early twenties, I met people who helped me see the importance of understanding how God has "wired" people. This led me, then, to consider my personality, natural interests, and what gave me the most satisfaction. It became increasingly clear that I was a "doer" type: quite organized, with a love of study, teaching, and coaching. I was not musical, not a social person, and not given to public speaking. What do I do with this mix of things?

Secondly, since I had a natural interest in daily news, travel, different peoples, and global affairs, I began to see a world in need—not only in need of a Savior but of temporal help, as I observed injustice, poverty, and suffering. It made sense to go where the needs were the greatest. William Carey said that "every Christian should live with an open Bible and an open map."

Thirdly, I tried to listen to what God was saying not only through his Word but also through other people who shared their experiences and wisdom with me. The natural world provided me a source of understanding of who God is through his creation. In my youth I would spend days in the wilderness, where I remember God clearly speaking to me through mountains, waterfalls, wildlife, and trees and the sun, moon, and stars. Such natural revelation taught me who God is and led me to his Word for special instruction about what that means to me.

So what of a "call to missions"? I don't think that is the right question. In recent years, teachers such as Tim Keller, John Piper, and J. D. Payne have developed modern expressions of what I have experienced. It is not about "missions activity"; it is about God's eternal mission and purpose and how he has created me and placed me in today's world.

Here are some helpful questions to ask: What is God saying to you through his Word and respected Christian leaders? What is going on in the world and what are the needs of this broken world? Who are you and how are you wired with gifts, experiences, skills, etc.?

How did that lead me into the missionary endeavor? By the time I finished university with a business degree, I had received positive reinforcement relative to teaching competency. While working as a fish plant manager in Alaska in the summer and as a teacher in the winter, I began to look outward. Where could a person like me serve God's purposes in the world? I talked to people "in the know," read about the greatest needs in the world, and processed everything with my wife. This decision-making process led me to the Amazon rain forest.

Why there? Well, there was a need for a teacher like me, and it was considered an unreached area at the time. It was a "wild and wooly place"— something that appealed to me. And people around me whom I respected affirmed this as a good idea. This wasn't a "needle in a haystack" approach to finding God's will, but the result of a person honestly and humbly seeking to obey God and his heart that all peoples come to worship him.

I readily admit that this process wasn't as easy as stated in a few hundred words. There was much prayer, along with times of patient and anxious waiting. But a wise counselor once told me, "Just make a decision based on what you know of God's truth and the world and get moving, praying that if it is wrong that God will clarify it and redirect." I have tried to pass that along to young people every chance I get.

Larry W. Sharp is vice president emeritus of Crossworld (www.crossworld.org) and founder and director of training of IBEC Ventures (www.ibecventures.com).

Notes

[1] David Sitton, "Don't Complicate the 'Missionary Call,'" *Desiring God* website, http://www.desiringgod.org/articles/don-t-complicate-the-missionary-call, July 27, 2011.

[2] Garry Friesen with J. Robin Maxson, *Decision Making and the Will of God* (Sisters, OR: Multnomah, 2004).

[3] Os Guinness, *The Call* (Nashville: Thomas Nelson, 2003), 34.

A Call to Missions

Jurg VanDyk

My call to full-time ministry started in the Warm Heart of Africa on Christmas Day in 1994. Two other young men and I, all in our late twenties, were sitting around a fire having a braai (barbeque) at a mission station. For many months the three of us had planned this vacation—an overland trip through Southern Africa, as well as spending a week on the shores of Lake Malawi. An aunt of mine spent some of her childhood years in Malawi, where her father, a Dutch Reformed minister, served for many years as a missionary in Nyasaland, known today as Malawi. Part of the plan was to spend some time on the Nkomo mission station where my aunt's father had served so many years ago.

During our time at the mission station we had a look at a water purification system that a young engineer was building to provide clean water for the mission hospital and base. The three of us, all engineers, were very impressed with the work. Back at the braai fire, I pondered about the work this young engineer was doing on the mission field. It was there, watching the flames of the fire, that the Holy Spirit lit the flame of missions in my heart.

Back in South Africa, after our overland trip, life gradually returned to its normal routine: going back and forth to work and attending church on Sundays. The only thing that changed was that almost every Sunday I was challenged by the Holy Spirit during the sermon. I had never had a desire to be in ministry—and definitely not full time—but now I experienced a tug at my heart that I'd never experienced before. I certainly wasn't ignorant about missions. When I was a child, we always had visiting missionaries and evangelists in our home; it was a joy for my parents to host visiting preachers. But I had become an engineer now, and my career was planned.

As an engineer, one works with facts and figures that need to add up to the correct answer, or else the result could be a loss of profits or even disaster. I could not simply rely on these feelings that I was starting to feel in my inner being. I had to be sure, and I was very specific when I said to the Lord that I never want to doubt whether or not I am called. He would need to make it very clear to me.

During my quiet time on a Sunday morning in early March of 1995, I read this well-known passage: "And I heard the voice of the Lord saying, 'Whom shall I send, and who will go for us?' Then I said, 'Here I am! Send me.' And he said, 'Go, and say to this people: "Keep on hearing, but do not understand; keep on seeing, but do not perceive"'" (Isa 6:8,9).

My immediate response was, "No, Lord! No! I don't want this passage; everyone gets this passage." In the following weeks I experienced inner turmoil as I wrestled with my feelings. What was the Lord saying to me? I was unsure and unsettled because of my insecurity and unwillingness to say yes to God's call on my life.

A couple of weeks later I had progressed in my quiet time Bible reading to Ezekiel chapter 33, and it was as if a ten-ton truck hit me in the face:

> So you, son of man, I have made a watchman for the house of Israel. Whenever you hear a word from my mouth, you shall give them warning from me. If I say to the wicked, O wicked one, you shall surely die, and you do not speak to warn the wicked to turn from his way, that wicked person shall die in his iniquity, but his blood I will require at your hand. (Ezek 33:7,8)

I was on my face before the Lord . . . "No more Lord, I will go!" As I write this more than twenty-two years later, I can still feel that intensity and the emotions that flooded through my soul as those words from the book of Ezekiel were spoken to me by Yahweh that day. How could I not heed such a word from my God? There were no more calculations to be made; I had nothing more to say, for the final word had been spoken!

I heard the call. So now what? I agreed to go, but where to now? It took almost two more years before I was ready to move. During that time, I completed building my current house. I was led to be baptized, although I had already accepted the Lord as my personal Savior in 1985. And I met the love of my life, my dear wife Minda, which I have thanked the Lord for ever since.

I had planned to go to Bible school in Cape Town the following year, but I was busy working for a civil engineering company on a project that had already overrun its completion date. I felt that it wouldn't be right to just walk away from the project before it was completed. This meant that I had to postpone going to Bible school for six months.

Upon the completion of that project, I was nominated to run the biggest project our company had at that time. This would have been the next step in my engineering career, putting me on the trajectory I had planned and worked so hard for. The project was a stadium that was upgraded years later for the 2010 World Cup soccer tournament in South Africa—an opportunity of a lifetime. Two months into that two-year project, I knew I had to make a decision. If I had chosen to do that project, there would always be another reason not to be obedient to the call. I knew that if I couldn't walk away from this opportunity, I would never be able to do it.

I remember so well the day that I informed my boss of my decision to resign. He walked into the office that morning, and while he was busy on the computer I prayed for the courage to drop the bomb. "I need to resign," I heard myself say. And at that moment I felt a burden drop to the ground.

Without looking up and with his fingers above the keyboard, my supervisor asked me why. Some months earlier I had the opportunity to share the gospel with him, and we talked till late one night about having a relationship with God. I told him that I was on my way to Bible school. He looked at me and said, "Jurg, it wouldn't even help to double your salary; this is something bigger!"

I completed my Bible school training and then started a mission organization called Global Mission South Africa (GMSA), where I served in Mozambique from 1999 until 2014. Then The Evangelical Alliance

Mission (TEAM) approached me to help in Chad in 2015; and since 2017 I have been serving as Director for New Initiatives and Special Projects in Africa with TEAM.

Jurg VanDyk, with his wife Minda and their three children, is currently based in South Africa, serving with TEAM.

CHAPTER 4

The Missionary Call

But I Don't Feel Called!¹

Neal Pirolo

Paul the Apostle said, "Do not be unwise, but understand what the will of the Lord is" (Eph 5:17, NKJV).

Volumes have been written on the subject of God's will. Yet before they go out of print, others have taken their place. And we still want to read more about this elusive something known as "God's will for my life."

We may say, "The Lord told me," and this is the point where we begin preparation—until something goes wrong or it becomes too hard. Then we say, "God changed his mind." No, we don't say that. It sounds . . . so . . . un-God-like. We do say, however, "He closed that door," which is saying the same thing. And at this point we bring God down to the capricious level of man. A word of wisdom, a word of knowledge, a prophecy to confirm his will, yes; but the revolving door of God's will, no—never!

Common yet Unwise Approaches to Seeking the Will of God

- *Finger pointing and promise card dealing.* Out-of-context-Scripture is a dangerous game to play in decision making. I knew of a man who was seeking the Lord for a wife. As he was reading Peter's letters, he read, "Grace be unto you," which for him became a promise of his wife's name. It worked! But one could also "finger point" to this combination: "Judas went and hanged himself" and then a flip of the page to "Go thou and do likewise."
- *Search for a sign.* Though, again, signs have been used in God's guidance of men (the wise men), our vulnerability to natural or supernatural phenomenon puts them, if used by themselves, in a very precarious category.

- *"Lord, bless my plans."* We in North America regard individualism as a highly valued ideal. Though heroes like Buffalo Bill and Babe Ruth have been replaced by the latest sports figure or space traveler, it is still the unique "I did it my way" type of hero that makes them stand out. Is it any wonder, then, that the American Christian approaches God with his very own plans? The focus of *call* is not on *me and my plans*, but *his will be done*, and my participation should be within that sovereign will of almighty God.

- *Do your own thing.* After all, God isn't that interested in your plans, right? Unfortunately, others have capitulated to this way of thinking and have fallen prey to the spirit of this age by saying, "Live by the Good Book, but beyond that use your own God-given judgment." It is impossible for me to understand or believe that the One who attends the funeral of every sparrow does not have a greater care than that in the plans of my life.

We need to be wise and desire to walk in our day-by-day decisions as Christ did, who said, "We must work the works of him who sent me" (John 9:4), as well as "I do nothing on my own authority, but speak just as the Father taught me" (John 8:28).

In a sequence of three "calls," I would like to present a firm grasp and a precise answer to the excuse "But I don't feel called!"

A Call to Mission

God reveals himself in the Word as an outgoing, missionary God:

"Say this to the people of Israel: 'I am has sent me to you.'" (Ex 3:14)
"Whom shall I send, and who will go for us?" (Isa 6:8)
"For God so loved the world . . ." (John 3:16)
". . . not wishing that any should perish . . ." (2 Pet 3:9)

God is involved in the lives of people, so that all may call him Father. Jesus went out to all sorts of people. The children sat on his knees; the prostitute washed his feet with her tears; the religious leader sought his counsel by night; he touched and healed the leper. Jesus refused to be bound by human social barriers. The comfort, teaching, and power of the Holy Spirit is with us now, and even to the end of the world. He is a Person who reaches out to people. The individuals whom this reaching-out God chooses and calls must become outgoing people as well. Jesus said it succinctly: "As the Father has sent me, even so I am sending you" (John 20:21).

The mission of the church is outreach. Once a newly formed local church (or movement of churches) gets over the initial euphoria of being established, it needs to get down to the business of the kingdom. Since God is a missionary God, his church must be a missionary church. Every Christian accepted a call to mission when he/she became a follower of Christ, whether he/she realized it or not.

The church of Jesus Christ is a militant body. There is no room for detente, no allowance for peaceful coexistence with other religious traditions. Yes, the gospel of Christ is an all-inclusive message of hope, for whosoever will may come. But it is an equally all-exclusive doctrine; no man comes to the Father but through Jesus.

Jesus said, "All authority in heaven and on earth has been given to me. Go therefore and make disciples of all nations ..." (Matt 28:18,19). These marching orders have never been rescinded. The church does not need to wait for additional guidance before it goes out to make disciples. Both in your hometown, and in the surrounding counties or states, and to the most hated and despised of all people (Samaritans), and to all the nations.

In this general sense, then, every committed Christian, as a disciple of Christ, is called to the mission of the church, known as the Great Commission.

A Call to the Body of Christ

In an equally clear analogy, all Christians are called to exercise some function in the local fellowship of believers. The Spirit distributes, as he chooses, a diversity of gifts. As the individuals exercise the gifts within the body, it becomes evident to them all which gift(s) they have been equipped with by the Holy Spirit. As they function within that body, those spiritual gifts are developed.

In a most dramatic way, Acts 4:36 shows us how Joseph, who had joined himself to the body of believers in Jerusalem, having come from Cyprus, when his gifting was recognized, was given a new name: Barnabas, which means "son of consolation, exhortation, encouragement, comfort." That is quite a gift—thank you, Holy Spirit!

Scripture is also clear that, from God's perspective, the gifts that man looks on as the more prominent, are less. And the less honorable, more feeble, uncomely parts are to be given greater honor, that there should be no schism in the body (1 Cor 12:21–25).

"
> A missionary is a Christian
> called to make disciples of all nations;
> one who manifests social, professional,
> and spiritual gifts appropriate to bridging
> cultural distinctives; one who is open to the
> location change necessary to fulfill that *call*.

"

The Lord places certain apostles, prophets, evangelists, pastors, and teachers (each with their giftedness) in the body "to equip the saints for the work of ministry" (Eph 4:12). The end result is that every believer is perfected to fulfill some function in the body of Christ. Some become *mouths*; some a listening *ear*; others serve as the *smellers* of trouble; and even the appendix that seems to be just *hanging on* to that lower intestine—are all needed for their respective function. There is no such thing as a vestige organ in the body of Christ.

Do I have to draw out the parallel? Some pastors look over their congregation and declare some members to be a vestige! But as they learn more about how the spiritual body functions, fewer and fewer parts are "nonessential" for the body to perform its calling.

A Call to a Location

Everyone is born to live somewhere (not a very brilliant declaration, but it had to be said somehow). We grow up and become a part of that culture.

We experience our countercultures, but the hippies of the 60s became the upwardly mobile of the 80s. They settled down in their 3.4 bedroom houses in the suburbs with 2.3 children and 3.2 cars, etc. And today they are the boomers who are starting to retire. Enculturation did its work for the perpetuation of society.

Though we do not change a person's name anymore, like Joseph to Barnabas, we should feel free to challenge members of the body of Christ to change locations. When church leadership begins recognizing the giftedness of someone as they relate to people of other cultures, their facility with language, their ability to communicate the simplicity of the gospel, their heart beating with God's, we should be encouraging that person to pursue a career in missions outside of their birth culture.

The Missionary Call

As these three *calls* are merged into one, they constitute a missionary call.

A missionary is a Christian called to make disciples of all nations; one who manifests social, professional, and spiritual gifts appropriate to bridging cultural distinctives; one who is open to the location change necessary to fulfill that *call*.

But it is at this point that many lose out, for they have somehow been trained to think, "Not until I hear a voice from heaven" or "When I see the handwriting on the wall." We cannot counter that with a simplistic, "Go where the needs are," for there are thousands of needy ministries around the world asking for helpers to come alongside. How, then, do we get from "here" to "there"? From where we are at the moment to where God wants us to be?

A look at the book of Acts with this question in mind will give us at least six different ways that *call to location* occurred, and could occur today:

1. **Supernatural Direction.** Acts 13:2 is clear that church leaders heard the Holy Spirit say, "I want Barnabas and Saul." Later, in Acts 16:9, Paul had a vision of the Macedonian man appealing him to "Come over and help."

   Several years ago, a friend of ours was attending Prairie Bible Institute in Canada, a school with a strong cross-cultural vision. Direct supernatural guidance came to his friend the first night he was there. He had a dream that a plane appeared in a cloudless sky and began skywriting a message in one word: "NEPAL." Upon graduation and through an amazing set of circumstances, he was invited by nationals to this otherwise difficult-to-get-into country.

2. **Sanctified Common Sense.** Paul's second journey, according to Acts 15:36, was initiated by a sensible and responsible plan to go back and check up on how the brothers were doing in the cities they had previously visited.

   From the vast number of unreached people groups that have been identified in recent years, even delineating their degree of openness to the gospel, a friend of mine made a logical determination to prepare himself to minister to one of them. Within a year of this reasonable decision, he and his family, with their church's blessing, were able to leave to fulfill this commonsense calling.

3. **Circumstantial Guidance.** Following the martyrdom of Stephen, there were no Christians in Jerusalem who cried out, "But I don't feel

called!" When the persecution came, they split, left town, scattered to the nations (Acts 8:1; 11:19). Also, when Emperor Claudius commanded all Jews to leave Rome, Aquila didn't "go into a season of prayer" with Priscilla over it; they left. (Acts 18:2)

A pastor friend in central California established a thriving ministry among a group of Mexican migrant workers. When he heard they had been picked up and deported back to Mexico, his first response was disappointment. However, when I pointed out that he had just sent out his first missionaries, his countenance brightened.

4. **Invitation by Believers.** It appears the Macedonian *man* turned out to be a *woman*. Her name was Lydia, a seller of purple cloth, from the city of Thyatira. When she and her household were baptized, she pleaded for Paul and his team to stay in her home there in Philippi (Acts 16:14,15). The church's desire for Paul to stay in Ephesus was very strong, yet he desired to keep to his schedule so that he could arrive in Jerusalem for the Feast of Pentecost. Therefore, he asked the elders to meet him in Miletus instead. (Acts 20:16,17)

Today, Third-World Christians are standing on a "Macedonian shore," crying out with a new Macedonian call, saying, "Come over and help us. Teach us the Word of God in such a way that we can go out and teach others." God is faithfully raising up Third-World Christians as the new missionary force, so the very best thing we in North America can do to respond to their invitation is to go.

5. **Sent by a Church.** When the church in Jerusalem heard of the revival going on in Antioch, they sent Barnabas to check it out (Acts 11:22). A key to responsible action and accountability was the church's initial involvement with the missionary call.

Today, church leadership is often the last to know when one of their members decides to go cross-cultural. It is best when church leadership is proactive in identifying, training, sending, and supporting those members of the congregation who are gifted in ministry to the uttermost parts of the earth. Even young churches can participate in God's will of guiding missionaries. Over the past many years, I have worked with many individuals wanting to go to the unreached fields of the world. Without exception, those who have a strong sense of their church's backing go with a greater confidence. Though some have gone without this, and have done quite well in the field, there is always an "emptiness" in their feeling of moral support.

6. **Sent by Missionary Leaders.** It is clear from Luke's writings that as Paul's ministry team grew he became responsible for their work by sending them here and there (at one point eight men were traveling with him). One example is when Timothy and Erastus were sent to Macedonia from Ephesus. (Acts 19:22)

When we first applied to Wycliffe Bible Translators, we requested to be sent to Columbia. We had been there, talked with the principal, and we had a good feeling about the place. However, when the Wycliffe board decided to accept me as a missionary teacher, they saw a greater need for us to go to Peru. Out of submission to authority, we allowed them to guide us in this way.

One Final Thought

In a chapter of this length, it would be futile to think we could cover the enormity of this subject, knowing God's will, with all of its ramifications. Subjects like these should draw us to the whole counsel of God. However, this one final thought, I believe, encompasses all considerations of his will for my life:

Let the peace of Christ [the inner calm of one who walks daily with Him] be the controlling factor in your hearts [deciding and settling questions that arise]. To this peace indeed you were called as members in one body [of believers]. And be thankful [to God always]. Let the [spoken] word of Christ have its home within you [dwelling in your heart and mind— permeating every aspect of your being] as you teach [spiritual things] and admonish and train one another with all wisdom, singing psalms and hymns and spiritual songs with thankfulness in your hearts to God. Whatever you do [no matter what it is] in word or deed, do everything in the name of the Lord Jesus [and in dependence on Him], giving thanks to God the Father through Him. (Col 3:15–17, AMP)

The peace of Christ given by God's will is not pictured in the calm, pastoral scene of sheep by still waters. It is rather a picture of a raging river of life coursing between its banks through a mountain gorge across the open plains. There is deep-flowing, sure motivation that keeps surging in spite of the surface splashing of uncertainty. The winds of adversity can whip up the waves to whitecap ferocity, yet the river keeps moving by the force of the current. His peace in my heart is that current, assuring me that I am in the flow of his will.

Neal Pirolo is founder and director of Emmaus Road International (www. eri.org) and author of *I Think God Wants Me to be a Missionary, Serving as Senders Today, The Reentry Team,* and several other books. He and his wife, Yvonne, have been serving in ministry for over forty years.

Note

[1] Most material in this chapter was taken from Neal's book, *I Think God Wants Me to Be a Missionary* (San Diego: Emmaus Road International, 2015). Permission granted.

Connecting to the Pipeline

1. As a missionary mobilization team in your church, share how you have heard God's voice in the past or how you have sensed his call on your life.

2. Whether or not you know it, your church has a tradition and/or doctrine regarding how God speaks today. Sometimes we use terms like *general revelation* or *special revelation*. We may identify as cessationist or continuationist. You may be reading this from a Reformed theological viewpoint, a dispensational theological viewpoint, or any number of other theological perspectives. Take some time as a mobilization team to discover where your church stands on the issues of how God chooses to call people to the mission field. This will become very important as you process and interview candidates later on.

3. What are some common experiences that you read about in these missionary stories?

4. Discuss some ways your church can provide "quiet spaces" and "spiritual margin" in the lives of your future missionaries to hear from the Lord.

5. What is the difference between *call* and *clarity*?

6. Is *clarity* "to this place" and "for this purpose"?

7. Can we know *clarity*, or should we just accept the *call*?

Part 2

Obstacles: Learning to Overcome Hindrances to the Call

Newton's third law of physics, "For every action, there is an equal and opposite reaction," can be applied to our spiritual lives as well. If we advance toward fulfilling the Great Commission and seek to deploy people who are called by God to go and serve, then we can expect spiritual warfare to take place. Our enemy is not always blatant, but he is subtle and cunning.

In this section, we discuss potential obstacles to people hearing God's voice, and the first two may seem surprising—family and the church. Many times, these two entities represent obstacles for the same reasons: fear, misunderstanding God's purposes, focusing on the temporal instead of the eternal, pursuing what makes us happy instead of what makes us holy, etc.

We took a positive approach in regard to revealing obstacles in family objections, asking missionary parents and grandparents to describe what they did to raise their kids differently. However, our approach for revealing obstacles in the church is direct and head-on. Our desire is for readers to be informed, enlightened, and encouraged, but we also want to challenge the status quo. While there are many obstacles in addition to those we highlight here, these are consistently rated at the top of the list: family, church, finances, short-term trips diverting from long-term efforts, and underestimating the power of God in transforming the lives of his people.

CHAPTER 5
Family Objections

Parenting with a Purpose

Peggy Bright

For twenty years, I prayed for my daughter Abby to hear God's voice calling her to be a missionary. It seems like just yesterday she was born prematurely and the nurse shared with me the news that my newborn had some heart complications. The first time I saw Abby was through an incubator, all wrapped up in bandages, with tubes, wires, and monitors all around her. Only parts of her face were showing, but I remember that her skin was a mixture of bright red and dark blue. My prayer was very simple: "God, please save my baby and I will raise her to be used for your kingdom."

I can imagine that is similar to what Samson's mother and John the Baptist's mother prayed. They devoted their jobs as mothers to raise their children so that the Lord could use them in magnificent ways. That is what I wanted too. I always wanted to have children, but more than anything I wanted my child to have meaning and purpose beyond just living a good life.

I grew up on a farm in Nebraska. We had a good family and I loved my life there, even though we didn't have much money. Right after graduation I married my high school boyfriend. Kevin joined the military and we moved to Leavenworth, Kansas. Three years later he was discharged and we moved again . . . and again . . . and again—just trying to find work. I was able to get a decent job, but Kevin could never find anything long-term.

On our sixth wedding anniversary, Kevin was so distraught coming home after losing yet another job that he lost control of his vehicle and crashed into the center median of the interstate. Though he survived the crash, he suffered major brain damage and has been unable to care for himself during the many years since then. He lives in an assisted care facility and cannot recognize any of his friends or family.

Within a week of Kevin's accident, I found out I was pregnant with Abby. My life was changing and I had nothing to cling to except my faith. For all practical purposes, I was going to be a single mom. However, I was committed to raising Abby in a way that would honor my Father in heaven and that would help her understand that she has a purpose in this life.

Thank God for my church. They cared for me through difficult times and made sure that we were never in need. Abby didn't grow up with all the latest gadgets and toys. She wore hand-me-down clothes. We didn't have cable TV, or go to the movies on Friday nights, or eat out at fancy restaurants. But we had wonderful friends at church who made sure we were invited to holiday parties and other events through the years. When Abby discovered her love for soccer, our friends bought her a uniform, shoes, and equipment; and they even paid for lessons and a team membership.

The church was very active in the community, so Abby and I didn't just receive help but had opportunities to serve as well. One of the first things we signed up to do together was to serve in the food line at a homeless shelter when Abby was only five years old. She was barely big enough to set the tables before the clients arrived. Her job was to set out the plasticware. One of the volunteers taught her how to arrange the spoons, forks, and knives; and she was very diligent to stand on a chair and make sure the fork was on the left, the knife was on the right, and the spoon was next to the knife. Over the months and years that we did this together, Abby learned how to fold napkins and make creative designs. The soup kitchen was almost turned into a gourmet dining experience because she put so much care and attention into the place settings.

Abby became the "belle of the ball" to the homeless visitors. She spent time with them, talked to them, and even remembered their names, which is very important to those who live on the street. I'm afraid that most of us adults don't realize how important it is to get to know someone who is down and out by name. Abby was intuitive enough to know that although these people may have been dirty on the outside, they had enormous worth and value on the inside.

One day on our way to school we saw a homeless woman standing on the side of the road with a cardboard sign that said "New in town. Hungry. Please help." We didn't have any money to spare, but I wanted to teach Abby the lesson from Jesus' instructions to "Give to the one who begs from you, and do not refuse the one who would borrow from you" (Matt 5:42). So we invited Sarah to get in the car, and we took her to a fast-food place on the next block. We bought her a meal, got to hear her story of how she began living on the streets, and were able to tell her what resources were available in the area. We also prayed for her.

Yes, Abby was late to school. Yes, I invited a stranger into my car. Yes, we ate fast food. All of these things caused my friends and family to question my ability to make good decisions as a mother. But they needed to understand that I was raising my daughter for a purpose. There are more important things in a child's life than being on time for school one day—like being obedient to the words of Jesus, who wants us to feed the hungry. While safety and security are important for a mother to provide for her child, ministry to a stranger in need can have eternal rewards (Matt 25:34–40).

My first mission trip with Abby was to Honduras, where we served in an orphanage for a week, when she was twelve years old. In the mornings, we painted walls, cleaned bedding, and prepared meals. In the afternoons, we hosted a Bible camp for the kids and the community.

Abby really stepped into the role of a missionary even at her young age. She could have been out playing soccer with the kids, but she chose to stay with the volunteers as we worked on the building. She took an active role in preparing for the Bible lessons and in organizing the activities, which included a soccer camp. The kids in Honduras all played soccer with bare feet and worn-out balls. Even though they were really good at playing the game, Abby was able to teach them some fundamentals and lead them in practicing with drills.

The next year, as a thirteen-year-old, Abby was one of the leaders and took lots of initiative in planning the trip back to Honduras. She organized a collection drive to take athletic shoes, soccer balls, cones, and jerseys to the kids in the village. By the time she graduated from high school, Abby had traveled to six countries on mission trips and was very active in the leadership of the church youth group.

Abby just turned twenty years old and is about to graduate from Bible school with a degree in intercultural studies. She has already been visiting missionary sending agencies and trying to discern God's will for where she will go next. She has a heart for those who are hurting and wants to share the good news of Jesus with people who are unreached. Recently, I heard her talking about unengaged people groups in Central Asia and how she may be able to use her love for soccer to reach young people through sports outreaches.

Even though I raised Abby on purpose to be a missionary, the reality is just now beginning to set in that she will be leaving me soon. She has been my world for twenty years, and I will have to let her go.

We read in Scripture how Hannah raised Samuel—her only child at the time—to be used by God. We don't hear many sermons about parents who raise their children for a purpose. Sermons about loving your children, protecting them, and making sure they know the Lord are all well and good; but maybe we should hear more about raising children with the intention of sending them to live in hard places and do the Lord's work. I am sure Mary, the mother of Jesus, would agree with me.

Peggy Bright (pseudonym). Her daughter serves in a restricted access nation.

The Influence of a Grandparent

Fawn Brents

It was 1963. Every Sunday morning found me in the same row of chairs at Pleasant Grove Bible Church, usually standing between my grandparents, singing all five stanzas of a hymn from the Broadman Hymnal. On one side of me stood my grandmother, Eva, a petite four feet eleven, singing softly. Eva had a cleft palate. Because of her speech impediment, people couldn't understand the words she sang. But I did. And I knew she believed them. On my other side stood Grandpa Sid, towering at six feet two. He belted out every note and word of the hymn with confidence. He believed what he was singing, and his wholehearted delivery made me believe it too.

In that sheltered place, I felt like a small sapling planted between two giant oaks, protected and supported by the expectation that I would one day be like them. Memories like this anchored me through my parents' divorce and turbulent teens. And forty-three years later, when our first grandchild came along, I knew what grandparents were supposed to do.

In our early years of marriage, my husband, Charlie, and I served in Ecuador, South America, with Gospel Missionary Union. I remember the day I told my grandparents that God had called us to Ecuador. They were generous givers who had supported other workers. But my grandmother's response to our news was the revelation of a silent prayer that she had never shared with me. She said, "I have prayed that God would put it on your heart to someday serve him as a missionary."

Her answered prayer often gave me confidence of God's direction in the years that followed. Our four years in Ecuador gave us a passion for missions and a desire to pass it on to our fourteen grandchildren.

I've come to see that being a grandparent is a privilege that holds great responsibility. Charlie and I have an obligation to pass the truth of who God is on to our children and grandchildren. It is an investment of time and treasure, with the potential for big returns. Eternal ones. Our hope and prayer is that the generations that come after us will put their confidence in the Lord. If we miss this, we will have failed as grandparents.

Psalm 78:5–7 says:

He established a testimony in Jacob and appointed a law in Israel, which he commanded our fathers to teach to their children, that the next generation might know them, the children yet unborn, and arise and tell them to their children, so that they should set their hope in God and not forget the works of God, but keep his commandments.

The psalmist refers to "the children yet unborn." Sid and Eva did not know that when they were teaching me the ways of God, they were teaching their great-great-grandchildren what it looks like to follow Jesus.

In our living room, next to my favorite chair, sits a stack of important books and papers: my Bible, my journal, and prayer letters from missionaries around the world. It's where I start the day. When our grandkids spend the night, they curl up with me to begin their day in that chair—me with my coffee, them with a cup of something warm. In those early morning moments, I have their full attention. They love to hear a Bible story and look with me through my stack of most recent prayer letters. I tell them about faraway countries and people hungry to know about Jesus. They see the faces and hear stories of missionaries around the world. I'm praying that God uses these moments to open their hearts to follow Jesus whatever the cost.

We love to see our grandchildren come to visit, but the visits remind us why God gives children to the young. The same inquisitive mind that listens to my stories with rapt attention is thinking of a thousand things to do that all require endless energy. Gene Perret, writer and producer for *The Carol Burnett Show*, said it best: "On the seventh day God rested. His grandchildren must have been out of town."[1]

I know grandparents who have opted out. They have decided that it's too much work and they are too busy to spend time with their grandchildren. Today, grandparents are younger than ever before. The average age of a first-time grandmother in the US today is fifty years old.[2] For most grandparents, this is the prime of life. Earning income is at its highest, and as a young and often healthy empty nester there is freedom to travel and pursue new interests and even a second career. But in his book *Grandfathering: Live to Leave a Legacy*, Dr. Dan Erickson offers this warning: "Do not fear failure; fear you would spend your life succeeding at what does not matter."[3] Grandparenting matters.

Being an engaged grandparent will disrupt your routine, make your house messy, and leave you exhausted after an overnight visit. But it's worth it. Someone once said, "All you get to take to heaven with you is the Word of God and the souls of men." The temporal for the eternal is a good trade. I want my grandchildren to see what it looks like to live a life of faith in the living God. I'm far from perfect, but God doesn't require perfection, just faithfulness and a little creativity.

Twice a year I visit an orphanage we support in Guatemala. Our personal involvement with the children there has provided a connection to missions for our grandchildren. Twelve years old is the magic age when each of our grandchildren get to go and visit the children at Casa de Mi Padre, in Santa Cruz del Quiche.

Our oldest grandson, Tayven, was the first to be commissioned from our family. This year is Emma's turn. Next year Andrew. After that it will be Samantha, then Adrey, Evey, and Jessa. The excitement of commissioning the last grandchild fuels anticipation for the next. Thanks to photographs and Facebook, they know the names and personal stories of each orphan. Our hope is that at an early age this generation will catch the vision for overseas missions. We are clearing a path and planting seeds that we trust will bear good fruit.

In preparation for the trip, the children select a verse that expresses what they hope God will do in their lives during the trip. We suggest an age-appropriate book to carry on the plane that gives them fresh thoughts to meditate on from God's Word. We instruct them to bring a journal to write down what God teaches them while they are there. And we ask them to be prepared to give their testimony while they are there and also in church when they return.

This year the other grandchildren are writing notes to the kids at the orphanage, and Emma will deliver letters of encouragement from our other grandchildren. Emma is our missionary, sent out from our family this summer. Mom, Dad, aunts, uncles, cousins, and siblings are praying for her. We are praying that Emma's life will be forever changed.

While the long-term results of our family-sending experiment are not in yet, the investment looks promising. We are watching the next generation put their hope in God. They are learning to give, to pray, and to go.

Fawn Brents and her husband, Charlie, served with Gospel Missionary Union in Ecuador for four years. She has been a real estate broker-officer with Kansas City Real Estate for over twenty years.

Notes
1 Gene Perret, www.azquotes.com/author/91716-Gene_Perret.
2 American Grandparents Association, www.grandparents.com/money-and-work/saving-and-investing/the-power-of-the-grandparent-economy
3 Dr. Dan Erickson, *Grandfathering: Live to Leave a Legacy* (Grand Rapids, MI: Credo, 2014).

CHAPTER 6

The Church

A Missional Heresy

David J. Wilson

"We Are All Missionaries—Right?"

We often hear this from people who should know better: elders, deacons, pastors, and even some missionaries themselves. The truth is, we are not all missionaries. As Christ-followers, we are all called to be witnesses. However, some are called to do ministry locally while others are called to do missions elsewhere.

Just to explain, I'm not interested in endorsing the overuse and abuse of titles. When we get to heaven, there will be little need for titles, so I don't believe we should spend much time clinging to earthly titles here. However, we need to have a clear understanding of words, because words have meaning. There are consequences to the church and to the worldwide expansion of gospel. As you read this, take a moment to ask for discernment from the Lord to see if there have been any carelessness and misrepresentation of the Lord's work in the church.

In this section of *Pipeline*, we are highlighting potential obstacles to God's people hearing his voice calling them to be missionaries. We will look at this misunderstanding practically and biblically. We will also explore some of the root causes for this misuse of the word *missionary* so that we will know how to handle the next person who makes this proclamation.

The problem in misusing the word *missionary* in the church is that there is a dumbing down of what it means. To explain this simply, let's consider the use of titles as it relates to other professions. Just because you give someone an aspirin for their headache doesn't make you a doctor. Nor are you a baseball coach when you shout criticism at a pitcher during a ballgame. Why would we call someone a missionary who simply shares their faith with a neighbor or coworker or maybe does a few good deeds for strangers down the street? It's like saying "I am a car" just because I am hanging out in my garage.

As evangelical believers, we would agree that all Christians should be actively sharing their faith and serving people in their community, workplace, and church. Paul tells us in Ephesians 4:11 that God called some to be apostles, some to be prophets, some to be evangelists, and some to be pastors and teachers. Therefore we see that there are a variety of different roles—and yes, even titles—for people to fulfill within the body of Christ. As we will see later, the title of *missionary* developed later in the progression of the church to fulfill a specific need and task, just like the roles of evangelists, pastors, and teachers. For a full examination of the word *apostle*, see Denny Spitters and Matthew Ellison's work in *When Everything Is Missions* regarding how the term relates to the missionary-sending enterprise.[1]

The term *mission* is not found in Scripture, yet its concept permeates both the Old and the New Testament. The Latin word *missionem* means "the act of sending" and was first used to describe Christian activity in 1598 when the Jesuits sent members abroad to set up centers for Christian work in other cultures. The word *missionary*, therefore, comes from this root as "one who is sent."

This is an important distinction for a clear understanding of the word *missionary*. If someone claims to be a missionary, yet doesn't have a church or sending agency, can they truly be a missionary—one who is sent? Sent by whom? The word itself demands that they be *commissioned, ordained, accountable to, and under the authority* of some sanctioned or approved entity. Some would say that they are *sent by God*, which is correct, but the New Testament teaches us in Acts 13:1–3 that God confirms the call of missionaries (Paul and Barnabas in this case) through the authority that he gives to the church.

For a brief synopsis, the word *mission* implies a task in which God sends a person whom he has called to introduce another group of people to salvation in Christ. The word *missionary* describes the person who is sent. The mission of the church is to deploy missionaries into all parts of the world until everyone has the opportunity to hear and respond to the message of Jesus. This is the basis of the Great Commission.

'' The mission of the church is to deploy missionaries into all parts of the world until everyone has the opportunity to hear and respond to the message of Jesus. This is the basis of the Great Commission. **''**

Before Jesus gave us the Great Commission, we have a few examples of God's people in the Old Testament hearing and responding to the Lord's call to serve those in other nations:

- Abraham—to be a blessing to all people on earth
- Jeremiah—to be a prophet to all nations
- Jonah—sent to call the people of Nineveh to repentance

These are unique Old Testament figures, because they are "sent ones." Other Old Testament figures were operating from a model based on attraction, or what theologians would call "centripetal." This means that the people of Israel were to serve as a magnet and as an example for all to "come and see." Isaiah instructed Israel to be a "light to the Gentiles." The primary vision and mission was that the world was expected to come to Israel to receive salvation, but Israel was not necessarily sent out to the world.

This all changed in the New Testament, when a new mission was birthed to be an outward vision and focus, theologically known as "centrifugal." God sets up the first "sending agency," the church, which replaced the nation of Israel as the keeper and protector and proclaimer of the gospel. Jesus gives this entity a mandate to do four things:

- go into all the world
- make disciples
- baptize in the name of the Father, Son, and Holy Spirit
- teach disciples to obey all he has commanded

The change is made from a "come and see" salvation to a "go and tell" proclamation of redemption and forgiveness of sins. This Great Commission mandate is not optional and represents the last instructions given by the Lord Jesus. To seal the instructions, he promised that he would be with the church until the end of the age.

Paul and Barnabas are prime examples of missionaries who were called by God and sent out by the church in Antioch. We see in Acts 13:1–3 that

God spoke through the Holy Spirit to the church leaders concerning these missionaries:

> Now there were in the church at Antioch prophets and teachers, Barnabas, Simeon who was called Niger, Lucius of Cyrene, Manaen a lifelong friend of Herod the tetrarch, and Saul. While they were worshiping the Lord and fasting, the Holy Spirit said, "Set apart for me Barnabas and Saul for the work to which I have called them." Then after fasting and praying they laid their hands on them and sent them off.

Paul and Barnabas were sent out as "prototype missionaries" from the church at Antioch. This is one of the few passages of Scripture that give us vivid clarity on the differences between missionaries and church leaders such as apostles, prophets, evangelists, pastors, and teachers (Eph 4:11) and others mentioned in passages such as 1 Corinthians 12. Here we see three important elements that go into the missionary calling. First, missionaries are called by God to a particular task. Paul and Barnabas were set aside for the task that the Lord had called them to. Second, God confirmed this calling to the church leaders. This sending entity, the church at Antioch, heard from the Lord directly and was instructed by God to set them apart for the task. Third, the church took responsibility and accountability for them by commissioning them with fasting, praying, laying on of hands, and then providing for their needs when they sent them off.

The task is a primary consideration when we begin to understand the importance of the work of a missionary. There are "means" and there are "ends." There is a wide variety of means in mission work. The modern missionary is creative, innovative, and daring. There are endless possibilities to adapt, improvise, and overcome the obstacles that are set before cross-cultural global workers. Missionaries must gain access to countries that are closed. They should provide value to their new communities. They are constantly seeking ways to bridge the gaps of culture and contextualize their message to fit an ever-changing world. Some choose to conduct business as mission. Others will work through social justice causes. Many are engaged in Bible translation work. And still others will target a specific group of people like Hindus, Arabs, college students, human traffickers, prisoners, etc.

Paul and Barnabas were sent to reach people who were not only far from God but far from the church in Antioch. And they were very different from those church leaders who were sending people on this mission journey. They had a different language, different heritage, different culture, and different ways of thinking. They were different in practically every way, and these ancient missionaries had to adapt, improvise, and overcome in every way as well.

The means are varied, but the ends are very specific . . . which brings us back to the Great Commission of our Lord Jesus:

- go into all the world
- make disciples
- baptize in the name of the Father, Son, and Holy Spirit
- teach disciples to obey all he has commanded

This is the mission of the church. Regardless of the method, whether you make disciples to plant a church or plant a church to make disciples—the "ends" are far more important than the "means." God spoke directly to the church leaders at Antioch and made them primary participants in this missionary endeavor.

We should see that this is a serious work that required much thought, prayer, support, recognition, and endorsement by more than just the individual. Mission work is a communal effort, and that is often blurred and corrupted by our modern Western culture that places a high value on individuality. In some mission circles and churches there is a tendency to celebrate the lone trailblazer and self-made pioneer who goes out all alone to accomplish a task. Biblically, however, we are taught to serve alongside one another and on behalf of the church. As the African proverb states, "If you want to go fast, go alone. If you want to go far, go together."

So, according to this passage, can someone call themselves a missionary if they are not sent by some authorized entity like the church? Can they truly be on mission if their primary task is anything other than making disciples of those who are unreached? Perhaps a more critical and strategic question for tomorrow's missionaries to ask is this: What is the difference between people who are unreached and those who are unengaged with the gospel?

Missionaries are called to go to difficult places, exchanging what they know for something they do not know. They cross barriers: national borders, cultural differences, language procurement, and even socioeconomic variations. They study for years and acquire experience that qualifies them for a specific type of work. They must learn a new language, adapt to a new culture, sell their belongings, and move their family to places that are often hostile to their presence. Sacrifice is the predominant trait, because many times their families suffer as a result of their calling.

The children of North American missionaries often leave the sterile, secure learning environment of their Western schools for substandard schools in the Majority World. Aging parents are sometimes left in need of care while the missionary is far from home. Home visits are infrequent and generally are not a vacation, but rather what is now being called "home assignment," where the agency expects them to be on speaking tours to inform supporters of their activities.

When on the field, missionaries are held accountable for their actions by the church and their agency. They set goals, which must be measurable and are evaluated for their effectiveness. They are grouped into teams for support and encouragement. This is more than just being Christ's representatives. They have assignments, tasks, duties, and a "mission" for which they are responsible.

For someone to say that "We are all missionaries" is to bring disrespect to the memory of an American doctor who served for thirty years in Afghanistan and lost his life in 2010 when a group of Taliban hijacked his convoy heading out to treat patients in a remote village. His wife still lives there and brings hope and heart-wrenching forgiveness to people who are far from God.

Who can compare themselves to Jim Elliot, who surrendered his life on a river beach in the jungles of Ecuador in 1956? And even more so, can there be such a thing as a "local missionary" when compared to Jim's wife, Elisabeth, who decided to stay and work toward reconciliation with the natives that took her husband's life so that they could receive the gospel?

What about Hudson Taylor, David Livingstone, William Carey, and all the early missionaries who packed their belongings in their coffin because they were leaving on a steamer to travel for weeks and even months to arrive at their final destination? They knew they wouldn't be coming back home, but they endured much hardship so that the gospel could be proclaimed to the ends of the earth. When someone says "We are all missionaries," do you see this kind of sacrifice in their lives?

Today, many missionaries spend much of their time trying to get visas for their ministry post. Rather than going to school for Bible degrees, they study for a trade that will earn them business visas to restricted access nations (RANs). Real missionaries encounter an intentional lifestyle change because they know God has called them to do something very special, something that is different from most other people. Yes, all Christians are called to do "ministry," but not all are called to be "missionaries." Ministry is done locally in our Jerusalem and Judea. Mission is done globally in our Samaria and to the ends of the earth (Acts 1:8).

The word *missionary* is easily abused for a variety of reasons: pride, arrogance, profit, naïveté, ignorance—sometimes even for financial gain. We all know that people will be more likely to give money if it is for missions.

In the church, money is a huge issue. Just imagine, if we are all missionaries and if everything is missions, then it would be logical to take funds from the mission budget to build the playground at the church. How can this happen? The explanation is easy; 51 percent of the people who live in your community are from other countries and you need a place to invite them and their children to play. Certainly you have heard people say, "Why do we need to go to *them*, when *they* are coming to *us*?" That means that the funds will now go to enlarging your local church instead of expanding the kingdom of God in places like Yemen, Bhutan, Laos, or West Africa. The warning here is that the institutional church, just like the humans who inhabit it, will always take the path of least resistance unless its leaders fully surrender to the hard work of obedience to the call of God and the Great Commission.

Matthew Ellison tells a story about a children's pastor in a church in Portland, Oregon, who gave an announcement about a short-term mission trip to an "unreached people group." The price and convenience was very attractive—free, and no need for a passport, flight, hotel, or time off work. The pastor explained, "They're right here, in our basement! We need your help with the children's ministry. Come join us and reach this unreached people group."[2]

This is not just about semantics. This represents real abuse, with real world problems, which affects the eternal destinies of billions of people around the world who have no relevant access to the gospel of Jesus Christ.

Other abuses of the missionary title come from people who just want recognition or notoriety—a baptized form of Christian pride. For those who are uninformed, the title of *missionary* conjures up feelings of mystery, intrigue, and clandestine adventures of Christians trudging through the jungles, smuggling Bibles, and surviving major hardships. To draw a secular example, it could be compared to someone claiming to be a secret agent, spy, or even a special operator in the military. The person is seeking a form of attention that is not duly earned.

And for some, the abuse comes from plain ignorance. Very few people sit down and consider their words and the effects they may have. In the church, we give license and grace in good measure. When it comes to doctrine and theology, we have clear lines that help us understand God better, the world better, and our purpose in life better; but outside of that we are a little inconsistent in our practice of faith. If we are going to be serious about the Great Commission, the last words and mandate of our Lord, then we need to shore up our understanding of how we will be making Christ known among the nations.

Missionaries are professionals who have a calling, a task to accomplish, an authority structure for accountability, and a message to proclaim to the world. We need to see them in the same way we see medical professionals who earn degrees and seek board certification, attorneys who pass the bar exam and are held accountable to strict legal standards, and educators who must be employed through institutions that maintain a high level of accreditation.

A good evangelical will understand the concept of "the priesthood of all believers"—that every Christ-follower has been called by God to be "a witness." The Lord has also empowered every believer with the Holy Spirit. In fact, according to Acts 1:4 and 1:8, the early disciples were not to go out into the world until the Holy Spirit had come upon them. Some were called to go and do mission, some were called to stay and do ministry, but all were called to "witness."

Let's be satisfied with the distinction between "ministry" and "mission" and not try to exalt one over the other. The purpose of this chapter is to identify distinctions between the words we sometimes carelessly use and to help the church give honor to whom honor is due. Paul, our model missionary, is the one who said:

> And he gave the apostles, the prophets, the evangelists, the shepherds
> and teachers, to equip the saints for the work of ministry, for building
> up the body of Christ, until we all attain to the unity of the faith
> and of the knowledge of the Son of God, to mature manhood, to the
> measure of the stature of the fullness of Christ, so that we may no

longer be children, tossed to and fro by the waves and carried about by every wind of doctrine, by human cunning, by craftiness in deceitful schemes. Rather, speaking the truth in love, we are to grow up in every way into him who is the head, into Christ, from whom the whole body, joined and held together by every joint with which it is equipped, when each part is working properly, makes the body grow so that it builds itself up in love. (Eph 4:11–16)

Next time you hear a pastor or church leader say, "We are all missionaries," don't just go along in agreement, but take a moment to talk about your favorite missionary in a distant land whom you support and share with them a recent newsletter that talks about their work. You may just be unveiling the true implication of the Great Commission for the first time. Invite them to join you in supporting that person or others who need to raise their support to complete their task. And then, as you are leaving the church, stop and take down that sign that says "You are now entering the mission field." Clichés and platitudes can do more harm than good.

David J. Wilson served in the local church as mission pastor for over twenty years. In November 2016, he joined Avant Ministries in Kansas City, MO, as director of church relations.

Notes

[1] Denny Spitters and Matthew Ellison, *When Everything Is Missions* (Orlando: Bottomline Media, 2017) 70.

[2] Ibid., 100.

CHAPTER 7

Money

Five Keys to Raising Support[1]

Dr. Steve Shadrach

"I want to serve God and be obedient to his leading in my life, but I don't want to RAISE SUPPORT!"

If you have said or thought these words, you're not alone. In fact, most people living a donor-supported lifestyle will admit that at one time they probably had feelings much like this. Although the choice to live and minister on support may not be a popular one in North America, where independence is a high value, it is required if you are going to work for many Christian ministries or mission agencies. For those who are surrendered to the will of God in their lives, it isn't a question of whether you will raise support but of whether you will be obedient. When that question is answered, support raising just becomes one aspect of the job that God is calling you to in obedience.

Yes, starting from scratch and putting together your support is a huge challenge, but many people have come to see it as a real blessing. Even though stresses and pressures are involved in raising and maintaining a personal-support team, I wouldn't want to live any other way! The bonds I have formed over the years with our supporters are priceless. The stories of God building my faith during difficult times could fill a book. And most of all, I have reported to ministry assignments with a sense of destiny and authority. Why? Because I (and sixty-plus donors) have paid a dear price to get me to that ministry. I had better take it seriously and give it my all. That's real accountability.

> For those who are surrendered to the will of God in their lives, it isn't a question of whether you will raise support but of whether you will be obedient. When that question is answered, support raising just becomes one aspect of the job that God is calling you to in obedience.

As church leaders, you will be helping missionaries decide the best way to fund their ministry. Should they be a "tentmaker" and work a job while ministering, or should they raise part or all of their personal support? Both are biblical, but if they're going to raise support they will probably have some doubts, fears, and questions. Assure them with these words: "YOU ARE NORMAL!" I still get stomach butterflies each time I pick up the phone to make a support appointment.

If missionary candidates want to be successful, they are going to need some guidance. I've listed five keys to raising a personal-support team. This is one of the most exciting adventures (i.e., roller-coaster rides) that I have ever experienced, so you are in a great position to help them hold on tight!

The Five Keys to Raising Your Personal Support

1. **Understand the Biblical Basis.** Take some time to study the Scriptures for yourself so you will know exactly what God thinks about asking others to give to you and to your ministry. Some choose just to pray and trust God to bring the funds in. The great George Muller did this to support his orphanages in nineteenth-century London. But it is just as biblical and requires as much or more faith to personally invite others to invest. Either way, we have to understand that God is the source of our funds, not the donors or our plans or hard work.

   Scott Morton of The Navigators, in his excellent book *Funding Your Ministry*, highlights five examples and teachings from the Old and New Testaments about the validity of God's ministers being supported by others:

   A. The example of the Levites (Num 18:24)—The Israelites gave their tithes to the priests for support.

   B. The example of Jesus (Luke 8:2,3)—Many people supported Jesus and the disciples.

C. The teaching of Jesus (Matt 10:9,10)—A kingdom worker is worthy of his support.

D. The example of Paul (Acts 18:3–5)—He stopped working as a tentmaker to preach full time on support.

E. The teaching of Paul (1 Cor 9:1–18)—He had the right to be supported by the churches.

Once you have a biblical perspective on this topic of asking for and living on the support of others, check one more thing: Evaluate your own giving. Before you can ask anyone else to give, you have to be committed to investing sacrificially in kingdom work on a regular basis. Let's practice what we preach!

2. **Kill the Giants in Your Own Mind.** Remember the twelve Hebrew spies who went into the Promised Land to take a look before the whole nation was to enter and claim what God had given them? Only Joshua and Caleb came back ready to invade. The other ten spies were so terrified of the giants they saw in the land that they confessed, "We became like grasshoppers in our own sight, and so we were in their sight" (Num 13:33, NASB). Instead of trusting God and moving out with courage, they let fear paralyze them. How they viewed themselves affected how the giants viewed them.

It is the same with support raising. The confidence level we have in our God, our vision, and ourselves can make us—or break us! All of us have different "giants" in our own minds that will keep us from beginning and persevering in the process of assembling a full support team. These are some common "giants" we must conquer:

A. Missionary candidates might think support raising is really just begging.

B. They might think they don't represent a worthy investment.

C. They might think support raising is just a "necessary evil" that must be endured.

D. They might think people are rejecting *them* (or their ministry) if they say no.

You must kill these giants one at a time as you fill your mind with the Scriptures and believe what God has said about you and your calling. Then you can courageously march in and take the land! Just as God had prepared the land for the people simply to go in and take it, we need to believe that God has prepared the hearts of the donors and we need to walk boldly in faith to find those givers and ask them to join us in our vision.

3. **Pray and Plan Well.**

   A. **Pray.** Author S. D. Gordon said it well, "Prayer is the real work of the ministry. Service is just gathering in the results of prayer."[2] We need to bathe ourselves and our donors in prayer before, during, and after this support-raising journey. God will go before you. He will also build a love for your donors as you pray for them individually.

   B. **Create Your Budget.** Include everything you need for your personal needs, giving, saving, and ministry expenses. Seek to balance a lifestyle that will allow you to maximize your effectiveness with the people you're reaching, but also be above reproach from your donors regarding the stewardship of your finances. If you happen to have school debt, simply include the required monthly amount owed and keep going. Your donors will admire you for keeping your promise to pay it back. Plan on and commit to raising at least 100 percent of your budget *before* you even report to your assignment. Have a "*when* I raise my support" attitude, not an "*if* I raise my support" attitude.

   C. **Namestorm.** Now that you have turned the whole process over to God, you are ready to begin your planning. Write down *every* person you have ever known during your lifetime. Don't play Holy Spirit by saying, "Oh, that person would never give." You'll be surprised by a few who will give—and by a few who won't! Also, think of people who have a heart for student work, missions, or whatever group or area you are targeting. List churches, Sunday school classes, foundations, and corporations. The bulk of your support, though, will come from the individuals you've spent time with over the years.

   D. **Map Out a Plan.** Divide up all the people according to the cities they live in. Then label each person "hot," "cold," or "medium" depending upon whether they probably *will* give, they probably *won't* give, or they *might* give. Next, pray and attach an amount that you would like to ask them to give. Don't use a one-size-fits-all plan; instead, base the amount on what you perceive they are able and willing to give along with the kind of relationship you have with them. You might feel more comfortable suggesting a range of giving rather than a specific amount. Either way, know that the tendency for most support-raisers is to ask for too little, not too much. Remember, there is no cash-flow problem in heaven. Americans give billions of dollars to charity each year. I believe God has instilled in every person a desire to give, and you are simply helping them invest in eternal things, and thus build up their treasure in heaven. Go for it!

E. **Plan Out a Map.** Figure out what city you will go to first, second, etc. Schedule it out on your calendar. If you want to send a letter in advance telling people what you are doing and that you will be calling, do it. But the key is to call each person in advance of the trip in order to set up an appointment. During the call, don't let them say yes or no to giving—your only objective is to make an appointment with them. Seek to line up all of your "hot" prospects first, your "medium" prospects next, and finally (if you still need more appointments) the "cold" prospects.

4. **Ask Them Face-to-face.** This is the key. James 4:2b says "You do not have because you do not ask God" (NIV). The word *ask* is used in the Gospels 113 times. God wants to teach us about asking—him and others. I have looked at surveys regarding *why* people give, and the number one reason is always because someone asked. It's not unspiritual or fleshly to ask. It is good, biblical, and faith-building to ask. Let's not hide behind our fears. Let's walk toward them and render them powerless! The worst thing people can say is no.

If you choose instead to cut corners, take the quick, easy route, and just send out a fund-request letter or make a group presentation, you might have a 10 percent response rate. If you send a letter followed by a phone call asking for support, you might get 25 percent of people to say yes. But if you are willing to sit down eyeball-to-eyeball with others and lay out the incredible ministry vision God has given you, usually well over half of the folks pull out their checkbooks to join you as ministry partners!

This approach takes time and money and courage, but it communicates to the donor that they (and your vision) are so important to you that you must meet with them in person. Don't be fooled: *How* you go about securing their commitment will determine the amount, consistency, and longevity of their giving. My research shows that ministries that train their staff to ask for the gift (in person) raise their full budget in half the time of groups that simply share the need but don't ask. We have not—because we ask not. Sound familiar?

5. **Cultivate the Relationship.** Here are the ABCs for having a long and fruitful relationship with your supporters:

A. Remember, it's not fund-raising, but "friend-raising." You can have an incredible ministry in the lives of donors, and you might be their only connection to Jesus Christ or the Great Commission.

B. Consider tithing your ministry time to your support team: prayer, writing, calling, ministering.

C. Thank before you bank (when a new person or new gift comes in). Be prompt and professional in all of your correspondence and record keeping.

D. Regularly mail, or email, well-written newsletters. Share how your donors' investments are paying off, along with some specific prayer requests. Occasional postcards, phone calls, texts, and visits are great too. Beware: The main reason people drop off of support teams is because they don't hear from their missionary.

E. Win, Keep, Lift. When you win a donor, they are now on your team. Keep them on the team by caring for them and cultivating them. Periodically, ask them to consider lifting (increasing) their monthly or annual gift to you. Cru had a campaign years ago in which they asked people to give one million dollars to their ministry. Almost 250 people said yes! Research showed, though, that the very first gift that each person had made to the ministry years earlier had been, on average, a mere ten dollars! Someone had taken the time to win, keep, and (over the years) lift them.

People will stick with you for life if you appreciate them and keep them informed. View them as vital partners in your ministry and you will gain not only life-long supporters, but friends too. One day you will turn around and realize how blessed you have been and that you wouldn't want to live any other way. Trust God and begin this exciting adventure today. You will never regret it!

Dr. Steve Shadrach is the executive director of the Center for Mission Mobilization, (www.mobilization.org), and the founder of Support Raising Solutions, (www.supportraisingsolutions.org). These organizations train Christian workers all over the world how to raise personal-support teams.

Notes

[1] Much of this chapter has been taken from Steve Shadrach, *The God Ask: A Fresh, Biblical Approach to Personal Support Raising* (Fayetteville AR: CMM Press, 2016). Permission granted.

[2] S. D. Gordon, *Quiet Talks on Prayer* (Echo Library, 2007).

CHAPTER 8

Short-term Mission Trip Strategy

Train and Debrief for Short-term Trips

Kendra Cervantes

If you have picked up this book, you are on a journey that is beyond the average lay person. You have probably read other missiological books, know about the lives of famous missionaries, and may have had training in leading short-term trips. I am no missiologist, but my story is the reason why it is crucial that you do more than read these types of books—that you truly invest in the lives of each individual whom you direct on to a short-term team.

What about training? Oh, the missionary will do that when they get there, right? Wrong! Let's get real. If we do have some sort of training in place, it consists of a few disorganized meetings, handing out a journal, telling them to have a three-minute, five-minute, and fifteen-minute (for those who *really* care) story of their time overseas, throwing a pizza party when they get back, and looking at some funny pictures.

You never know what someone is going through until you ask. You never know what they are thinking, or what moves their heart, until you treat them as a real human being with true emotions, fears, a history, a future, and a soul. As mobilizers and church leaders, we are responsible to be a proactive resource to real people, and to facilitate their training and debriefing processes.

From concrete mixing to mime evangelism, my journey is more common than you think.

> As mobilizers and church leaders, we are responsible to be a proactive resource to real people, and to facilitate their training and debriefing processes.

My Journey

13 As I sat on my couch at thirteen years old, sick with the flu, I read my Bible. It was then that I, someone who had been in church since the age of eight, first grasped what Jesus did on the Cross. Later that year, after going on my first mission trip, I fell farther from the Lord than I ever imagined. I was ashamed and embarrassed. How could I sin, but have had such an amazing time serving Jesus in Mexico? I thought I had been called, but maybe that was a mistake. "Surely missionaries don't fall into sin like this," I concluded.

12 I was number twelve in line at the Departamento de Trámite de la Dirección Nacional de Migración in Uruguay. I stuck tight to my team leader's wife as she barreled through the crowd to find our way to the waiting area. The room felt like it was closing in on me, like I had blinked my eyes and was in a dream. I sat on the hard, plastic bucket chair, my head spinning trying to grasp how this place, filled with chaos, had anything to do with my residence in the country as a missionary.

I spoke so little Spanish, and had no idea what was next. I was fearful and felt alone, all the while being surrounded by my teammates who seemed to be taking everything in stride. I couldn't be the weak one; I couldn't say that this was making me confused and unsure. I had to process on my own. While I had *incredible* team leaders, something inside me, some sort of identity shame, told me to keep it in. I had a Spanish last name after all, Cervantes . . . and I couldn't speak the language of the most famous Spanish writer, Miguel de Cervantes.

11 Proverbs 25:11 says "A word fitly spoken is like apples of gold in a setting of silver." Jennifer poured her wisdom into us. After serving for two months in Guatemala, she saw that a friend and I were struggling with leaving Central America. In a casual conversation, she asked us if we were OK, and we had the courage to tell her we weren't. She gave us question after question to process, not taken from any book but from her life experience living abroad. She cared and didn't want us to experience shock when we came home.

After returning to campus, neither my friend nor I wanted to speak to anyone else; no one had lived through what we did. We withdrew for a couple of weeks from any meaningful conversation, trying mentally and spiritually to unpack everything we had lived through. Eventually, with no help from any human being around us, we started leveling out again. I was never the same after that; I had changed forever, but no one who knew me could see it on the outside. My soul bore a scar, a deep spiritual scar that nine years later is still hard to describe.

Ten puzzle pieces. At a cross-cultural training center, I sat on the floor in my group counseling class with a puzzle I had made as part of an exercise to share the most hurtful parts of our lives with our group. We had to process; we had to get it out. Ten puzzle pieces was all it took to silence the room. After pouring out my heart, the room sat silent. Why couldn't one missionary—many of whom were mobilizers, former church leaders, or on-field missionaries—help me process what I shared? The silence that day in the counseling room was deafening.

Nine days was all it took, after she returned home from Africa, to get an enormous tattoo of the continent on her side—a tattoo that stretched from her armpit to her waist. Nine days changed her life forever. Nine days! While this wasn't me, what was this girl going through that she made a decision based on nine days that will change her life forever?

At 8 PM I received a text message from my dad. A business card from the FBI had been left for me. I had received word to call the office and speak with someone in "CT." I thought it was a joke, but after we did some checking with the police, we learned it was not a joke. I was told I was on a terrorist kill list. WHAT?! WHO, WHEN, WHERE, WHY, HOW? . . . How? . . . short-term trips. Do we stop to count the cost? I mean, we say we do, but do we? Do we realize our responsibility in sending out missionaries to handle matters of life or their own possible death?

Seven classes a day. I taught seven classes a day back-to-back for two months while in my internship. Seven classes . . . it was a lot! Edith was there, seventy-seven-year-old Edith. She sat with me; she asked questions; she told me it was unhuman not to cry; she said, "Let it out, kid." Edith was really there. Edith knew how important it was to help me process.

Six trips to Mexico. During those six trips I was pulled over by the police, forced to pay a bribe, screamed at, confronted by a gang, cut by a piece of glass, scared for the life of a child, and hospitalized after getting a parasite from pork tacos. Not once over those six trips did our team have meaningful follow-up when we returned home. Fourteen years later, if I think hard enough, I can feel the depth of the needle injected into my body that helped me stop vomiting.

Five months was all it took for the Camino Global mobilizer to convince me to join the agency for long-term service. In five months, this mobilizer changed the next five years of my life.

Four adults who no longer speak to each after serving in Africa together for two weeks on a church trip.

Three demonic nightmares that literally brought me to my knees.

Two hours later my former youth leader called me back; she had called my bluff. She bought me a plane ticket and paid for my registration. Was I really going to the Urbana Missions Conference? But I was damaged goods. What could the Lord want with this nineteen-year-old's life that he couldn't find in someone much more spiritually qualified?

One heart completely devoted to the work of Jesus. One missions success story who statistically shouldn't be here today. One short-termer who still thinks back to her very first trip and how she could have done better. One woman who through it all never had any formal short-term mission training or debriefing.

We all come with an immense amount of baggage, no matter how colorless we believe our testimonies to be. And so do our short-termers. We grab an unsuspecting student or follow up on an email, and, in many cases, change a life completely. As mobilizers we are stewards, doorkeepers to an exciting world that can lead to great spiritual success—or deep spiritual pain. Will you be the church leader or mobilizer who joins the ranks of the hundreds of the well-meaning mission leaders whom I have interacted with over the last twenty years who says little to nothing, or will you put into practice the things that you have learned even if your agency or church isn't?

Kendra Cervantes served with Camino Global on a church planting team in Montevideo, Uruguay, for two years. In 2012 she joined the staff of her church as office manager and later as director of mission, sending out over one hundred short-term missionaries and overseeing the church's partnership with missionary families and organizations. She has since served as the director of communications for a pregnancy resource center and now as an office manager.

CHAPTER 9
Inadequate Assessment Processes

Least Likely to Succeed

David J. Wilson

Thinking back on my days as a teenager, I recall a section in my high school yearbook called "Senior Superlatives." This is where predictions were made on the future of select students based upon their past performance in school. Some serious students were celebrated as "most likely to succeed" and become a doctor, lawyer, engineer, etc. Others who were known for their kindness and nurturing spirit received recognition for being "most likely to get married and start a family" or "most likely to join the Peace Corps and save Ethiopia from a famine." Yet other superlatives were more comical and even sarcastic, like "most likely to get lost in his own house" or "most likely to fall *up* a flight of stairs."

In our fallen humanity, even as adults we often judge people and put them into categories that fit our own bias and preconceived ideas about how they will either succeed or fail in life, work, and ministry. Sometimes we use reason, science, and research methods to justify and analyze people. Personality tests like the Myers-Briggs Type Indicator have become standard conversation starters at Christian conferences. (I am an INTJ, by the way.) When someone asks, "What are your spiritual gifts?" we all know to recite the top three gifts that appeared on the inventory we took a couple years ago. And when we go into a job interview, we should be prepared to provide the results of our most recent "StrengthsFinder" assessment.

One of the obstacles that exists within the context of the sending agency and the church is that some missionary candidates are overlooked because they don't fit the prescribed mold of what we think a missionary ought to look like or act like. Looking for the ideal candidate, we rely heavily on personality tests, psychological evaluations, and leadership profiles, all of which are very good things. However, we must realize that although these are helpful tools of evaluation that measure human ideals, they don't necessarily take God's ideals into consideration.

In his enduring work, "Predictors of Missionary Success," Dr. William G. Britt revealed some surprising results as he studied cross-cultural workers, missionaries, Peace Corps volunteers, and military personnel to determine a portrait of a successful missionary.[1] Just as one illustrative example, predictor number nine in Britt's work deals with the concept of social poise. Workers who were found to exhibit a high degree of social poise were observed to be less successful in a cross-cultural setting, according to the study. Those who exhibited a lower degree of poise in social situations in their home culture were rated more successful overseas.

In his chapter in the book *Mind the Gaps: Engaging the Church in Missionary Care*, Britt states: "Perhaps applicants who impressed referents enough to be marked high on social poise were a bit too fastidious for a different culture where American cultural norms and expectations were not observed."[2]

One might conclude that if someone is called by God to be a missionary in a "foreign" culture, then the Lord has uniquely gifted that person to fit within a different cultural milieu and not necessarily be seen as "poised" within their culture of origin. As we look at missionary candidates, we can apply this principle to other areas of the person's life. This is not intended to discount evaluation methods and tools, but merely to open the possibility for churches and agencies to be sensitive to the work of the Holy Spirit through unlikely people.

Perhaps God's candidate-selection process is quite different than ours. In this chapter we will discover from Scripture how the Lord sent people who just did not fit the expected mold.

Believe it or not, a high school yearbook has many things in common with our Scriptures. For one, it is a reference book of actual historical events that happened to real people who occupied a specific time and place. These people were all learners on a journey of discovery (disciples, if you will). In the yearbook, these learners recounted their jewels of wisdom, which were passed down from their teachers, who spent time investing and entrusting their knowledge to a new generation. They chronicled not only their victories but also their defeats, along with lessons learned. The high school yearbook tells the story of a group of people with a common goal (graduation) and a shared experience (living life together).

There is, however, one profound difference between our holy Scriptures and the high school yearbook: Instead of celebrating people who were regarded as *most* likely to succeed, the Bible is filled with people who were considered *least* likely to succeed.

Taking a look at biblical characters, consider the unusual way that the Lord has used unlikely people to accomplish his purposes. Time and again, the children of God fail to recognize their true potential because they are caught up in the earthly deception of personal strength, human competence, and worldly wisdom.

Over the years, I have often prayed, "Lord, make me into the kind of man that you would want to write about." At first that seems to be a very lofty prayer and an unattainable goal, until you actually study the lives of men in the Bible! In the words of Paul to the Corinthians,

> Consider your calling, brothers: not many of you were wise according to worldly standards, not many were powerful, not many were of noble birth. But God chose what is foolish in the world to shame the wise; God chose what is weak in the world to shame the strong; God chose what is low and despised in the world . . . so that no human being might boast in the presence of God.... As it is written, "Let the one who boasts, boast in the Lord." (1 Cor 1:26–31)

The Apostle Paul will be the first character we consider in this chapter, simply because he understood this concept and made statements like "I am the least of the apostles" (1 Cor 15:9) and "I am the very least of all the saints" (Eph 3:8). Let's take a close look at "God's yearbook" and see these people as God sees them. Others may judge them as "least likely to succeed," but God uses the foolish, the weak, the low and despised in the world, so that he may be exalted.

❝ Instead of celebrating people who were regarded as *most* likely to succeed, the Bible is filled with people who were considered *least* likely to succeed.

Paul—Least Likely to Reach Out to Gentiles

I'm trying to imagine what it was like for the early believers to accept the presence of Paul, "persecutor of the church." They saw him approve of the martyrdom of Stephen and they knew that he ravaged the house church movement. According to Acts 8:3, as Paul entered "house after house, he dragged off men and women and committed them to prison." Actually, the book of Acts lists his brutality four different times (8:3, 9:1, 22:4, and 22:19). His actions must have had significant reverberations among the believers as they tried to worship the Lord in groups as well as share their newly found faith with other Jews. How could this man ever be welcomed by the church? And even more so, how could he be a representative of the movement?

Apart from his actions as a persecutor of the church, his behavior as a zealot for the Pharisaical law would certainly disqualify his calling to go to the Gentiles. Paul's sect of Judaism, the Pharisees, held to a strict interpretation of the oral tradition of the Law of Moses, particularly as it related to cultural and social interactions with the Gentile world. Unlike the Sadducees, they were resistant to the Hellenization of their faith and practice. They took great precautions to avoid interaction with those who were unclean, according to their traditions, for fear of losing their purity. Paul even described himself later on as "circumcised on the eighth day, of the people of Israel, of the tribe of Benjamin, a Hebrew of Hebrews; as to the law, a Pharisee; as to zeal, a persecutor of the church; as to righteousness under the law, blameless" (Phil 3:5,6). So how can this "Hebrew of Hebrews" be called by God to go to people who have no station or class standing in his worldview?

It is quite possible that Paul's appearance was unimpressive. In 2 Corinthians 10:10, he quotes his adversaries: "For they say, 'His letters are weighty and strong, but his bodily presence is weak, and his speech of no account.'" An early Christian document called the *Acts of Paul*, while certainly not possessing authority on par with that of the New Testament, describes Paul as: "A man of middling size, and his hair was scanty, and his legs were a little crooked, and his knees were far apart; he had large eyes, and his eyebrows met, and his nose was somewhat long." When you take all of this into consideration, in addition to the fact that he was single (1 Cor 7:8) and maybe had some physical deformity (2 Cor 12:7, Gal 4:13,15), Paul does not seem to represent the ideal candidate that most mission agencies are looking for today.

Fortunately, the Lord does not call people based on an earthly standard of behavior, belief system, or bodily appearance. One of my favorite clichés is "God does not call the equipped, but he equips those whom he calls." This is certainly true of Paul. Many scholars have tried to calculate the number of years from Paul's conversion on the road to Damascus to the moment when he is actually preaching to Gentiles in Galatians; that appears to be about seventeen years. That is a very long time for candidate preparation, cultural adaptation, and missionary methods training, but the time was worth it because he made a significant impact for God's kingdom.

David—Least Likely to Be a King

In the Old Testament, the prophet Samuel found himself in a precarious position to anoint a new king while the reigning king was still alive. Take a look at some of the words the Lord uses as he guides Samuel in this selection process for the next king:

> "Fill your horn with oil, and go. I will send you to Jesse the Bethlehemite, for *I have provided for myself a king among his sons.*" And Samuel said, "How can I go? If Saul hears it, he will kill me." And the Lord said, "Take a heifer with you and say, 'I have come to sacrifice to the Lord.' And invite Jesse to the sacrifice, and *I will show you what you shall do. And you shall anoint for me him whom I declare to you.*" (1 Sam 16:1–3; emphasis mine)

Here the Lord says to Samuel that he has "provided" (*ra'eh*) a king for himself, meaning in Hebrew that he has inspected, seen, looked at, and chosen someone already for the task. This root word was also used with Abraham on Mount Moriah in Genesis 22 when God provided the ram to be used in a sacrifice because he is *Jehovah Jireh* ("God is our provider").

In this narrative in which God is selecting the next king, we see Samuel in the role of investigator, seeker, and discoverer of God's will. Although the ruddy shepherd boy David didn't fit the narrative from Samuel's perspective, this prophet of God was sensitive to the Lord's direction and remained focused on finding his provision. The story highlights a parade of sons from the house of Jesse who appear before the prophet, each of which is considered by Samuel but ultimately vetoed by the Lord. When those sons who presented themselves as strong, good-looking, rugged, intelligent, and capable appear before this selection committee of one, the Lord says to Samuel, "Do not look on his appearance or on the height of his stature, because I have rejected him. For the Lord sees not as man sees: man looks on the outward appearance, but the Lord looks on the heart" (1 Sam 16:7).

As the parade of sons draws to an end, Samuel seems to be in a state of limbo since the Lord has not revealed his anointed one. But Samuel knew that the Lord sent him specifically to the sons of Jesse, so he asks, "Are all your sons here?" And then Jesse, the father of many sons, reveals his opinion on whom the Lord is seeking: "There remains *yet the youngest, but behold, he is keeping the sheep*." (1 Sam 16:11; emphasis mine)

Here the father of David exposes his bias about whom God can use and whom he cannot use. David was the youngest, he was "ruddy," and he spent all his time out in the field with the sheep. Jesse didn't even think to bring in this boy for consideration, and his initial reaction, "But behold, he is keeping the sheep," tells us that he was trying to reason with the prophet not to even consider this "candidate."

This scene sounds like selection committees in which candidates are evaluated by means of what we see, how we experience a person in social settings, and the way we use our natural instincts to determine someone's abilities. Even though Samuel was a prophet, he had an earthly disposition; yet he was mature enough to listen to the Holy Spirit—that still, small voice—and he was able to evaluate with spiritual insight and discernment so that he could see what God saw—the heart.

Not only was David an unlikely king in the beginning, but later, after his sin with Bathsheba—specifically the murder of Uriah—he was also voted "least likely to be a man after God's own heart." But in the New Testament, we read: "[God] raised up David to be their king, of whom he testified and said, 'I have found in David the son of Jesse a man after my heart, who will do all my will.' Of this man's offspring God has brought to Israel a Savior, Jesus, as he promised." (Acts 13:22,23)

David's life was a portrait of both success and failure, and his character is on display for all to see throughout the book of Psalms. He lets his heart be open for examination as he pours it out in faith and dependence on almighty God. Psalm 51 clearly demonstrates the dual nature of his weaknesses as well as his strengths. This psalm did not give David the title of king, but it is likely one that helped him qualify for the even greater title of "a man after God's heart":

> Have mercy on me, O God, according to your steadfast love; according to your abundant mercy blot out my transgressions. Wash me thoroughly from my iniquity, and cleanse me from my sin! For I know my transgressions, and my sin is ever before me. Against you, you only, have I sinned and done

what is evil in your sight…. Create in me a clean heart, O God, and renew a right spirit within me. Cast me not away from your presence, and take not your Holy Spirit from me. Restore to me the joy of your salvation, and uphold me with a willing spirit. (Ps 51:1–4, 10–12)

Gideon—Least Likely to Lead an Army

We know the Sunday school story of how the Lord used Gideon and his three hundred men to defeat the Midianite army of 135,000 men. Gideon is celebrated as a man who was fearless and faithful to the impossible task that God had called him to do in his name. This is the ultimate story of the underdog winning amid dreadful odds and proving to a harassed group of people that there is a God in heaven who deeply cares for his people.

Yet the story of Gideon begins with a below-average man, from an insignificant family, living among a disadvantaged nation of people who are in hiding. When the angel of the Lord appears to Gideon and calls him into service, he replies, "Please, Lord, how can I save Israel? Behold, my clan is the weakest in Manasseh, and I am the least in my father's house" (Judg 6:15).

The story of Gideon is found in the book of Judges, chapters 6–8. It represents one of the many times that the Israelites did evil in the sight of the Lord. Because of this, God sent the Midianites to oppress them for the purpose of drawing them back into his favor. The people of God were hiding in the mountains and caves and living as captives in their own land.

We first encounter Gideon as he is threshing wheat on the floor of a winepress. Normally wheat was threshed on a hilltop so that the grain would drop to the ground as the wind carried away the chaff. However, a winepress was enclosed and sunken in order to process grapes (not grain) and capture the juice as it ran off the press. This was a back-breaking and time-consuming way to separate the wheat from the chaff. But just like everyone else in Israel, Gideon had to work this way to keep from being harassed by the Midianites who would have waited for him to finish his work on the hillside and then steal the grain.

This is why the angel's initial greeting to Gideon is so amusing: "The Lord is with you, O mighty man of valor." He is hiding and doing manual labor the hard way, yet he is greeted as though he is a conquering warrior. Gideon didn't see himself according to his potential, but God knows who the real Gideon is and will begin the process of molding him into that mighty man of valor, beginning with a reevaluation of self.

Gideon begins asking the Lord lots of questions, which is a very good place to start. However, the Lord demands action from Gideon to conquer his fears and insecurities.

> And Gideon said to him, "Please, my lord, if the Lord is with us, why then has all this happened to us? And where are all his wonderful deeds that our fathers recounted to us, saying, 'Did not the Lord bring us up from Egypt?' But now the Lord has forsaken us and given us into the hand of Midian." And the Lord turned to him and said, "Go in this might of yours and save Israel from the hand of Midian; do not I send you?" (Judg 6:13,14)

So what is this "might" that Gideon is exhibiting to the Lord? First, he is a hard worker. Instead of staying in the cave, he is actually working by collecting the grain and then doing what he needed to do to produce food for himself and his family. Second, he is knowledgeable about all the deeds of the Lord as recounted by his fathers. Third, he is spiritually hungry to see the works of God performed in his time, just like they were before. And fourth, he is humble and aware of his own weakness, which is one of the greatest strengths that any man of God can have. The Lord affirms this humility by assuring Gideon that he (the Lord Almighty) will be with him: "Do not *I* send you?" (emphasis mine).

Throughout the story, Gideon exhibits a weak and imperfect faith, which only proves that he is human like the rest of us. His personal encounter with the angel of the Lord was not enough to encourage him in his bold and life-threatening mission. He was constantly seeking signs. The Lord tested Gideon by calling him to destroy his father's altar of Baal, which he did, though under the cover of darkness. Scripture says that "because he was too afraid of his family and the men of the town to do it by day, he did it by night" (Judg 6:27).

Gideon asked the angel of the Lord for a sign (Judg 6:17), which was fulfilled when some meat and cakes were consumed with fire from a rock (v. 21). Gideon asked for a sign related to a fleece of wool—not once, but twice (Judg 6:36–40). And, after the Lord spoke to him, he still desired a sign of confirmation when he went down to the Midianite camp to spy out what the soldiers were saying (Judg 7:9–15). Each time, he was showing his human propensity to doubt God's calling. Sometimes God shows displeasure in these types of requests, as in the Gospel of Luke when

Zechariah seeks confirmation of John the Baptist's birth and the Lord strikes him speechless until the birth as a consequence (Luke 1:20). But in the account of Gideon, God shows patience and placates this "mighty man of valor" by answering each request.

Likewise, God is still calling fearful yet humble people to leave the protection of the winepress and live their lives out in the open where the Spirit of the Lord can separate the wheat from the chaff. Faith is not the absence of fear, but the presence of God's power. From his earthly perspective, Gideon was correct in his self-assessment. The Lord did not call the smartest, the strongest, or the most heroic to deliver Israel from this oppressor's grip. God calls people like Gideon precisely because they are not any of these things. In the absence of intelligence, strength, and bravery, the Lord provides his people with his presence to accomplish his purposes.

The Scriptures are filled with people who would be voted least likely to succeed, and this chapter would be endless if we considered people like Jacob the deceiver, Peter the hot-tempered fisherman, Moses the stuttering spokesman, Abraham and Sarah the elderly parents, Rahab the harlot, and even Jesus the son of a carpenter, born in an obscure part of the world.

In our day, as we raise a new generation of missionary candidates and process missionary applications, we should actively engage our minds by using the modern evaluation methods available to us. But we should never rely on these academic methods exclusively, since God is still moving in the hearts and minds of the least likely characters.

Like the prophet Samuel, we need to engage our spirits to be sensitive to God's Spirit. Granted, one of the best predictors of missionary success is previous "fruit-bearing." Just as in financial investing, careers, and other areas of modern life, the past is one of the best indicators of the future. Still, with our abilities to evaluate personalities, establish the ideal profile of desirable candidates, and develop a portrait of people we want to send overseas, two critical questions must be asked during interviews (and should be verified by references):

1. Describe how you sense God *calling* you to this ministry/mission field.
2. What have you done in the past that has *prepared* you for this calling?

Moses would say, "I spent forty years on the backside of the desert." Paul would say, "It took me seventeen years to understand God's heart for the Gentiles." Gideon would say, "The God that delivered my fathers out of Egypt has appeared to me and has shown me his way. Even though I am afraid, I will step out in faith, because he is with me."

Conclusion

This subject of being *least likely to succeed* has interested me more and more over time because the older I get, the more I am aware of my own incompetencies. When I was a young seminarian, my youthful enthusiasm was a great cover for my lack of ability. My dependence upon the Lord was high because I had the excitement and energy of being a new pastor, doing new things and learning new skills. As I grew in my abilities, I can look back and see that I rested more on my own understanding of ministry than on the Lord's gracious provision. As my abilities increased, my dependence on God decreased—that is, until difficulties arose. Then I was forced to wrestle with my own failures and shortcomings in light of God's divine wisdom and guidance. Now I can see that times of hardship are also times of refinement by the Lord.

I once heard a missionary speak about his ministry in terms of a weight scale. On one side of the scale were his abilities, talents, and expertise. On the other side of the scale were his weaknesses, faults, and insecurities. The idea was that neither side of the scale should outweigh the other, because God can use both sides in equal measure.

It is good to know that many of the people whom God chose to write about in the Scriptures were not beacons of perfection. They were real people, with real struggles and real failures.

Consider these famous quotes about failure by successful people:

> *I have not failed. I've just found ten thousand ways that won't work.*
> —THOMAS EDISON
>
> *The only real mistake is the one from which we learn nothing.*
> —HENRY FORD
>
> *Success is not final, failure is not fatal:*
> *it is the courage to continue that counts.*
> —WINSTON CHURCHILL

So how do you define a successful missionary candidate? And what do you do with perceived failures in a person's life? Maybe God sees success and failure a little differently than we do. That young shepherd named David didn't have the outward appearance of a king; but rather than

> God likes to take the people who are
> *least likely to succeed* in human terms
> and fill them with his Spirit so that they
> can demonstrate his glory and greatness
> to a world that is in need of a Savior.

looking at the outside, God sees the heart. Going into battle with superior numbers is how earthly wars are won, but God's wars are won with people like Gideon who are faithful and dependent upon God's provision only. When it comes to someone's track record and past character, we only need to look at Jacob and the Apostle Paul to realize that God's business is all about changing people, from deceivers and persecutors to heirs of promise and proclaimers of good news.

God likes to take the people who are least likely to succeed in human terms and fill them with his Spirit so that they can demonstrate his glory and greatness to a world that is in need of a Savior. My final encouragement here is that we take care not to overlook people just because they "don't fit the mold."

David J. Wilson served in the local church as mission pastor for over twenty years. In November 2016, he joined Avant Ministries in Kansas City, MO, as director of church relations.

Notes

[1] William G. Britt, "Pretraining Variables in the Prediction of Missionary Success Overseas," *Journal of Psychology and Theology* 11, no. 34 (1983): 203–11.

[2] William G. Britt, "Predictors of Missionary Success," chap. 4 in *Mind the Gaps: Engaging the Church in Missionary Care* (Redlands CA: Believers Press, 2015), 45.

Connecting to the Pipeline

1. Do you see any obvious obstacles in your church culture that will affect candidates' hearing God's voice calling them to the mission field?

2. Are there any subtle obstacles that need to be addressed in a loving, redemptive, and gentle way?

3. When you hear the word *missions*, what is the first thing you think about as it relates to money? Have the team list those thoughts on a whiteboard and try to identify potential obstacles.

4. Have a frank and honest discussion with your team to evaluate your church's practice of short-term mission trips. Arrange to meet with the person in your church who is responsible for mission trips and try to develop an alignment between your long-term and short-term strategy.

5. Make a list of all the biblical and historical characters you can think of who defied all odds and expectations and accomplished things that were deemed impossible for them to do. Are these people exceptions to the rule, or are they establishing a pattern?

Part 3

The Local Church: Developing a Mobilization Team

Different churches are organized in different ways. Some are pastor led; others are elder/deacon led. But the one common denominator is that they are all organized. In the missions world, one of our favorite concepts is "contextualization." That is our trade-craft—it's what we do. So in this section of *Pipeline*, we will discuss how to contextualize missions within the context of your local church's specific organizational culture. If your church has committees, when you read the phrase "form a team," just translate that phrase to your context and "form a committee." If you read "get permission from your elders," but you don't have elders, then just exchange that idea with getting permission from whatever authority structure your church has.

The ideas developed here are not necessarily intended to be models for you to follow, but principles for you to adapt to your specific church. Some of the writers in this section come from a megachurch perspective. Others come from a medium-sized urban church perspective. And still others come from smaller, rural churches. The one thing they have in common is a well-formed strategy that works in their particular church. Learn from them and make applications that are appropriate to your setting.

CHAPTER 10

Developing a Mobilization Model

The Sending Church

David J. Wilson

In the summer of 1961, the coach of the Green Bay Packers walked into training camp with a football in his hand and the fundamentals of the game in his head. Professionals who had been playing the sport for the majority of their lives were subjected to a lecture from their coach that covered everything about the game, starting at page one of the playbook. Coach Vince Lombardi began his lecture with the now famous words, "Gentlemen, this is a football."

The year before, the team had suffered a tragic loss in the postseason, forcing them to think about that loss for many months before coming to training camp. This opening lecture on such an elemental level may have felt like a waste of time to these seasoned professionals, but it was critical for the coach (and his players) to get back to the fundamentals of the game. That year, the Green Bay Packers won the NFL championship. And then they went on to win five of the next seven championships. Because they had previously neglected the simplicity of the game, they needed to go back to the fundamentals. This rudimentary lecture caused them to begin thinking deeply about what mattered most—and it worked!

Everyone has a different perspective on "church," so we need to explore the simple, yet profound, fundamentals of this institution. What better place to start than with the words of our Lord, who is the ultimate authority? Jesus is more than just our coach when it comes to understanding the church. And unlike Vince Lombardi, Jesus provided us with an earthly perspective as well as an eternal view when he gave us his "This is a church" speech, as recorded in the Gospel of Matthew. There are only two places in Scripture where Jesus mentions the church (Greek, *ekklesia*):[1]

And I tell you, you are Peter, and on this rock I will build my church, and the gates of hell shall not prevail against it. I will give you the keys of the kingdom of heaven, and whatever you bind on earth shall be bound in heaven, and whatever you loose on earth shall be loosed in heaven. (Matt 16:18,19)

If your brother sins against you, go and tell him his fault, between you and him alone. If he listens to you, you have gained your brother. But if he does not listen, take one or two others along with you, that every charge may be established by the evidence of two or three witnesses. If he refuses to listen to them, tell it to the church. And if he refuses to listen even to the church, let him be to you as a Gentile and a tax collector. Truly, I say to you, whatever you bind on earth shall be bound in heaven, and whatever you loose on earth shall be loosed in heaven. (Matt 18:15–18)

By taking this brief (and only) description of the church given to us by our Lord and Savior, we see that there are some significant implications for the Great Commission, which Jesus gave to us after his resurrection. First of all, the church belongs to Jesus. He says, "I will build *my* church." The church is *his* body, and it is described as *his* bride in the epistles and Revelation. Second, Jesus is a builder of his church and his followers are allowed to keep the keys. He has given us the responsibility to manage and steward this institution. Third, there is a mysterious connection between this earthly institution and the heavenly realm, indicating that this is not just a club to belong to but a binding covenant that merges the temporal with the eternal. Fourth, there is an accountability for each other and a responsibility to others for living together in love, unity, and on purpose. Action is involved in the church that Jesus is describing here. He is building and giving us the keys (Chapter 16), then he is giving us the authority to bind and loose (Chapter 18). It appears Jesus is expecting us to do something significant with those keys he has given to us.

With this basic and fundamental understanding of Jesus' church, we will explore what it looks like to be that kind of engaged organization in our time. We will also take a look at how to fulfill his Great Commission through his authorized sending agent, the church. We recognize that the church belongs to Jesus. We acknowledge that he is the builder and we

"
> A Sending Church is a local community
> of Christ-followers who have made
> a covenant together to be prayerful,
> deliberate, and proactive in developing,
> commissioning, and sending their own
> members both locally and globally,
> often in partnership with other churches
> or agencies, and continuing to encourage,
> support, and advocate for them
> while making disciples cross-culturally.
"

are merely the managing stewards of the keys. With awe and wonder, we commit ourselves to the binding nature of this covenant that bridges the gap between this temporal world and the eternal kingdom of almighty God. And we will seek to encourage each other to be about our Master's business by being more than just a sedentary church, but to become a "sending church."

Thanks to the Upstream Collective, we have this working definition: A Sending Church is a local community of Christ-followers who have made a covenant together to be prayerful, deliberate, and proactive in developing, commissioning, and sending their own members both locally and globally, often in partnership with other churches or agencies, and continuing to encourage, support, and advocate for them while making disciples cross-culturally.

In his book *The Sending Church Defined*, Zach Bradley unpacks this statement into easily understandable segments, which helps churches reengage in their primary objective—the Great Commission.[2]

If we start with this baseline definition of the church, it seems reasonable to take a closer look at how a three-strand partnership (see Ecclesiastes 4:12) between the church, the agency, and the missionary can be most effective.

A quote from the late Dr. Ralph Winter should stir us to continue his work of uniting the church, the agency, and the missionary: "Our efforts today in any part of the world will be most effective only if both of these two structures [the church and the agency] are fully and properly involved and supportive of each other."[3]

There are many ways to develop a partnership, and most agencies want to deepen the relationship between their missionaries and the churches that send them. Likewise, local churches are beginning to see amazing fruit and return on their investment (ROI) when they reach out to dialogue with the leaders at sending agencies. There is a growing movement within agencies to designate staff who are dedicated to church relations. They are creating programs, conferences, and other avenues to connect with the church and develop deep and strategic partnerships for kingdom expansion.

As an exercise to get this discussion started, here is a brief outline of the potential roles and responsibilities for each of the three important members of this three-strand relationship between the church, the agency, and the missionary.

Three-strand Partnership: Church, Agency, and Missionary

"Though one may be overpowered, two can defend themselves. A cord of three strands is not quickly broken." (Eccl 4:12, NIV)

1. Church
   a. Sending—primary partner, stakeholder, and participant of the Great Commission
   b. Selecting—affirming the character and competence of a missionary
   c. Praying—before the field, on the field, ministry contacts, family at home, reentry
   d. Mobilizing—short-term trips, mid-term opportunities, and long-term support
   e. Nurturing—providing a spiritual community as a base of primary support
   f. Resourcing—ensuring the missionary is well equipped (What are their ministry needs?)
   g. Caring—holistic support contributing to effective ministry through *missionary care*
   h. Communicating—ensures a clear and transparent understanding between partners
2. Agency
   a. Supervising—overall on-field oversight, leadership, and accountability
   b. Facilitating—recognizes the centrality of the church as the sender while preserving the mutually deferential roles of each participant

    c. Organizing—provides the administrative services that free the missionary to focus on ministry

    d. Consulting—offers timely consultation to the church on major decisions regarding personal, family, and ministry difficulties and decisions

    e. Caring—holistic support contributing to effective ministry through *member care*

    f. Communicating—ensures a clear and transparent understanding between partners

3. Missionary

    a. Calling—an overwhelming confidence that God has this purpose for their life

    b. Performing—conducts the ministry on behalf of the sending church and the agency to meet mutually desired goals

    c. Deferring—ultimately responsible to the sending church, while on-field supervision and accountability is delegated to the agency

    d. Reporting—provides regular (monthly/quarterly) and honest (achievements and challenges) reports to the church, agency, and ministry partners

    e. Conferring—with both church leadership and agency leadership on major issues

    f. Caring—holistic support contributing to effective ministry through *soul care*

    g. Communicating—ensures a clear and transparent understanding between partners

Notice that the last two roles and responsibilities for all three partners are similar. It should be noted that all three bear some, but not all, responsibility for care and communication. It helps to make the work more robust and intentional when all three are in unity and sharing the workload.

Patrick Johnstone warns those in the agency to be careful not to leave out the influence of the church:

> Possibly the most defective partnership is that between mission agencies and local churches....The centrality of the local church in missions needs to be emphasized, and agencies must be more accountable to their supporting churches for their ministries and use of workers. However, both are vital components of the church and must work together.[4]

Missionary sending agencies are very busy places, staffed by people who are highly experienced in matters related to cultural influence, global security, and international gospel impact. Most who serve in the agency have the ability to discern a broader understanding of those nightly news stories we hear about from obscure corners of the world and seem so mundane to the majority of people in North America. Anyone who visits the headquarters of most sending agencies can attest that their international insights are surprising, profound, and very revealing, just by hearing their stories of living abroad.

As in all professions, the greatest asset can also be a severe weakness. As it relates to partnership with churches, many agencies know what is best for missionaries and are capable of making swift decisions that make the most sense. But, unfortunately, in an attempt to be expeditious, decisions have often been made in a vacuum, without consulting with the local church partners; and that is not a best practice. Understanding the roles and responsibilities of each entity can help to bridge this gap in communication.

Similar to sending agencies, churches are busy places too. And when it comes to sending missionaries, they like to see a return on their investments (ROI) and need to be intimately involved in the Great Commission by sending their own people. Like the agency, the church has strengths and weaknesses; but when balanced with a strong partner, we can enjoy a lifetime of fruitful ministry together with our missionaries. When it comes to strengths, the church has a vast array of volunteers and resources that are readily available if properly deployed. Unfortunately, one of the more recent weaknesses of the church that needs to be discussed is the concept of outsourcing.

Is Outsourcing Mission to the Agency the Right Approach?

Outsourcing has become a way of life in the business world because it cuts down on cost and time for workers. In the local church, outsourcing and subcontracting can be very good for administrative functions such as payroll, insurance, retirement, etc. However, as the guys from *Simple Church* would say, this is not appropriate for other functions of the church:

There are some tasks a church must never outsource because these tasks are embedded into what Jesus envisions a church being and doing. Sadly, because many churches drift toward complexity, they have outsourced the mission of God. They let others handle mission. They tout how much they give to a mission agency as their commitment to missions. They place pictures of missionaries on their bulletin boards and boldly declare their mission mindset. We applaud missions giving and missionaries on bulletin boards. But, these expressions must not be all the church does for those outside of herself.[5]

As a pastor, I have seen the church outsource to parachurch organizations discipleship areas such as women's ministry (Beth Moore Bible studies, etc.), men's ministry (Promise Keepers, etc.), and student ministry (InterVarsity, Cru, etc.). I have also seen theological education outsourced to Bible schools and seminaries. In-depth Bible study at the local church level is often sacrificed to the prevailing winds of practical, topical, and application-based teaching from the pulpit. While this approach is good for evangelism and new-believer formation, time must be set aside for local church members to go deeper into the Scriptures. Just one conversation with a Bible professor at the university or seminary level will reveal that most of their new students are fundamentally biblically illiterate. And these students are coming from relevant and active churches. Similarly, global mission is often exclusively outsourced to the missionary sending agency. Some churches opt to just *pay, pray, and stay out of the way.*

So if the church outsources discipleship to the parachurch, then outsources theology to the Bible school, and finally outsources mission to the agency, then what is left for the church to do? Perhaps this is why there are so many disputes, conflicts, and controversies within local churches across our nation. I love the quote from Jean-Paul Sartre that says, "Only the man who isn't rowing has time to rock the boat." Apply this concept to the church and you have a breeding ground for disengaged people who have a calling on their lives, but no outlet to be properly engaged.

To illustrate the necessity for church engagement, think for a moment about the topography of the Holy Land. You have the Sea of Galilee, which feeds the Jordan River, and then the river empties into the Dead Sea. The Sea of Galilee is a stunningly beautiful and vibrant lake that is teeming with fish and surrounded by lush vegetation. As it feeds the Jordan River, it transfers that life downstream, causing the river to host all forms of life-giving sustenance. But then something happens when the Jordan reaches the Dead Sea. All of that goodness stops and is basically—killed. It's called the "Dead" Sea for a reason. So with all the same good stuff flowing in, why does it die? Simply put, the Dead Sea has no outlet! There is no place for all this water, minerals, and life to go. It soaks up all the good things that make the other bodies of water full of life; but with no place to go, it becomes a stagnant pool of lifeless, selfish, unmotivated, passive, and nonproductive existence—lifeless living!

Does this resemble the local church in any way? Do pastors and church leaders constantly "pour" into believers lots of good, life-giving information only to have a room filled with people who have potential but no outlet for using what they know? Where does all that knowledge go when the church is not proactively and intentionally engaged in discipleship, theology, and mission?

I regret that we must title this chapter "The Sending Church." It should simply be called "The Church." But because of the church's propensity to outsource critical elements of its existence, local churches that are fulfilling the Great Commission must be assigned a descriptive adjective like "Sending" to distinguish them from those counterfeit institutions that just go through the motions: meeting on the weekends, singing a couple of songs, talking about God, taking up a collection, and trying to make people feel good about themselves as they go back to their weekly routine of lifeless living.

Sam Metcalf, in his book *Beyond the Local Church*, observes: "In North America, the fastest-growing segment of the population, categorized according to religious affiliation, are the 'Nones,' meaning those who are done with formal religious affiliation."[6] When asked, "What is your religious preference?" they check the box labeled "None." So it isn't that the next generation is disinterested in faith, but they aren't going to be content with living a lifeless faith. And that is a great thing! We should have hope in this. We should be overjoyed with the potential of kingdom expansion in the generations that come next. And we should also be very wise in how we, as the church, respond and engage with them. That is why we need the adjective *sending* added to *the church*.

Most missionary agencies are dedicated to reaching the unreached with the gospel of Jesus Christ through the planting of churches, doing business as mission, transforming communities through development, and a variety of evangelism and justice work. They seek to formulate a partnership between the local church here in North America and the missionaries who sense God calling them out of their comfort zone to go into all the world. Some agencies are willing to allow the local church just to outsource missionary deployment to the sending agency, but there is a movement to change that. Many are striving to engage the church properly and actively in every aspect of missionary deployment. From training to retirement, and all points in between, agencies are going back to the foundational roots to recognize that the Great Commission still belongs to the church. They are motivated to be a support network that advocates, empowers, and enables the local church to accomplish its mission here on earth.

For the sake of sticking with the fundamentals in this discussion, the three main functions of a sending church in relation to sending missionaries cross-culturally are *cultivating*, *commissioning*, and *caring*.

Cultivating

Back in 1966, Dick Pearson wrote a powerful little book called *Missionary Education Helps for the Local Church*. Here is a quote to help us discover God's design for church-based missionary mobilization:

> A brief study of Christ's limited post-resurrection words, recorded in the Gospels and Acts, will clarify that world missions is not a part of the church program; it *is* the program for his Church. The church is responsible to present world missions as God's priority in *every area of church life*, so that those who should be foreign missionaries will be exposed, challenged and encouraged to go overseas, and those God calls to stay home will have a correct view of the foreign mission field and the significance of their participation from the homeland.[7]

Pearson described practical ways that churches in the 1960s could cultivate in church members a heart for the global harvest. Many of these are still relevant today—simple things like:

- Regularly scheduling missionary speakers
- Hosting an annual missions conference
- Adopting a special Christmas offering to benefit a global missionary effort
- Including missionary prayer requests in the Sunday worship folder
- Sending birthday and anniversary cards and gifts from the children's ministry
- Displaying photos of supported missionaries and a map on the wall
- Highlighting a story about a famous missionary in the sermon
- Showing a missionary documentary in small groups
- Encouraging the memorization of mission-related Scriptures

- Most important—form a missionary education committee (or better—*a mobilization team*)

These are all intended to help keep the global mandate of the Great Commission on the hearts and minds of people so that they will be sensitive to the "still, small voice" of God, who is continually calling and wooing people to join him in his work among the nations. The formation of a church-based mobilization team is a critical step to sending the next generation of missionaries from the local church. This team should focus on intentionally and proactively preparing, maturing, and discipling young people to be deployed to places that are difficult, yet in much need of the gospel.

To use Zig Ziglar's old saying, "If you aim at nothing, you will hit it every time." It is important for the church to have something to aim at, and to have a goal in mind for young people (and older people as well).

If we believe that being on mission is the goal of the church, then we need to plan for it. Formulate a team or committee that has marching orders to raise up the next generation of pastors, missionaries, and other church leaders. Smaller churches might have three or four people who are committed to the task, while larger churches might have ten to twelve people. This group should meet regularly, plan a budget, study missions and missionary methods, and carry out a plan that includes mission promotion to children, youth, adults, and even outsiders. When a church gets serious about developing a pipeline for sending people *out of the church*, God will begin to send people *into the church* to grow and develop their capacity for being good "senders."

Like J. D. Greear says, "A church is not a group of people gathered around a leader, but it is a Leadership factory . . . that stirs up the gifts of God in people." He describes how a church should have a process to challenge and empower people so that they will have the courage to step out in obedience to Christ. That needs to be the new metric for success in the church, rather than the misdirected goal of measuring numbers in the seats and dollars in the plate. Greear says that in his church, "We measure our success by our sending capacity, not just our seating capacity."[8]

Commissioning

Once the church is actively engaged in cultivating the spiritual growth and development of people to live a life of service to the Lord, it is amazing what happens next—they start seeing fruit! Christ-followers, both young and old, begin hearing the voice of the living God calling them to the nations. The whole notion of a mobilization pipeline is that "If you build it, they will come" (just like in the movie *Field of Dreams*).

The church needs to understand the concept of "commissioning" as it relates to the Great Commission. As the modern-day expression of the body of Christ, or the bride of Christ, the church has the divine charter of fulfilling these parting words of our Lord and Savior Jesus Christ. Marv Newell, in his book *Commissioned: What Jesus Wants You to Know as You Go*, describes the five mission statements given by Jesus for his church:

1. **John 20:21**

   Jesus said to them again, "Peace be with you. As the Father has sent me, even so I am sending you."

2. **Mark 16:15**

   And [Jesus] said to them, "Go into all the world and proclaim the gospel to the whole creation."

3. **Matthew 28:18–20**

   And Jesus came and said to them, "All authority in heaven and on earth has been given to me. Go therefore and make disciples of all nations, baptizing them in the name of the Father and of the Son and of the Holy Spirit, teaching them to observe all that I have commanded you. And behold, I am with you always, to the end of the age."

4. **Luke 24:44–49**

   Then [Jesus] said to them, "These are my words that I spoke to you while I was still with you, that everything written about me in the Law of Moses and the Prophets and the Psalms must be fulfilled." Then he opened their minds to understand the Scriptures, and said to them, "Thus it is written, that the Christ should suffer and on the third day rise from the dead, and that repentance for the forgiveness of sins should be proclaimed in his name to all nations, beginning from Jerusalem. You are witnesses of these things. And behold, I am sending the promise of my Father upon you. But stay in the city until you are clothed with power from on high."

5. **Acts 1:7,8**

   [Jesus] said to them, " . . . But you will receive power when the Holy Spirit has come upon you, and you will be my witnesses in Jerusalem and in all Judea and Samaria, and to the end of the earth."

Newell explains that "Jesus gave these mission statements to his disciples on five different occasions, in five different addresses, at five different geographical settings, with five different emphases." The order listed above is the chronological order that Newell suggests. In summary, he says, "Without question these five mission statements of Jesus make up the missional Magna Carta of the church, from its inception, for today, and into the future."[9]

The Great Commission belongs to the church, and therefore missionary mobilization is a mandate that the church needs to take very, very, very seriously. Acts 13:1–3 is likely the best example of a church in the New Testament sending missionaries.

> Now there were in the church at Antioch prophets and teachers, Barnabas, Simeon who was called Niger, Lucius of Cyrene, Manaen a lifelong friend of Herod the tetrarch, and Saul. While they were worshiping the Lord and fasting, the Holy Spirit said, "Set apart for me Barnabas and Saul for the work to which I have called them." Then after fasting and praying they laid their hands on them and sent them off.

As it relates to the role and responsibility of the church in sending missionaries, consider these three lessons from the church at Antioch: First, the missionaries were called by God to a particular task. In this case, they were called to preach the gospel to the unreached. Second, God confirmed this calling to the church leaders. This sending entity, the church, heard from the Lord directly and was instructed by God to set them apart for the task. Third, the church responded by ceremonially "commissioning" them by fasting, praying, laying on of hands, and then sending them off. Pastors and mission leaders need to be fully invested in the success of their church's missionaries by sending them well prepared and fully supported spiritually, emotionally, and financially. Consider these three elements:

1. **"After fasting and praying."** This represents a physical and spiritual demonstration of corporate support to discern the will of God in this decision. The decision to support Paul and Barnabas came with serious thought and consideration of all the implications, not just intellectually, as they surrendered to the will of the Lord. This had profound implications for the spiritual conditioning of those being sent.

2. **"Laid their hands on them."** The laying-on-of-hands ceremony is a powerful demonstration for modern missionaries. The church leaders at Antioch were communicating to Paul and Barnabas, "We are a part of you, and you are a part of us." Today, as we commission missionaries, just as in pastoral ordination, there is a passing of the

mantle to a new generation—a mantle that has been passed down for two millennia. With this gesture the church is communicating that their new missionary is an extension of the corporate mandate for the church.

3. **"Sent them off."** Though this seems to be a brief add-on phrase, for the missionary this statement can mean either success or failure on the field. Depending on the sincerity of the church, this expression can mean either "get them moving" or "help them succeed."

Missionaries need the tangible demonstration of support that comes in primarily one key form: money. Paul and Barnabas wouldn't have voyaged very far if they were broke, even in those days. It took money to get on a boat and head for a distant land. It took money to eat, travel, and stay safe. The church likely took an offering and collected supplies that were necessary for such a journey, and then threw a farewell party.

Continuing with conjecture, we can assume that people who had previously traveled to these places, or even lived there, spent time with Paul and Barnabas to help them prepare for a change of culture. Others likely agreed to take care of family members, belongings, and other matters of business and home.

Caring

Missionaries are worthy of their pay, and they need to raise a living wage that includes a home to live in, a vehicle to drive, food to eat, clothes to wear, medical care, retirement planning, education for children, and ministry expenses. Within the walls of the missionary sending agency, far too often there are groans and sighs from God's faithful servants as they receive the news that their church has stopped sending financial support. For a variety of reasons, churches make career-ending and ministry-impacting decisions simply by cutting back on their missionary support. This brings us to the third function of the church in this triad of the Great Commission—caring.

Although the long-term care of a missionary is not just about money, that does have profound significance. In his book *The Treasure Principal*, Randy Alcorn reminds us that Jesus is constantly guiding his church and his followers to consider an eternal perspective when it comes to money.[10] In Matthew 6:21, Jesus says, "Where your treasure is, there your heart will be also," so it would be very difficult for a church to support a missionary but fail to provide for them financially. Some churches may decide just to pray for the missionary or visit them on the field, but unless the church is fully engaged with the missionary's work through supporting them financially, they cannot be considered a "sending church."

Apart from money, church-based missionary care is a relatively new and exciting trend among churches that send missionaries. Churches are reengaging to be full participants in the Great Commission by taking intentional and proactive steps to ensure the viability and resiliency of missionaries on the field. Neal Pirolo's classic book, *Serving as Senders*, identifies six areas of support for churches to consider as they care for their global workers:

- Moral Support
- Logistics Support
- Financial Support
- Prayer Support
- Communication Support
- Reentry Support

In each chapter, Pirolo takes one of these areas piece by piece to provide "senders" with ideas and inspiration for a lifetime of care. Simple things like communication can be an incredible gift for a missionary who is serving in a distant land. Pirolo says:

> It is hard to imagine the importance of communication from home until you have been there. When a person or family arrives on the field to establish their new routine, real loneliness can set in—a feeling of isolation, of being out of it.... The content of your communication is vital. Say things that really matter.... Share your thoughts and feelings.... Get involved in their lives on the field as much as you can.... Ask questions about their lives and respond to what they have said in their previous letters to you. This is especially encouraging because it shows that you really read their letters and are interested enough for some follow-up conversation about it.[11]

By reading books like this on missionary care, you can help guide others in your church to offer best practices with ideas, inspiration, and proactive care. Another book that is designed to offer best practices for churches as they care for missionaries is *Mind the Gaps: Engaging the Church in Missionary Care*. I had the priviledge of leading a church-based missionary care team to write this book to share our experience in caring for missionaries and to offer a model for other churches to consider. *Mind the Gaps* will help sending churches talk through a philosophy of ministry, develop a confidentiality policy, study the strategic focus of the church to find a good fit for the missionary, and make connecting the missionary to the whole congregation a priority. Here is an excerpt:

> *Forgotten.* It's a word that too often describes how missionaries may begin to feel as they are living far from their home of origin. When they first leave for the field, it is often with a wonderful commissioning and send-off with the prayers of people who know them, love them and appreciate what they are doing. But as the years go by and the busyness of life overtakes those in the home church, memories can fade and good intentions of staying in touch can fall by the wayside ... churches change ... pastors and staff leave ... members move away and new members come who don't know the missionary.[12]

For these reasons, and many others, it is important for the sending church to establish a missionary care team, separate from the mission committee, whose sole purpose is to monitor, manage, and coordinate care with the missionary sending agency. Missionary care cannot be the responsibility of just one person (i.e., a pastor or individual church member), but rather of a team of people who can withstand the many changes that every church experiences over time. Also, a team approach brings energy, enthusiasm, and ownership to a broader group of people as they seek to develop relationships with missionaries and their agencies.

Memorandum of Understanding (*MOU*)

Because of the complexity of the modern missionary movement today, understanding the authority structure of your organization is essential for a vital and dynamic relationship between the primary partners (church, agency, and missionary). Some agencies have a hierarchical model of leadership. This is quite common in large denominational sending organizations and in agencies that rely on using expert resources. Other agencies recognize the role of the church as the leader, assuming the mantle of authority for what happens on the field while the agency provides administrative services and logistical support. And yet a third model exists where the missionary on the field is the primary decision-maker. (Of course, there are a myriad of hybrid models, but only one can sit in the driver's seat.)

Regardless of the model being used, establishing an MOU will solve many disagreements that are bound to happen, since it isn't a matter of *if* problems arise but *when* they occur. This MOU document will serve as a guide to settling disputes with utmost civility and efficiency. Humility should be the first point of reference in the MOU; but in the heat of the moment when these three entities have divergent opinions, relationships can be strained if a clear understanding of the authority structure isn't well defined.

Perhaps the solution to most problems that may occur is to have a dynamic and robust relationship from the very beginning. That is why many sending agencies offer frequent events in which they invite church leaders to come and meet agency leaders. Most organizations have someone on their staff who serves in a role loosely defined as a director of church relations and whose primary responsibility is to make sure that the church, agency, and missionary are well connected.

One of the best things a church that is serious about raising up the next generation of missionaries can do is to contact a sending agency. If you aren't already in a relationship with an organization, you can start by taking an inventory of your church's shared legacy: What is the DNA of the church and what are you known for? If your church has a heart for Muslims, then contact an agency like Frontiers that specializes in reaching Muslims. If your church has a deep love for the Bible, then perhaps you can partner with Wycliffe to see the Scriptures translated into another language. Are there people from Kenya in your congregation? Then maybe the Lord is leading you to plant a church with Avant in Kenya. Do you have medical professionals in your church? Take a look at all the hospitals that Samaritan's Purse runs around the globe. Is your church heavily influenced by business leaders? Crossworld specializes in sending business professionals to make disciples through the marketplace. East Asia? OMF. Europe? GEM. Unreached/Unengaged? Pioneers.

Later in this book you will find a section written by missionary sending agency representatives to highlight their work and how the church can help send missionaries to the field through their organization. There are hundreds of sending agencies in North America alone, and many more outside of the US and Canada. Peggy Newell put together a book called *North American Mission Handbook: US and Canadian Protestant Ministries Overseas* to help in your search for a good partner.[13]

Regardless of its size, your congregation can make a dramatic impact in the world by partnering with an agency. The Lord will multiply your efforts when the church, the agency, and the missionary are in proper alignment and working toward a common cause and a strategic goal.

The "sending church" is not just an idealized description of what could be, but a real possibility for your church. Also included in this book is a section written by leaders of churches that are currently engaged in proactive and intentional mobilization of their congregation. We have been careful to include small, medium, and large churches that are focused on the world and working to keep the Great Commission on top of their priority list. These churches know the fundamentals, keep things simple, and strive to make Christ known among the nations. Because of their relationships with missionaries and agencies, they can confidently say on Sunday morning, "This is a church!"

David J. Wilson served in the local church as mission pastor for over twenty years. In November 2016, he joined Avant Ministries in Kansas City, MO, as director of church relations.

Notes

[1] Wayne Grudem, *Systematic Theology* (Grand Rapids MI: Zondervan, 1994), and Millard Erickson, *Christian Theology* (Grand Rapids, MI: Baker, 1998).

[2] Zach Bradley, *The Sending Church Defined* (Knoxville TN: The Upstream Collective, 2015) 3, www.theupstreamcollective.org.

[3] Ralph Winter, "The Two Structures of God's Redemptive Mission," in *Perspectives on the World Christian Movement* (Pasadena, CA: William Carey Library, 2009), 244–53.

[4] Patrick Johnstone, *The Future of the Global Church: History, Trends and Possibilities* (Downers Grove IL: InterVarsity, 2011).

[5] Thom Rainer and Eric Geiger, *Simple Church: Returning to God's Process for Making Disciples* (Nashville TN: B&H Publishing, 2011), 249.

[6] Sam Metcalf, *Beyond the Local Church: How Apostolic Movements Can Change the World* (Downers Grove IL: InterVarsity, 2015).

[7] Dick Pearson, *Missionary Education Helps for the Local Church* (Palo Alto CA: Overseas Crusades, 1966), 2.

[8] J. D. Greear, *Gaining by Losing: Why the Future Belongs to Churches that Send* (Grand Rapids, MI: Zondervan, 2015), 101–6.

[9] Marvin J. Newell, *Commissioned: What Jesus Wants You to Know as You Go* (St. Charles, IL: ChurchSmart Resources, 2010), 22–24.

[10] Randy Alcorn, *The Treasure Principal: Unlocking the Secret of Joyful Giving* (Colorado Springs CO: Multnomah, 2005), 46-60

[11] Neal Pirolo, *Serving as Senders: How to Care for Your Missionaries* (San Diego CA: Emmaus Road International, 1991), 121–24.

[12] David J. Wilson, *Mind the Gaps: Engaging the Church in Missionary Care* (Redlands CA: Believers Press, 2015), 82.

[13] Peggy Newell, *North American Mission Handbook: US and Canadian Protestant Ministries Overseas* (Pasadena, CA: William Carey Library, 2017).

CHAPTER 11

Building a Mobilization Team

Rites of Passage

David J. Wilson

What if Your Church Decided to Be Intentional about Fulfilling the Great Commission?

Regardless of the size of your church, you can be part of making Christ known among the nations. In the chapters that follow, you will hear from church mission leaders from small rural churches, large megachurches, and all sizes in between—all of whom are being proactive in their cultivation of missionaries. The common denominator isn't the numbers of people sent but the impact the church has on the ones who are sent.

The "pipeline" is a metaphor for the strategic and organized deployment of missionaries who come from churches, unite with a sending agency, and ultimately serve sacrificially on the mission field. We could also substitute the phrase "rites of passage" for the "pipeline," but somewhere along the way the evangelical church has lost this important concept.

Rites of passage are still common among institutions like fraternities and sororities and military and civic organizations. A few church traditions have kept this concept of development for their youth and new converts. The Catholic Church retains rites of passage with baptism, catechism, and first Communion. The Jewish traditions of bar mitzva and bat mitzva still help young people move along the pathways of their faith. The Mormons (LDS) keep the concept of rites of passage with their elderships, Melchizedek priesthood, and the ever-present two-year mission after high school.

It seems like evangelicals have completely eliminated this concept, by not only separating from these faith traditions theologically but also avoiding elements of practice. Just because we don't agree with their message doesn't mean that we can't learn from their methods. In fact, these practices may be just what we need to rediscover in an effort to get sending churches reengaged in the Great Commission.

As we develop this framework for mobilization in the local church, we need to be aware that churches come in all shapes and sizes, so keep in mind that these are principles and not a program. Each church we interviewed had a process of taking someone from the baseline of no faith in Christ to someone who has completely surrendered their life to serve. We identified and labeled four incremental steps in this process: First Step, Next Steps, Step Up, and Step Out. We also highlight the six elements from our survey and research that we found in the most successful sending churches: Education, Events, Exposure, Expectations, Experiences, and Excursions.

The first priority to being a sending church and developing these mobilization rites of passage is to pray. The Lord Jesus, in Matthew 9:38 and Luke 10:2, compels us, with an imperative verb, to "pray earnestly to the Lord of the harvest to send out laborers into his harvest." It is important for us to understand our different roles as we endeavor to build this pipeline. According to Jesus, our role as believers is simply to *pray*. The Lord's role is to *send* the laborers.

The Lord's Mobilization Strategy: We Pray and He Sends

When we approach mobilization with this fundamental understanding, all the stress of evangelism, discipleship, recruitment, mentoring, and candidate preparation just melts away because we begin to realize that the results are in the Lord's hands, not ours. Our job is to be faithful, and he will make us fruitful.

Now what if we pray and he sends, but we have no idea what to do with all the people who are hearing his voice calling them to the nations? That may describe the condition of the average evangelical church today. We are so thankful for the church leaders who agreed to write chapters for this book to share their vision, strategy, and implementation of ministry. You can learn from their experience and apply it to your own church context.

In this chapter we will be laying the fundamental groundwork for establishing an intentional and proactive ministry of church-based missionary mobilization. Many leaders in the mission agencies that participated in our research have essentially said, "The church really needs to understand that by the time their candidate reaches the agency, it's too late for character development, biblical literacy, and ministry skills. We need to help local churches start to think globally when it comes to preparing their young people."

To get started, the local church should first develop a ministry team with the specific purpose of mobilizing the next generation of missionaries. When the team is developed and fully functioning, they can establish rites of passage for their congregation that will serve as spiritual markers in the lives of disciples and future pastors and missionaries. As in all areas of church life, if something is important we usually organize a committed group of people to get the job done. Is the Great Commission important in your church? If so, let's get organized . . .

Designing a Church-based Mobilization Team

After prayer, we start by recruiting people who are devoted to the task. The policies, practices, and priorities should come later, as a result of the discussions from the group that is tasked with mobilization responsibilities. Some leaders may want to establish policy first and then find people who will do the work, but that may not be very wise. When a group of lay people from the church are given the vision and the authority to develop that vision, they become owners of the process. Their investment will be much stronger and deeper than if they are just sitting on a committee making decisions.

The selection of team members is especially important when you consider the lives of those whom they will be nurturing to live a life of sacrifice in service to the Lord. Some on the team need to understand what it's like to live cross-culturally. Others need to be well read with a serious mind for studying and recommending resources to help people mature. The team also needs people with organizational skills to coordinate events as well as keep the team on task.

When it comes to the mission/ministry experience of team members, we need to do some counterintuitive thinking. Yes, the team needs individuals who have already been involved in missions and have a fully devoted heart for reaching the nations for Christ. But an argument can be made to recruit people from the church who have never been involved in missions, perhaps someone with some of the skills listed above but no experience serving the Lord cross-culturally. The reason for including someone like this is to represent and speak on behalf of those who have not been engaged in the Great Commission before.

Those of us who serve in global ministries don't like to admit this, but there is *always a reason* why people are not involved. Sometimes the reason is fear of working with those who are different—such as foreigners, the poor, people who come from a different culture or speak a different language, or people with contrary beliefs. Other times they don't see the need to reach out beyond their comfort zone. Also, to put it bluntly, some people see missionaries as just plain weird. (A friend of mine says he likes being weird for Christ.) Regardless of their reasons, people are not engaged in missions, so the team needs someone with a realistic viewpoint to overcome objections by others.

Another counterintuitive consideration is to make sure you recruit busy people. Sometimes we can lean toward a flawed assumption that we should seek out people who have plenty of time on their hands, thinking that this is a good way to get people involved. But frankly, there are often *good reasons* why people aren't very busy. However, busy people are generally well organized, successful, and effective in their lives. In addition, if they catch the vision they are capable of reprioritizing and will make every effort to turn their success in life into significance for the kingdom of God.

You may want to consider a wide variety of skills and professions. Here are some examples to get you thinking about those in your church: former missionaries, missionary parents, missionary candidates, event planners, administrative assistants, human resource personnel, salespersons, life coaches/career advisors, pastors (youth, children, college), entrepreneurs, real estate professionals, teachers.

Here is one last consideration for recruiting team members. Today's missionaries are more likely to be team players than lone rangers who blaze a solo trail on the mission field. The vast majority of missionaries who go out through an agency today are placed on a team to accomplish a task that is much larger than what one person can do alone. There is still pioneering work to be done by individuals, but the "team concept" is overwhelmingly in the majority. Because of this, the mobilization team needs people who are team players and who understand the importance of working together with others.

In the North American church, we love to celebrate self-made individualists who made it on their own. However, that is not realistic on the modern mission field. When cultivating people to become modern missionaries, you need team members who are personally involved in a team themselves. This will help ensure an authentic representation from the leadership level.

Once the team is assembled, they can begin developing policies, practices, and priorities in the form of a POEM (Philosophy of Effective Ministry). Just as a sample, here is something put together by one local church:

The purpose of the Mobilization Team is to prepare cross-cultural missionaries with the skills, knowledge, and character required for effective service, in the context of our church, so that we can affirm the Holy Spirit's calling on their lives, and fulfill our responsibility as their "Senders" when we match them with a compatible global partner agency.

When evaluating missionary candidates, there are three desired outcomes in the quality of the person that will be sent:

Spiritually Mature—Able to sustain and nourish a close relationship with the Lord

Relationally Healthy—Developing skills in conflict resolution and maintaining appropriate interpersonal relationships

Culturally Adaptable—Has experience with building bridges in another culture to become more incarnational as a servant of the Lord

This is just an illustration of a well-conceived POEM, but it will be a good starting place for your newly formed mobilization team to have some meaningful discussions as you begin to get organized. Take your time and give lots of thought in regard to the future as well as the present.

This may seem theoretical or even impractical, but over time you will continue coming back to your original ideals as a point of reference when you face difficult decisions. Say, for example, someone in your church comes to your group to ask for your help in mentoring a youth intern. Because you state the purpose of preparing "cross-cultural missionaries" in your POEM, you have the ability to say no, which will help to limit your local obligations while maximizing your focus on the nations.

At this moment, you may not have any candidates in the pipeline, so it may be helpful to study those whom Jesus recruited and how he engaged them in ministry.

The Steps of Jesus

During his earthly ministry, Jesus gave us great examples of shared ministry, partnership, and organization. He didn't do ministry alone, and even today he chooses to share his ministry with us. Consider these examples from the life of Jesus, and you will see that he actively engaged his followers in the work of sending laborers in four different ways: First Step, Next Step, Step Up, and Step Out.

First Step: Good Works First Impressions

"Follow me." This represents one of the first encounters that Jesus had with his disciples. Though it was simple, it had profound impact and consequences. The rabbi/disciple relationship was common in those days, and the disciples of Christ knew that they were being recruited to learn from a teacher by walking, talking, and serving together on the dusty road "classrooms" of Palestine.

Here is something we need to consider, though. Jesus knew that the Cross was coming, but his disciples weren't aware of that. When Jesus was selecting men to be by his side, he knew that he was recruiting them for more than just learning. He was preparing them for a life of sacrifice and for a life of service to a heavenly kingdom on a resistant earth. As David Platt says in his book *Follow Me: A Call to Die. A Call to Live,* "The road that leads to heaven is risky, lonely, and costly in this world, and few are willing to pay the price."[1]

Within the local church, our primary role as leaders is to equip people to follow Jesus and to be his disciples. There are numerous pathways for discipleship to happen: Bible study, fellowship, home groups, special events, service opportunities for the community, etc. The *First Step* is often the entry point into the church, and that point varies from church to church and from community to community.

Keep in mind that today the entry point is rarely the front door on a Sunday morning. More and more people are coming to church "through the back door" these days. Although we no longer live in a church-centered country, people are still finding their way to the church, many times through venues other than Sunday morning services. The back door of the church could be the website, special holiday events, weddings or funerals, or an invitation to a small group Bible study in a home.

It is important that those coming in through the back door experience a "good works first impression." What I mean is that the church should provide low investment/high impact opportunities that will be attractive to guests and new believers, like a food drive for low-income families, a school teacher appreciation banquet, or something else that helps guests see that the church is concerned about serving outside its walls. These *First Step* opportunities should be designed to draw people in to give them a taste of what Jesus meant when he said, "It is more blessed to give than to receive" (Acts 20:35).

Unfortunately, some churches stop at this step and it becomes the end, instead of a means to the end. Jesus didn't call his disciples to follow him just to walk and learn, but to serve and to change the world. Good works are good, but they are not the best. They can become a distraction from the greater purposes of the church. If they are used properly as a means to an end, however, through them God will transform lives, communities, and the world.

Next Step: 3+ Christians

Once Jesus' disciples accepted the call to follow him, he began to use them in a variety of ways. He sent some to run errands; some organized boats for passage across the Sea of Galilee (Matt 14:22); some prepared a room for them to participate in Passover (Luke 22:7–13); and some organized transportation—namely a donkey (Matt 21:1–3). Even Judas had a job on this ministry team: He was in charge of the moneybag (John 13:29). It seems as though Jesus was constantly testing his team in this discipleship stage. Jesus likely knew that Judas was a thief, yet he still allowed him to participate in his ministry team.

When designing *Next Step* opportunities for the church, picture a funnel. You begin with the larger body that is engaged in doing good works and generally participating in the life of the church. Some will want more than just general participation. Some will be content with attending services, Bible study, and fellowship events, but others will want to experience more of what it is like to serve the Lord. As a pastor on our church staff, we would identify people from the congregation who were what we called "3+ Christians." These were members who gave the church more than three hours per week. The first three hours were loosely identified with the worship service, Sunday school, and Wednesday night prayer service (the three pillars of many American evangelical churches).

The task for church leaders is to find ways of engaging these 3+ Christians in meaningful service either in the church or in the community. They can be greeters at the front door, serve on a committee, help in the nursery, volunteer at a local after-school center or homeless shelter, or even participate on a short-term mission trip. This is an intentional *Next Step* of service that meets a need in the church, builds confidence in the individual, and also gives pastors and leaders the opportunity to observe the person to see if they have an even greater potential for deeper ministry.

Yet again, these *Next Step* opportunities can become distractions to the larger purpose of the church. For example, dynamic conversations are taking place within the mission community about the rightful place of short-term mission trips. Is the cost of sending groups of people to exotic destinations around the world worth the price for once-in-a-lifetime experiences? Is there long-term benefit, or harm, in doing short-term trips? Who are the real beneficiaries of a short-term trip—participants or recipients?

These are fantastic questions to ask, and the church needs to wrestle with this before designing a trip. However, if the short-term trip has the goal of exposure for a smaller, select group of individuals to test the Lord and his calling on their lives, then it has a significant purpose. Not all short-term trip participants become missionaries, but most missionaries have at one point participated in a short-term trip.

Step Up: The Lord Will Provide

During the feeding of the five thousand, Jesus helped the disciples understand their role in his ministry while at the same time distinguishing his own role.

> Now the day began to wear away, and the twelve came and said to him, "Send the crowd away to go into the surrounding villages and countryside to find lodging and get provisions, for we are here in a desolate place." But he said to them, "You give them something to eat." They said, "We have no more than five loaves and two fish—unless we are to go and buy food for all these people." For there were about five thousand men. And he said to his disciples, "Have them sit down in groups of about fifty each." And they did so, and had them all sit down. And taking the five loaves and the two fish, he looked up to heaven and said a blessing over them. Then he broke the loaves and gave them to the disciples to set before the crowd. And they all ate and were satisfied. And what was left over was picked up, twelve baskets of broken pieces. (Luke 9:12–17)

Jesus engaged his followers in an extraordinary demonstration of provision based on the needs of the people upon whom he had compassion. They started out with only a few loaves and fish, but when they got organized Jesus was able to perform a miracle. Sure, Jesus could have done this on his own, but he intentionally chose to use the disciples and to make them a part of his ministry.

Here is where we need to bring the metaphor of the pipeline back into the picture. Jesus will provide, but it is our job to organize and get ready for the blessing that is about to come our way. If we build a pipeline that is capable of sending a few missionaries, then he will send a few missionaries.

If we build a pipeline that can accommodate a thousand missionaries, then he will send a thousand, plus a few extra. Our role is to organize people and to bear witness to the miracle that will bring glory to his name.

Pastors are notorious for trying to do ministry on their own. I recall a pastor confessing to me that he was feeling burned out because of all the hospital and nursing home visits he had to do. After listening for a while, I asked him what he really enjoyed in ministry, to which he replied, "Mentoring and equipping the saints for ministry." The obvious solution was to encourage him to mentor and equip a team of church members to serve in a visitation ministry. That way he could exercise his calling to be an equipper and others in the church could use their gifts of showing mercy. This would fulfill Paul's description of the church, whereby Christ "gave the apostles, the prophets, the evangelists, the shepherds and teachers, *to equip the saints for the work of ministry,* for building up the body of Christ, until we all attain to the unity of the faith and of the knowledge of the Son of God." (Eph 4:11–13, emphasis mine)

Rather than the mobilization pipeline within the church being the responsibility of just one person (i.e., the pastor), a team of people should have the primary responsibility of organizing the church to be a sending church. So many people in the church have incredible skills, talents, and abilities, but they aren't being properly engaged in ministry. If you get organized around a vision and invite these people to participate, they will not only step up but leap at the chance to turn their successful capacity into a significant ministry.

In every church, large or small, there are people whom God has given the gift of organization. They can catch the vision, see the task ahead of them, and implement the strategy—just like the disciples did during the miracle of feeding the five thousand. Every pastor/mission pastor would benefit from identifying those people and engaging them in ministry.

There is one last example of how Jesus engaged his followers.

Step Out: *Sending out the Seventy-Two*

After this the Lord appointed seventy-two others and sent them on ahead of him, two by two, into every town and place where he himself was about to go. And he said to them, "The harvest is plentiful, but the laborers are few. Therefore pray earnestly to the Lord of the harvest to send out laborers into his harvest. Go your way; behold, I am sending you out as lambs in the midst of wolves. Carry no moneybag, no knapsack, no sandals, and greet no one on the road. Whatever house you enter, first say, 'Peace be to this house!' And if a son of peace is there, your peace will rest upon him. But if not, it will return to you. And remain in the same house, eating and drinking what they provide, for the laborer deserves his wages. Do not go from house to house. Whenever you enter a town and they receive you, eat what is set before you. Heal the sick in it and say to them, 'The kingdom of God has come near to you.' But whenever you enter a town and they do not receive you, go into its streets and say, 'Even the dust of your town that clings to our feet we wipe off against you. Nevertheless know this, that the kingdom of God has come near.' I tell you, it will be more bearable on that day for Sodom than for that town." . . .

The seventy-two returned with joy, saying, "Lord, even the demons are subject to us in your name!" And he said to them, "I saw Satan fall like lightning from heaven. Behold, I have given you authority to tread on serpents and scorpions, and over all the power of the enemy, and nothing shall hurt you. Nevertheless, do not rejoice in this, that the spirits are subject to you, but rejoice that your names are written in heaven." (Luke 10:1–12, 17–20)

In this passage of Scripture, we see evidence of Jesus training his followers spiritually, relationally, and cross-culturally. He gives them instructions, vision, and encouragement. He also entrusts them with his message, his power, and even his kingdom. There will come a time when your mobilization team has to release people into a very dangerous world, and you may question if they are ready. The best part of this story is that Jesus didn't just send out the twelve, but he sent out the seventy-two to be "lambs in the midst of wolves." They were sent intentionally underprepared (no moneybag, knapsack, or sandals). And they were equipped to be rejected—"Even the dust . . . we wipe off against you."

Missionary mobilization is not about designing the perfect missionary, but about sending people whom God has chosen to represent his kingdom. We are not building indestructible robots; we are preparing people who are faithful, prepared, and resilient for a lifetime of service to the Lord.

In order to accomplish this goal, we need to send out people from the church to experience temporary difficulties. Just to wrestle with this concept, consider the state of Christian parenting. Many Christian parents are leading the way in perpetuating a climate of dependence on safety and security for their children by either placing them in private Christian schools or homeschooling them. My comments here are not meant to condemn this strategy, but simply to highlight a deficiency in our ability to nurture missionaries who will go to hard places in the world to reach the unreached. It's hard to imagine individuals who have been sheltered all their lives in a closely guarded and well protected environment being willing to go to a place like Yemen, Bhutan, Cambodia, or Libya.

Recently I interviewed a retired missionary who spent forty years (1957–1997) in the headhunter-filled jungles of Ecuador. When I asked what prepared her for that kind of life, she replied, "I had a hard life growing up. We were migrant laborers and my parents moved us kids around looking for work in the California orange groves. Most of the time my bed was under an orange tree with a root for a pillow."

If we are going to send people to reach the unreached, we need to understand that they are unreached for a reason. They are in hard places, and our people need to have some experience with hardships and suffering. We may be able to overcome this problem by creating some tension and some experiences that will help train our young people to endure hardships and overcome obstacles, but it must be intentional. Otherwise we will simply follow the path of least resistance. Ideas that could help include short-term mission trips, exposure to missionaries, the "30 Hour Famine," etc. Your team just needs to make "training in hardship" a priority, or else the missionary attrition rate will continue to rise. A theology of mission would be incomplete without a proper theology of suffering.

Rite of Passage

A rite of passage is a significant event or a transition period in someone's life that marks a change. A changed life for the kingdom of God is a beautiful thing. And that is our business as mission leaders. Every business needs a business plan. As Benjamin Franklin once said, "If you fail to plan, you are planning to fail!"

As we have been speaking to successful church leaders and interviewing them to discover their best practices, we noticed that most all of them were doing some of the same things. They spoke the same lingo, read the same books, attended the same conferences, and consulted with the same leaders. The ways they lead their churches were different, but many of the principles were employed as they sought to mobilize missionaries from within their church. They were all focused, intentional, and very proactive in developing their people for a lifetime of faithful service.

Included below are the six categories of ministry planning that we discovered from highly successful church mission leaders. Your team may want to develop and organize around these categories as you look at your calendar planning. We are providing you with just a few examples; there are so many more that you can apply. Most denominations offer experiences that will fit within the larger context and give your congregation lots of opportunities to get engaged.

Here are the six categories: Education, Events, Exposure, Expectations, Experiences, and Excursions.

Education

"Perspectives on the World Christian Movement" (www.perspectives.org) is likely the single most effective mission course that anyone can take. It is offered all over the world in churches, Bible schools, seminaries, and missionary agencies. When I speak to missionaries and ask them about their calling to the mission field, I hear three common responses:

1. a personal relationship with a missionary at a young age
2. a well-planned short-term trip
3. the Perspectives class

In addition to Perspectives, there are many other valuable mission education curricula, such as Henry Blackaby's *Experiencing God* and David Platt's *Follow Me*. These may not be specifically about missionary training, but they provide a general overview of God's heart for the lost and his focus on reaching the nations for Christ. Some mission education needs to be general enough to instruct a larger crowd, but over time you will also need training that will edify those who want to go deeper into their calling. Greg Carter wrote *Skills, Knowledge, Character: A Church-Based Approach to Missionary Candidate Preparation*, which is specifically intended to mentor and disciple missionary candidates within the context of the local church.[2]

Other education pieces include books like *Operation World* to start discovering the needs of the world and the missing pieces of our missionary sending efforts. You can study books together on missionary care, business as mission, community development, and poverty alleviation. Books that highlight a theology of suffering, such as *So Send I You* by Oswald Chambers,[3] can provide perspective for young people as they start reading biographies of missionaries. Some students may want to discover missionary methods and read books on church planting principles. The list is endless, but the idea is to make mission education a priority and a part of the regular routine of the church calendar.

Events

Every three years, the Urbana Conference (www.urbana.org) draws thousands of Christian young people to the largest mission-centered recruitment event in North America. Students are challenged by world-class speakers who are very intentional about mobilizing the next generation of missionaries. The highlight of the event is the exhibit hall that features hundreds of missionary sending organizations. Young people can roam the hall for days and interview all of the recruiters to see which agency is a good fit for them.

Most denominations have annual meetings and/or regular events as well, so your church would be wise to send some of your young people as delegates to participate. They can meet denominational leaders and find out what kind of mission opportunities exist through the global outreach arm of the organization. Sometimes the summer camps for students will highlight mission opportunities and bring in leaders who can help counsel young people.

Missionary sending agencies will often have an annual church partnership conference for churches that support their missionaries. If your church currently supports a missionary through an agency, contact the person at the agency who relates to churches to see if they have any events coming up.

Some churches choose to host their own mission conference. They invite their supported missionaries to come that week (or weekend), they offer a special speaker (often from a sending agency or Bible school), and have special events designed for a variety of age groups. As an example, here is what one church did just for the children's ministry:

The Church Missionary Airplane Experience

The men's ministry constructed a giant airplane out of PVC pipe and plastic wrap on the front lawn of the church (similar to a greenhouse nursery, but with wings!). Inside was set up with rows of chairs to resemble the passenger compartment of an airplane. The children were also given a passport that they colored and designed themselves. Volunteers took pictures of students, printed them out, and glued them to the first page. The passport contained blank pages for visa stamps, so there was a room at the church where the students had to go and answer questions about the different countries where they wanted to visit. Most of the countries on the itinerary were places where the church sent missionaries.

Once the children had the visa stamp, they were allowed to board the "airplane." While on the plane, missionaries from around the world taught the children about that country and the people group whom they served. After a while, the children deplaned and were escorted to a special room that was set up and decorated with pictures, artifacts, and even food from the country they just learned about. There they received a visitor stamp in their passport, and they were back on the plane for another "destination."

There are many creative ideas like this for churches to help highlight missions to children and begin the process of mobilization at the earliest possible age.

Exposure

Time and time again, we hear stories from current missionaries who describe pivotal moments in their childhood development when a real-life missionary came and had dinner at their home. It appears that having a personal relationship with a missionary is a significant indicator for mission involvement. Just as with short-term trips, not every person who knows a missionary personally will one day become a missionary themselves. But when most every missionary was young, they met someone who served the Lord in some far-off place. Our hypothesis is that knowing someone who is a missionary makes mission work normal.

If your church already supports missionaries, it would be an utmost priority for you to pay for them to come to the church regularly and speak to the congregation. Along with that, they need to visit Sunday school classes, small groups, home groups, and even have meals with families, just for the exposure to the next generation. When a church talks openly about sending people to distant lands and then brings in those people for personal updates and reports, missions goes from abstract to concrete, to flesh and blood—real.

If your church doesn't currently support missionaries, contact a local mission agency and schedule a speaker. When missionaries are home on furlough ("home ministry assignment"), part of their responsibilities typically includes visiting churches to share their story and represent the organization.

Expectations

Sometimes we can understand rites of passage in terms of prerequisites. In order for you to advance from one stage of personal development to another, you should prove yourself with a lesser degree of challenge and responsibility. For example, if someone wants to be supported as a missionary from First Church, they need to go through the missionary mentoring training (MMT). If they want to go through MMT, they need to serve on the mission committee. If they want to serve on the mission committee, they need to go on a short-term trip. If they want to go on a short-term trip, they need to go through the Perspectives class, etc.

You can customize your expectations based on your church's values and specific mission approach, but the important part of these rites of passage is that they build upon one another. If, for example, your church sends the high school seniors on a special mission trip to Israel every year, that is a special privilege that should be earned and anticipated by the underclassmen. They can earn this opportunity by participating in local outreach projects, serving in the children's ministry, reading particular books, or participating in certain classes and training programs during their earlier high school years. The middle school students will see this as something to look forward to and will strive to do all they can to participate in the future. You can also offer similar experiences for elementary students to look forward to in middle school.

Just think through the stages of development that are already happening with your young people and apply them to missionary mobilization.

Experiences

Some of the best experiences for the development of future missionaries happen away from the church campus. You can educate young people about the problems of poverty and homelessness, but until they actually walk the halls of a homeless shelter, prepare meals for low-income families, and shake hands with someone living on the streets, it will never be real. Every individual in every church needs to have personal, one-on-one experience with people who are normally marginalized, overlooked, and ignored. And they aren't hard to find. Church leaders need to provide contextualized ministry for church members in relation to those who ask for handouts in grocery store parking lots, at freeway exits, or on downtown street corners.

There needs to be wisdom as well as compassion that arises from a biblical perspective that can only come from the church. Steve Corbett and

Brian Fikkert's book, *When Helping Hurts*, sparked a valuable conversation in the missions world and in the church.[4] If contextualization is the cornerstone of mission practice, the nearest training ground is most major cities and urban neighborhoods here in North America. This concept is something that is caught rather than taught, so significant experiences are necessary for this missiological development of a Christian disciple.

Another experience that sending church leaders can provide for their disciples is road trips to visit missionary sending agencies and training centers. Scattered all over North America, these agencies allow visitors to come in for a tour and an explanation of what they do as a ministry. Just like parents who take their children on college visits to get onsite knowledge of the institution, agency tours can reveal many things that the agency values.

For example, if your church is located in the Midwest, you can take students on a tour of Avant Ministries in Kansas City, Missouri. By walking the halls, you will see that this missionary sending agency dates back to 1892 and has the primary purpose of planting churches among the unreached. You will see photographs and artifacts from some of their pioneering work among headhunters in Ecuador and the Berber people in the deserts of Morocco. Likewise, if you live in the southwest United States, stop by the headquarters of Frontiers in Phoenix. If you're planning a trip to Disney World in Orlando, you could visit a number of organizations, such as Pioneers, Wycliffe, and Cru.

These agencies love to receive visitors so that they can tell their story and provide future missionaries with a firsthand look at how to make missionary work a reality.

Excursions

Perhaps the most significant rite of passage a church can provide is a mission trip. As evangelicals, we may not agree with the message of the Mormons, but we cannot deny the impact of their mission method. The two-year mission is such an important rite of passage for them. All their young people look forward to going on their mission, and all the older people fondly remember their experience. I have frequently interacted with Mormons, and all of them have had their mission on the top of their minds as they discuss their faith development. This is comparable to Catholic baptism, first Communion, confirmation, and confession all in one. It is as important to them as circumcision and bar/bat mitzvah is to Jews.

There are two extremes regarding mission trips in evangelical churches across the country. The first extreme is the church that doesn't venture beyond its walls for any outreach at all, including short-term mission trips. This is sad and unfortunate, but it is likely the reality for a majority of churches in North America. It is a symptom of a much deeper issue that should be examined, evaluated, and prayed over.

The other extreme is a church that offers short-term mission trips like they are cold donuts on a Sunday morning. There is nothing special about them, because they are cheap and easy. They offer them from a menu of options, which is also sad and unfortunate for a variety of reasons—primarily because people in the church come to see the short-term trip as an end instead of a means to an end. Some people use the mission trip as a way of escaping their monotonous, unfulfilled, self-centered daily routine. It is like a cheap drug fix or a spiritual vaccine for those suffering from the disease of the institutional feel-good religion.

Nevertheless, there are some really good reasons to offer short-term trips. For the purposes of this book, the best short-term trip is the one in which participants survey a destination and meet people whom they may be sensing God's call to serve long-term.

There are a variety of mission trip options:
- Short-term trips (defined as a weekend to two weeks—basically using vacation time from work)
- Mid-term trips (defined as two weeks to three months—includes summer break opportunities)
- Semester mission trips (three to six months—taking a break from school)
- Gap year (six to twelve months—for students between high school and college or between college and grad school)
- Stint (twelve to twenty-four months—often for missionary candidates who have decided to serve as missionaries but are undecided on a destination)

There are many more options, depending on what agency you partner with, but these are the more frequently used industry standards from which to choose.

❚❚ Rites of passage can be powerful tools
to motivate people in the church
and bring excitement and enthusiasm
to a congregation. Your church can be the
solution to the pipeline supply shortages **❚❚**
that we are experiencing in missionary
mobilization, if you are intentional
and proactive about discipling people
to consider the nations.

Church-based Mobilization Is Not Just for the Youth

Mobilization is not just for young people, and a sending church should see the entire body of believers as potential recruits. Though many people accept God's call to missions when they are in their teens and twenties, some of our best recruits are people who have already learned significant life lessons. In fact, if we really want to make an impact in hard places, we need to focus our efforts on recruiting and mobilizing people who already have a college degree and workplace experience so that they can get work visas instead of missionary visas (which many nations no longer accept).

Another group of people you need to seriously consider is retirees. Bob Buford wrote an incredible book, called *Half Time*, about going from success to significance later in life.[5] In that same vein is a book written by mission agency executives Hans Finzel and Rick Hicks called *Launch Your Encore*, which gives specific attention to mobilizing seniors to the mission field.[6]

There are three major perks to a focus on mobilizing seniors. First, they have a retirement income, which reduces their need to raise funds. Second, many restricted access nations have special visa programs for people to retire in their country as a second home. Third, gray hair is an asset in most developing countries around the globe. While speaking with a friend from Liberia recently, we compared the value differences between our two cultures. Here in North America people buy hair products that conceal their gray hair, whereas there is a large market among West Africans for products that will gray their hair! They see age as a value for wisdom and experience, while we value youthfulness. (We also discussed the African value of extra body weight and larger waistlines, since being "plump" is a sign of wealth in nations that struggle to secure reliable food sources—but I won't divulge my North American bias, which we discussed, here in writing.)

Rites of passage can be powerful tools to motivate people in the church and bring excitement and enthusiasm to a congregation. Your church can be the solution to the pipeline supply shortages that we are experiencing in missionary mobilization, if you are intentional and proactive about discipling people to consider the nations.

As you read the following chapters written by church mission leaders, look for principles you can glean from them and apply to your specific church context. When Jesus commanded us to pray for the Lord to send laborers (Matt 9:38 and Luke 10:2), you may just be the answer to that prayer in your local church.

David J. Wilson served in the local church as mission pastor for over twenty years. In November 2016, he joined Avant Ministries in Kansas City, MO, as director of church relations.

Notes

[1] David Platt, *Follow Me: A Call to Die. A Call to Live* (Carol Stream, IL: Tyndale, 2013).

[2] Greg Carter, *Skills, Knowledge, Character: A Church-Based Approach to Missionary Candidate Preparation* (Valparaiso, IN: Turtle River Press, 2010).

[3] Oswald Chambers, *So Send I You: A Series of Missionary Studies* (London: Simpkin Marshall, 1930).

[4] Steve Corbett and Brian Fikkert, *When Helping Hurts: How to Alleviate Poverty without Hurting the Poor… and Yourself* (Chicago: Moody, 2009).

[5] Bob Buford, *Half Time:* Moving from Success to Significance (Grand Rapids, MI: Zondervan, 2007).

[6] Hans Finzel and Rick Hicks, *Launch Your Encore: Finding Adventure and Purpose Later in Life* (Grand Rapids, MI: Baker, 2015).

CHAPTER 12

Bethlehem Baptist Church

Preparing and Nurturing Long-term Global Partners

Todd Rasmuson

The global church can learn a lot from farm kids. I grew up in a small Iowa community, and many of my classmates participated in 4H. Many were young farmers who raised animals, grew fruit and vegetables, did crafts, and wore hats and scarves proudly displaying the green logo of the four-leaf clover. It would be years later that I would be curious enough to learn that the four H's are Heart, Head, Hands, and Health. Those four "H" words are useful to the kingdom as well.

During my eight years in rural Tanzania, I served as part of a team discipling rural leaders in Bible knowledge, attitudes of service, skills in agriculture, and aspects of a healthy home. Jesus was our main teacher, the Bible our main textbook, and discipleship relationships our main methodology. We were all about the four H's. We weren't seeking the glory of state fair ribbons, however. We were hoping to bring glory to God and to live with joy and satisfaction in following Jesus.

Now that I am a pastor of missions, the four H's have followed me. I serve at Bethlehem Baptist Church in Minneapolis, Minnesota, a church of about four thousand attendees with a passion to bless the peoples of the earth through Jesus. For many years John Piper faithfully taught our people to delight in God's heart for the nations and about our Father's plans to bless all his people. Many of us at Bethlehem have heard God's call to be part of global ministry, and we currently have about two hundred of our members and their two hundred children in more than forty countries of the world.

Additionally, we have about one hundred people in our "Nurture Program," our two-year preparation process to join them. The purpose of this chapter is to describe that program, capturing the key principles and parts so that other churches, regardless of size, can help prepare those God is calling to bless the nations through Jesus.

Bethlehem's Nurture Program was started more than thirty years ago by Pastor Tom Steller, currently an elder at Bethlehem and a faculty member of Bethlehem College and Seminary. My wife, Tamara, and I were two of the early students. Thus my description and analysis of the Nurture Program comes from the view of a student, a global partner practitioner in Africa, and now a teacher and pastor overseeing the program. It is not a perfect program; and like every good course or educational effort, it needs to be continually updated and revised to keep it fresh, relevant, and effective.

Heart: Faith in Jesus and Character Development

I begin with the most important of the four H's—the heart. Without a heart changed by God, we humans are incapable of consistently loving unselfishly, especially at the level of motives (e.g., Rom 3:23). Sin has rooted its way into us, and no matter how hard we try to maintain a list of good works, we stumble. Even if we think a thought of jealousy, unrighteous anger, or lust, we have blown it. In the court of a perfect, holy God, our only hope is a Savior. Thanks be to God that Jesus took our sins upon his shoulders, died with them on a Cross, and rose from the grave (e.g., Rom 5:8). We have the honor of nurturing hearts of faith by pointing others to Jesus and never tiring of the great gospel story of hope.

Out of the abundance of the heart, the mouth speaks (Luke 6:45b). If we hope to prepare people in our churches to share the good news of Jesus, we need to care about their hearts, their brokenness, their willingness to confess and forgive, and their love of God and others. Character matters, and our only hope is Jesus at work in our hearts.

So how do we nurture the heart of another? Jesus modeled the answer—disciple, walk with others in ministry and in life, ask questions, listen, love. The heart will overflow as we walk the journey with our Savior. In those overflow moments, we can provide correction, praise, insight, prayer, and a pointing to Jesus. Ultimately, our hearts belong to God, and he is the only one who can do the sustaining work of faith. However, we are not left powerless in the process to bless others. God has given those in the church his Spirit to work in us and through us, and we are part of his body (e.g., 1 Cor 12:12,13).

Specifically, we require that those in our Nurture Program become members of our church, actively serve in a small group, take classes in our church, participate in ministry opportunities, and interact with others in our church who are mission-minded. All of these experiences put them in places of trial and challenge that can increase the heat on the pressure cooker of their lives. When the heat comes, what will be exposed in their hearts, and how will we disciple them?

Head: Theological Understanding and Critical Content

Missions needs to be theologically driven and grounded in God's Word. The heart is a pleasure factory that will easily move to Satan's candy counter and forsake the amazing banquet prepared by our Father (e.g., James 4:1–4), so the head must be fully engaged. The Bible is the very words of God: an awesome feast to sustain our faith and inform our thinking for global work (e.g., Ps 119:105). Our churches are given the responsibility to teach and to build a solid foundation for global ministry on God's Word.

Specifically, we require coursework in systematic theology and in Bible study methods. In our church, we offer two semester courses in "Theological Foundations" and one semester course in "Mining God's Word." These courses have traditionally been taught by our elders, pastors, and/or long-time members of our church. Since we have launched a college and seminary, we have been blessed to have seminary professors and seminary students teach as well. All three courses are offered in a classroom and online.

Some of those entering our Nurture Program have taken coursework in theology and Bible study methods prior to coming to our church. Often we will waive some requirements, especially if we have observed them teach and/or talk about God in a variety of contexts. Sometimes people have had courses, but the content may not align well with Bethlehem's distinctives. It may be that some of our pastoral staff join us for a theological interview to see if we are unified in what the Bible teaches on these topics and others.

Before any of our Nurture Program participants are appointed as long-term global partners, they need to affirm our "Elder Affirmation of Faith." The document can be accessed at our church's website, https://bethlehem.church/elder-affirmation-of-faith/.

Besides systematic theology and Bible study methods, we believe that other content is critical to global ministry. Certainly we want all other content to be theologically informed too! We require that all of our Nurture Program participants take the "Perspectives on the World Christian Movement" course, and we have added a reading supplement and some discussion questions to address some theological and methodological concerns in the Perspectives course.

Additionally, we require the reading of books about peacemaking, cultural learning, spiritual warfare, suffering, and other topics as selected. The topics are subject to change based on needs we see in the global ministry terrain. After each book is read, Nurture Program participants write a reflection paragraph on the book, providing a few thoughts on its application to their possible future ministries.

Mission agencies have their requirements too, and we build time in our Nurture Program for our people to work on those, often during the phase of financial and prayer-partner development. Some agencies require specialty training (e.g., Wycliffe Bible Translators) that moves beyond our Nurture Program time line.

Hands: Evangelism, Discipleship, and Work

If the core command of the Great Commission is to "go and make disciples," we want to offer opportunities for our people to experience other cultures, do evangelism, and join the mess and celebration of discipling and being discipled. Toward that end, we require that people seek out a friend from another culture, share their faith with at least five others, and experience discipleship in small group ministry.

Business as Mission (BAM) has been a growing focus for many in our church, so we have encouraged people to connect with our BAM committee, gain work experience, and pursue specialized coursework and degrees that would prepare them for excellence in business. It is our expectation that our BAM global partners would be part of profitable business that adds value to cultures and integrates with church planting.

Health: Counseling and Care

None of us will reach perfect health until Jesus calls us home, but we want our people to strive for healthy lives (spiritually, emotionally, relationally, and physically). One of our partnering agencies told us, "Please keep working with your people on issues of brokenness. More and more of our candidates are interviewed by our agency and sent back to their churches

> **"** Until Jesus returns,
> the church has the responsibility
> and joy to send God's children,
> called by him, to bless the nations. **"**

to work on issues related to broken families and relationships, addictions, and emotional strength."

We host day-long retreats in our Nurture Program to come away and talk through issues that can overwhelm global partners and wreck ministries (e.g., team conflict, sexual brokenness, financial matters). We strive to help build resilience in our people, by God's grace, to prepare them for trials that will be present in themselves and in the new cultures coming their way. Many of our current global partners are teachers during our retreats and "mission fellowships," which are gathering times for those in our Nurture Program.

At the midpoint of our Nurture Program we require our people to complete a lengthy counseling intake form and meet with a trained biblical counselor to talk about their answers. My wife and I meet them for a pastoral follow-up to get to know them at a deeper level and to follow up on next steps related to growth areas. During the Nurture Program process, we work together on those issues—sometimes with successful growth and sometimes not. It may be that the time is not right for a person to pursue global ministry, and our churches need to provide care-filled counsel on other pathways to follow Jesus.

When a Nurture Program candidate gets to the mission field, member care continues from our church from a team including pastors, prayer and financial supporters, family, and their "Barnabas Support Team." All of our global partners are required to have a Barnabas Support Team of five to ten people committed to praying for them, providing practical helps, and serving as an ambassador for them in our church. Over the years, Barnabas Support Teams have played a critical role in keeping some of our families on the field.

One of the pastors of our church helps provide oversight to the Barnabas Support Team ministry, and we provide ongoing training to the teams to help them provide quality care to their global partners. When the issues become large, we turn to biblical counselors from our church, from their mission agencies, and from our city. The local church "owns" global partner care, but it is a team effort from many places.

Conclusion

Until Jesus returns, the church has the responsibility and joy to send God's children, called by him, to bless the nations. We can prepare our people well by nurturing their faith and pointing them to Jesus for critical heart work; by educating them with solid theology, Bible study methods, and other critical content; providing opportunities for practical ministry experience; and by giving ongoing care and counseling to promote healthy lives and relationships.

A farm kid may tell you that the goals of heart, head, hands, and health are "a ton of work." The four H's of our Nurture Program do constitute a weighty bit of effort, but the main work has already been finished by the King of kings. Death and sin will have no victory, and the names of all believers are written in the Book of Life. In our labor to prepare and nurture our people to bless the nations, Jesus is worth it all.

Todd Rasmuson is the minister for global outreach at Bethlehem Baptist Church (www.bethlehem.church) in Minneapolis, MN.

We thank Todd and those who serve at Bethlehem Baptist for providing us with access to their resource, "The Nurture Program," found on our website at **www.missionarypipeline.org**.

CHAPTER 13
Calvary Church

Mobilization Strategy

Steve Beirn

One of the more important aspects of global ministry in our church has been our philosophical approach to ministry. Our philosophy has allowed us to assert ourselves in making disciples of all nations. There are just two basic models of missions today in the local church. From these two models come scores of variations. The first model is represented by a sectioned pie. Each slice is a ministry of that church. Missions is one slice among many others. Circumstances or a change in church leadership will determine whether missions becomes a larger or smaller slice.

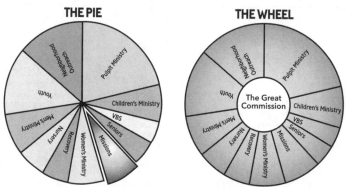

The second model looks like a wheel. This church has many ministry slices as well, but in the core of this wheel is a circle, a hub. That core is the Great Commission. Since the Great Commission is at the center, it can and should influence all other ministries of the church. It is placed at the center because of the magnitude of this global commission. The size of each ministry may change, but the core value that influences each never changes.

> Many people ask how a church can move from the "pie" to the "wheel." The answer is simple, but the implementation is challenging.

Many people ask how a church can move from the "pie" to the "wheel." The answer is simple, but the implementation is challenging. You can begin by selecting one or two ministries of the church and intentionally integrate missions into that program. This ignites interest and ownership in global outreach. Over time, enough integration takes place that the church can do some restructuring, and then making disciples of all nations becomes the core value instead of just one of the many things the church values. Keeping the Great Commission as the core value can become a challenge as well. Praying, discussing, and continuing communication of rationale for this ministry is important to maintain global ministry's place in the church. When well thought-out philosophy is in place, then mobilization can be more easily developed.

Our Mobilization Detail

When developing mobilization structure, you need to be able to answer several questions. The first question is, "Who are we mobilizing?" We identify the three basic categories: children, students, and adults. Every church should determine which category they will begin mobilizing first. The second question we ask ourselves is, "To what are we mobilizing?" For example, when we are approach a student or adult audience we focus in on specific goals to accomplish with that group. We are committed to three efforts:

1. The first is developing a personal connection with our missionaries.
2. The second is developing a stronger commitment to a world Christian lifestyle (we believe there is a difference between a Christian lifestyle and a world Christian lifestyle—just ask anyone returning from a short-term ministry overseas).
3. The third is developing deeper personal participation. This could mean anything from sacrificial giving to personally going overseas.

We have also changed our global emphasis from concentrated, time sensitive events to be age-customized efforts, integrated into the life of the church. We have thought out what we want people to do as a result of that event. Having an event just to have something on the calendar is not effective mobilization.

Our Mobilization Environment

We strive to influence our ministry environment in four different ways. The first is through our ministry message. Every church needs to communicate a high view of God. It should permeate the ministry. This will help our people develop a robust faith. Who would ever consider going to the ends of the earth unless he or she worshiped and served an all-knowing and all-powerful God?

The second way is through our trailblazers. These are people who are global ministry role models for our church family. They can be a young adult or a seasoned, retired person. They make obedience and passion for a needy world normative in the life of the church. They have taken personal ownership of the Great Commission. They cause us to ask the question, "How can God's heart for the world become more prominent in my life and in the life of my church?" This is a key way to model multiplication.

The third way to influence the ministry environment is through resources. The most obvious kind of resource is money. How can we develop a deeper faith walk as we trust God for finances? I am aware of a church that challenged people to give one dollar a day for missions. Now, more than fifty people enable their church to invest $1,500 per month in support of a ministry.

Finally, we should develop advocacy among our church leadership. They should not be asked to do the ministry of missions in the church. However, they should be prepared to endorse this ministry within the church. Building advocacy is an attempt to develop cooperation at every level of leadership with the church.

Our Mobilization Strategies

Our church has come up with three main mobilization strategies:

Cross Training

Over the last fifteen years, Calvary Church has had a church-based missionary preparation ministry called "Cross Training." It takes an average of at least three years to complete. It focuses on developing competency rather than credentialing. We want to see not only personal individual development but also a firm ministry partnership develop as we prepare to send them out.

At the writing of this book, we have twenty-two adults in this ministry. The preparation can unify our ministry vision, increase field effectiveness, and minimize attrition overseas. In order to enter "Cross Training" an individual or couple fills out an application and goes through an interview process with our leadership team and they are given a Cross Training Candidate manual.

We are known for creating four building blocks of personal development:

1. The first building block is assessment. This can help a person develop a strong sense of self-awareness, to understand their strengths and weaknesses. We always say that a better fit makes a better missionary.

2. The second building block is spiritual growth. This is an attempt to develop a ministry lifestyle through growth in spiritual disciplines such as self-directed Bible study, prayer, and sharing your faith.

3. The third block is ministry experience. This involves relating to and leading other adults. It is helping our candidates gain valuable experience in areas of life related to future ministry.

4. The fourth block is mentoring. This is a one-on-one relationship, meeting monthly the entire time they are in "Cross Training." The mentor can provide perspective and encouragement to their candidate so they can mature. Every mentor receives training prior to their first assignment. A church of any size can develop their own preparation track with these four building blocks.

Preferred Agency List

The second mobilization strategy is our preferred agency list. We highly encourage our candidates to look into and consider an agency from this list for ministry overseas. It is not a required list, but there are financial support incentives for going with a preferred agency. This list is reviewed every two to three years to ensure that we are working with organizations that value us. Our candidates know we are careful and intentional in all our working relationships. This list gives our candidates greater confidence in their future. There are five criteria for getting on and staying on the list. The first is an agency with a similar mission, vision, and values. If we are headed in the same direction it just may make sense to work together. The second is good field supervision of missionaries. The third is a commitment to member care standards of excellence. The fourth is valuing the local church. The fifth is thoughtful fiscal responsibility. Our church family is aware of this list (it can be found on our church website) and understands our commitment to be good stewards of all the resources God has given us.

Ministry Of Prayer

The third strategy in mobilization is often underdeveloped. It is the ministry of prayer. In Matthew 9:38 Jesus instructed us to "pray earnestly to the Lord of the harvest to send out laborers into his harvest." We have asked the question, "What would this look like in the life of our church?" The part that really haunts me is "praying earnestly." We have a two-year prayer emphasis where people sign up if they are willing to pray once a week for new candidates to join our "Cross Training" preparation track. They are given an update every two months. At the end of the two years we all have a breakfast together and review what God has done. Our goal is to get 10 percent of our congregation signed up and praying for new laborers. A simple prayer guide is also available to help remind everyone about key faith goals we would love to meet as God works. We have called the prayer emphasis *Petition*.

We have found that it is important to be open to creativity when trying to mobilize. For several years we planned a coffee shop week. We put out an invitation for people to be our guest for an appointment at a coffee shop with one of our mobilizers. We simply said that if they would like a starter conversation about missions they just sign up. Many significant conversations were the beginning of pursuing mission involvement.

Steve Beirn is the pastor of global ministries at Calvary Church (www.calvarychurch.org) in Lancaster, PA and author of *Well Sent: Reimagining the Church's Missionary-Sending Process*.

We thank Steve and those who serve at Calvary Church for providing us with access to their resource, "Cross Training" Candidate Manual, found on our website at **www.missionarypipeline.org**.

CHAPTER 14
Liberty Bible Church

Mentors Who Make Disciplemaking Disciples
Greg Carter

The local church is an amazing entity. When it works well, it is a grace-filled community, a base for social justice initiatives, an oasis for the harried and stressed, a locale for inspiring worship, and a beacon for orthodoxy in a shifting cultural quagmire.

Beyond all of these noble causes and experiences, the church perhaps shines best when it does the simple task of making disciples. Jesus, in the closing days of life on earth, called his disciples to multiply themselves locally, in nearby areas and cross-culturally, going as far as could possibly be imagined (Matt 28:18–20).

Two foundational thoughts of this chapter are that a local church needs to be making disciples: disciples who in turn make more disciples (2 Tim 2:2). These are faithful men and women who are committed to seeing future generations follow Jesus in knowledge and obedience. The second foundational thought is that local church leadership needs to be instructing its members on the kingdom of God around the world. An appropriate understanding of God's work in the world will be both an encouragement in seeing the big picture of his sovereignty as well as his call for service.

It will then be a reasonable hope that some of our disciplemakers, upon becoming aware of needs in the world, will be called to disciplemaking five thousand miles away. These are our future kingdom workers.

My personal premise is that local church mission leadership is capable and qualified to mentor its future missionaries in the critical areas of developing intimacy with the Father, building self-awareness/emotional health, developing ministry skills, and understanding cross-cultural issues.

> **"** My personal premise is that local church mission leadership is capable and qualified to mentor its future missionaries in the critical areas of developing intimacy with the Father, building self-awareness/emotional health, developing ministry skills, and understanding cross-cultural issues. **"**

The church produces workers for the harvest from within its body. It doesn't do this alone. There exists (albeit for the most part unrecognized and uncoordinated) a collaborative effort among the local church, the missionary sending agency, the theological school, and the specialized training organization. Together they weave a very complex process that moves the potential missionary from initial interest to onsite presence with confidence and capacity.[1]

The production of workers for the kingdom happens through a variety of manners and ways. Beyond the predictable programs and informal settings and occasions that bring about spiritual growth, is a requisite mentoring mentality that intentionally produces strong disciplemakers.

Mentoring is a preferred method for producing spiritual transformation that is foundational to equipping kingdom workers. A healthy mentoring relationship allows for the investment of a more mature Christian into the life of a younger (maturity level) believer.

An unfortunate challenge that the local church will quickly learn is that few of its members see themselves as qualified to be mentors. There is a faulty perception that the mentor is someone who "has her life in order" and thus has the platform to speak into someone else's life. An easy answer is that if this thought were true, none of us would be qualified to mentor.

A more reasoned response is that the mentee has a greater ability to hear and learn from someone who himself is still active in the process of being formed into the image of Christ. The value of a mentor who willingly offers herself in an open manner is far superior to someone who presents a facade of being neatly completed. Thus, descriptors of a person being recruited to become a mentor will include character qualities such as vulnerable, approachable, authentic, and transparent.[2]

A second area that causes some to decline the opportunity to mentor is a sense that "I don't know enough." That could be referring to missions, cross-cultural living, biblical knowledge, etc. And these could be valid potential limiting factors. However, a sharp observer has said that when considering a mentoring opportunity, don't ask "What do I have to offer?" but instead ask "How well can I listen?"[3]

The ability to ask good questions can't be over emphasized. The very nature of missionary life requires the ability to figure things out, in a whole host of areas. Rarely will the answers be readily apparent; the skill set of figuring out life is mandatory.

A mentor approach that asks the mentee leading questions is superior to telling answers. Good questions cause reflective thinking; they require assembling rationale for whys and hows. This methodology affirms the individual and his ability to draw on experience and wisdom from the Holy Spirit to arrive at good conclusions.

Asking good questions is an art. While you can find set lists of good questions (What can't you find on the internet?), the best questions come from the statement/answer that you just heard. The mentor who develops the ability of being a good question asker will be deeply appreciated by his mentee.

An additional answer to the person who would protest that she doesn't have her life together is the recognition that more is learned from watching someone rise from failure than cruise in success. We don't want people to fail simply to create a learning environment, but allowing people into our lives to see how we rectify past mistakes, errors, shortcomings (whatever we call them) is an incredible window on building maturity.

The Apostle Paul gives us a powerful response to our protestations of being unqualified.

> But [the Lord] said to me, "My grace is sufficient for you, for my power is made perfect in weakness. Therefore I will boast all the more gladly about my weaknesses, so that Christ's power may rest on me. That is why, for Christ's sake, I delight in weaknesses, in insults, in hardships, in persecutions, in difficulties. For when I am weak, then I am strong." (2 Cor 12:9,10 NIV)

The mentor understands that he will be developing his mentoree in these four areas:

- spiritual maturity, intimacy with the Father
- self-awareness/emotional intelligence (EQ)
- ministry skills
- cross-cultural skills

The mentor will use a combination of settings, experiences, and assignments to create the environment for the mentoree to gain capacity in each of the four areas. Thinking astutely, he will imagine the resources in his church and community that can be profitably marshaled for this process.[4] The mentor is not acting alone in his development of the future kingdom worker.

A. Intimacy with the Father[5]

Of all that we endeavor to accomplish with our mentee, the primary attribute to be developed is intimacy with the Father. This is especially so with men. Because men frequently default to finding their identity in their vocation, shifting this toward being a child of the Father is critical. An intimate relationship with God will steel the fledgling missionary to be resolute when life is difficult. He must be able to call on what he knows of the Father's love, affirmation, patience, forgiveness, calling, and empowering if he is to overcome the rigors of cross-cultural living. Without this intimacy, doubt will be a too familiar foe. He will question his decisions, his calling, the goodness and character of God, the unchangeableness of salvation only through Jesus.

The mentor will ensure that the mentoree understands and practices a variety of Bible study methods, has a habit of Scripture memory, and utilizes listening prayer. Understanding and using meditation and Sabbath principles are connecting pieces in developing intimacy.

Developing Your Mentors

Your mentor should have replicable personal practices and suggested resources to inform her mentoree. Encourage her to allow her mentoree to look into her life as she describes her own spiritual journey: what she has found to be effective in personal Bible study methods, Scripture memory, practices of meditation, and soul care. Help your mentor see that she is a catalyst rather than a definer of the approach and method.[6]

B. Self-Awareness

Several years ago ReachGlobal, the missions arm of the Evangelical Free Church of America, surveyed their city team leaders. The survey listed seventeen critical areas of competency for successful missionaries. Understandably, the area ranked as being most critical was spiritual maturity. In second place, and clearly outdistancing number three, was self-awareness.

In the past two decades there has been increased recognition of the need for self-awareness in order for teams to work together well. Self-awareness can be defined as an accurate assessment and understanding of my behavior, reasoning, speaking, gifting, and preferences; and, how all of these things impact those around me.[7]

A deeply rooted self-awareness in no way requires us to be a chameleon, shedding our values depending upon who we are around. It is the astute observation that others see and feel situations and information differently than I do. Therefore, how I present material, act, and speak will be moderated for the benefit of the greater good. Where I am a member of a team, good self-awareness will allow me to compensate for and accommodate those members who are naturally hardwired differently from me.

Self-awareness has value only when the possessor has the interest and desire to rein in default settings for the benefit of others. When each team member has the ability and desire to practice self-awareness, we will find harmony, deferential treatment, graciousness, patience, and submissiveness. Perhaps a bit of heaven on earth?

Self-awareness is learned; and the primary teacher is feedback. Few words can arouse more anxiety than hearing the statement, "Let me give you some feedback on that." For feedback to be helpful it needs to be undergirded with trust. Thus, the very first avenue for feedback ought to come from our spouse. No one in the world is as committed to me as my spouse; I need to trust her as she gives feedback to me. I need a solid level of personal security that enables me to hear what I cannot see and hear on my own.

Less gracious, more brutal and frank will be your children. If you can survive input from your family, you are ready to hear from others.

When giving feedback, remember these principles:[8]

1. *Feedback should be about behavior, not personality.* The first, and probably the most important, rule of feedback is to remember that you are making no comment on what type of person they are. Do not be tempted to discuss aspects of personality, intelligence, or anything else. Only behavior.

2. *Feedback should be as specific as possible.* Think about specific occasions, and specific behavior, and point to exactly what the person did, and exactly how it made you feel. The more specific the better, as it is much easier to hear about a specific occasion than about "all the time"!

3. *Feedback should be timely.* It's no good telling someone about something that offended or pleased you six months later. Feedback needs to be timely, which means while everyone can still remember what happened. Pick the right time. There are times when people are feeling open to

feedback and times when they aren't. An angry person won't want to accept feedback, even given skillfully. Timing is half of life.

Developing Your Mentors

You will want to give your mentors experiences that they can replicate with their mentees. These would include a spiritual gifts survey,[9] the DiSC assessment,[10] StrengthsFinder assessment,[11] and communication styles assessment.[12] Practicing positive feedback reporting will model this aspect to gaining stronger self-awareness. A reflective personality lends itself toward greater appreciation for self-awareness. Those without that natural benefit can still move the needle.[13] Helping them understand empathy[14] will improve their listening skills. Reviewing principles from the Johari Window will also enable them to do the same with their mentoree.[15]

C. Ministry Skills

Of the four areas to be developed, local church leadership probably is the most effective with teaching ministry skills.

Proactive churches should do training for its small group leaders on teaching and relational skills. Some have a counseling ministry where they disciple their members in biblical counseling methods. Those with active men's and/or women's ministries can be developing apprentice leaders for future leading opportunities. Personal evangelism should be valued from the pulpit and taught in an applied manner in smaller settings.

Developing Your Mentors

Likely you are selecting prospective mentors in your church who already have had significant ministry experience. Speak with each to learn where he has served and led in the church. Where you find gaps encourage participation so that they will feel competent to lead their mentees in those areas. Help your mentors see that they need to develop both leading and following skills in their mentees.

D. Cross-cultural Skills

Increasing ethnic diversity in America requires historic Anglo churches (where most missionaries still come from) to help its congregants gain proficiency in crossing cultural bridges. The Marriage Supper of the Lamb will have people from every tribe, language, people, and nation (Rev 5:9). Members of many of those groups are in our very cities, geographically near yet culturally distant. The local church needs to train its members to meet and become friends.

Decades of diversity training has not effectively addressed centuries of racially based superiority thinking and bias entrenched in today's society. Our church members live, breathe, and are influenced by this perversion. Good leadership will not allow this to go unanswered; it must respond.

It is difficult to imagine a church of integrity praying fervently for lost souls thousands of miles away and pouring personnel and financial resources into this, and yet able to ignore those same people when they move into our neighborhoods.

Developing Your Mentors

Your mentors need to rub shoulders with people who are not like them. No amount of books, sermons, movies, podcasts, etc., can replace the interaction from informal social contact. Only through this will they be able to move beyond the boundaries, consciously or unconsciously constructed, that dictate where we live, send our kids to school, and spend our "me" time.

Universities are a natural place to find people not like you. Seek out ethnic restaurants. Have your mentor visit the restaurant when the crowd has already exited; the lull in business will allow him to chat up the owner. Many cities have nonprofit organizations that promote and celebrate intercultural understanding. While they are not necessarily faith-based, churches would share many of the same central values.

We develop people for the kingdom. When we invest in our mentors, who in turn develop their mentees we are practicing disciplemaking. Some of our prospective mentees, will become missionaries, others will determine that God has called them to remain at home and hold the rope for those who go. And God's kingdom is built brick-by-brick through disciples who follow him in truth and obedience as transforming agents in their spheres of influence.

Greg Carter is pastor of global engagement at Liberty Bible Church (www. findliberty.net) in Chesterton, IN. He is also founder/director of Future Missionaries (www.futuremissionaries.com), and author of *Skills, Knowledge, Character: A Church-Based Approach to Missionary Candidate Preparation*.

Notes

[1] Greg Carter, *Skills, Knowledge, Character: A Church-Based Approach to Missionary Candidate Preparation* (Valparaiso, IN: Turtle River Press, 2010), 23–29. This collaborative relationship is more fully explained in this resource. Briefly, the school teaches courses in systematic theology, doctrine, cross-cultural communication principles, evangelism and mission strategies, anthropology, etc. The sending agency provides assessment of potential candidates, initial orientation, logistical support on the field, administration and oversight, etc. The specialized training organization provides training in fundraising/support team building, acquisition of language learning skills, serving on a multi-cultural team, etc.

[2] Laura Mae Gardner, director of international member care for Wycliffe, has compiled an excellent list of character qualities that she calls The Hardy Personality. See https://www.seminare-ps. net/mc/mc2005/04_Gardner_The%20Hardy%20Personality.pdf

[3] Stephanie Kaihoi, a ministry leader and mentor. A 30-Something, she is one of the great thinkers and practitioners of disciplemaking. (IMHO)

[4] As an example of resource people, here are a few of the ones I have "found" in my church/ community: A university professor who grew up as an MK and operates a consulting company in China, a free lance editor who assisted Dave Pollack with *Third Culture Kids: Growing Up Among Worlds*, a businessman who uses the DiSC assessment in his hiring process, a lay person who has a ministry in teaching spiritual warfare, a lay person with a strong personal practice of scripture memory, a lay person who teaches listening prayer, a university administrator of color who teaches on diversity, a local church-based organization that matches international students with area families, a non-profit that teaches English skills to newly arrived individuals. In each case these are tremendous resource people/organizations who can increase the capacity of your mentors in their respective areas.

[5] Discussing the concept of intimacy with a man will be a challenge. For most men the word intimacy primarily leads in one direction. The thought of being in an intimate relationship with our heavenly Father, while initially awkward, must be pursued. While I have considered using a different word, none are as descriptive as this one in conveying well the connection that needs to happen for a Christian man to be released from pursuing identity as found in the world and instead find it in God who richly affirms and satisfies.

[6] Precept Ministries International does an excellent job of teaching inductive Bible study methods. The Navigators, Inc. has a well regarded Topical Memory System. Two websites with scripture memory principles: http://unlockingtheBible.org/2016/04/how-to-memorize-scripture-Bible-verses/ and http://www.desiringgod.org/articles/scripture-memory-made-simple

[7] The Emperor's New Clothes, the classic children's book by Hans Christian Andersen, is an excellent view into self-awareness. Seeing through the lens of cross-cultural glasses allows the reader to ask why questions: why were the scoundrels able to get away with their scheme? Would the little boy be seen as a hero in every society?

[8] Content is adapted from https://www.slideshare.net/blackempress/communication-skill-66487276. Another good website is https://www.themuse.com/advice/5-steps-to-giving-good-feedback

[9] There are a number of spiritual gifts surveys available on the internet.

[10] DiSC profile, https://discprofile.com/. See also Uniquely You which combines the DiSC profile with a spiritual gifts assessment. https://uniquelyyou.org.

[11] Strengths Finder, www.gallupstrengthscenter.com/.

[12] Dr. Duane Elmer has an excellent communication styles instrument that has been widely used.

[13] T. J. Addington, *Deep Influence: Unseen Practices that will Revolutionize Your Leadership* (Colorado Springs: NavPress, 2014). Chapter 6 is an excellent chapter to review emotional intelligence.

[14] Brene Brown has an excellent short video that gives a quick picture of empathy. https://www.youtube.com/watch?v=1Evwgu369Jw.

[15] Understanding the Johari Window model http://www.selfawareness.org.uk/news/understanding-the-johari-window-model.

Chapter 15

Lincoln Berean Church

Equipping Candidates with Character and Capacity

Ryan Harmon

Since its inception in 1962, Lincoln Berean Church has aimed to be a globally engaged church. Over the years we have sent many of our own to serve as missionaries in foreign fields. Some of these couples and individuals are still engaged in faithful service twenty and thirty years after their initial deployment.

As a Global Outreach Team, we have been fortunate to work in a church where there is a high degree of buy-in from the staff and elders to be globally engaged. Our body has been quick to answer the call when there have been urgent needs around the world, financial or otherwise.

In the early 2000s our Global Outreach Team began to dream of even greater involvement in the work of raising and sending out more workers. While our church had always been quick to support missionaries, we found ourselves desiring to step into even greater intentionality and proactivity— we wanted to be a church that could be described as a sending church.[1] Our understanding of the Great Commission led us to the conclusion that we could not abdicate the work of missions to mission agencies if we were to remain true to the biblical conception of the local church. While mission agencies serve as a critical piece of the missions puzzle, without the active engagement of the local church, agencies will struggle to find ready candidates to send. As a result of our growing conviction that the local church must resist a reactive posture and embrace the mandate of active involvement in the sending of workers into the harvest, a paradigm shift took place for us and a significant increase in the number of missionaries we sent to the field occurred in the years that followed.

> *While mission agencies serve as a critical piece of the missions puzzle, without the active engagement of the local church, agencies will struggle to find ready candidates to send.*

In 2009, in partnership with Avant Ministries,[2] our church commissioned and sent six individuals to Gdansk, Poland, in a "Joint Venture" that aimed to see exclusively church-based teams engage in the work of establishing "Three-Self" churches (self-propagating, self-governing, self-supporting). Only eighteen months later, our church commissioned and sent our second team to Madrid, Spain. This team was made up of eight people from our body—one couple and six individuals. Our church's commitment to these teams was very high—promising substantial support along with a high degree of exposure to our church body. We were excited and our plan was to send three more teams in the subsequent three years. We were also cautiously optimistic about the philosophy that highly functioning teams, working in concert, could potentially accelerate the preparation and deployment process for future missionaries. Perhaps a true team environment would allow for a surge in missionaries who, while less formally prepared, could accomplish the task quicker since they were doing it together. These two joint venture teams were sent out with great hope and anticipation.

Reality Check

As time passed and our two teams engaged in the difficult work of cross-cultural ministry, the seemingly inevitable attrition among our team members began. Around the two year-mark, our team in Poland lost its first team member. In Spain, nine months had passed when our first team member returned to the US. Over the following years, this story would repeat itself again and again, each member leaving for different reasons. The reality of the difficulty of missions was being reinforced at every turn.

In spite of these difficulties, our church remained committed to sending out more teams and was on track to send its third team in three years when, on a walk in London, our team leader in Poland confessed that he had never engaged in anything as difficult as leading a team on a church planting venture. He continued to insist that if we were to send more teams, we would need to feel a high degree of confidence that the next leader(s) had the capacity and character to endure such an endeavor. Furthermore, he continued, our teams needed to be filled with people that local churches in the US would line up to hire due to their history of effectiveness in ministry—the mission field was not a good place to learn on the job.

This conversation essentially landed like a ton of bricks. Had our zeal to send out more and more workers resulted in sending workers whom we failed to prepare to accomplish the task? Had we unintentionally thrown the proverbial lambs to the slaughter? In some ways, it appeared that we had. If reality is what you run into when you are wrong, it hit us right between the eyes.

Retreat to Advance

With the London conversation fresh in our mind, we decided that while we were not any less enthusiastic about church planting or becoming a sending church, we could not allow urgency to trump prudence. Our guiding assumption had been that if someone loved God, was committed to the church, and had a passion for the lost, then they had the raw materials necessary for fruitful labor on the mission field. We had naively overlooked that with the dynamics of cross-cultural ministry being what they are, a rigorous course of preparation is nonnegotiable. Learning must still occur on the field, but it will take more of the shape of refining what is already present rather than creating what is not already there.

This conclusion, namely that our people do not come to us as ready-made missionaries, led us to slow down our pace, reevaluate our preparation program, and ultimately restate our goals. Pumping out numerous teams is nothing to glory in *if* the members of those teams are not equipped.

Renewed Emphasis on Preparation

Our learnings over the past five years have led to the conclusion that we must do a better job in equipping people in the areas of character and capacity. Both elements are absolutely critical to successful ministry on the field and, more precisely, successful *team* ministry on the field.

Character

One of the things that is most quickly revealed in the midst of culture stress is one's character. When speaking of character, we are talking about who someone *actually* is, not just who they can be at short intervals. In our context, the goal is character formation according to Christ, or more simply put: "To consistently act like Jesus requires a character like his."[3]

Christian author and philosopher, Dallas Willard, wrote extensively on discipleship and taking on the character of Christ. He had this to say regarding character: "Our character is that internal, overall structure of the self that is revealed by our long-run patterns of behavior and from which our actions more or less automatically arise."[4] Cross-cultural and team-related stress has a way of revealing our *long-run patterns of behavior* quickly and precisely. As one friend of mine noted after being on the field for a few years, "On the mission field you become the worst version of yourself!" Of course, what he was referring to is that the mission field has a way of allowing the true elements of character to be revealed—there's no more hiding.

It is because of this that we have made a concerted effort to develop ways of addressing issues of character in any potential missionary candidate. We must not assume that underlying negative patterns, patterns rooted in character, will automatically be resolved once one steps into a foreign context. In fact, quite the opposite is true. Character is critical and the local church is uniquely situated to address issues of character in potential missionaries.

Capacity

A pastor friend of mine once remarked that you cannot be what you are not already becoming! How many times have we assumed that we will be who we need to be once the correct situation arises. "I will share the gospel more once I have stepped onto the mission field; I will be more prayerful when I have the time to give to prayer; I will become more hospitable when life is less busy." We are all guilty of this type of thinking.

In spite of these wishful thoughts, once again reality reminds us that hoping for something rarely makes it so. Sharing the gospel is actually harder on the mission field! Inclinations toward prayer, if not fostered prefield, will not automatically occur once one passes through passport control. No, the seeds of what one needs to be on the mission field must be planted prior to departure. In fact, we would be wise to look for a track record of effective ministry prior to approving someone for foreign service.

Not New, but Difficult to Maintain

The reflections of our church are not new—nothing that has been stated above is earthshaking in its insight. What we have found to be true, however, is that it is difficult to maintain discipline in holding to these standards. Will our desire to send more people more quickly lead to our loosening of standards? Will we lower our expectations so that we can proclaim quick victories? This is a temptation every ministry faces, and maintaining discipline is not easy.

We have also found that emphasizing character and capacity means that we cannot expect people to come to us as finished products, but we must be willing to enter into long-term developmental processes with them. This poses other questions for us as a church: Are we willing to engage in the often tedious work of character development? Are we willing to be patient as potential missionaries develop skills over time? Are we willing to put in the time to actually mentor, even enter into an apprentice-type relationship, with those who are sensing a call to the field? Our answers to these questions will speak volumes about our commitment to preparation.

Conclusion

Lincoln Berean Church is in the very first phase of this new approach. We have yet to see what the outcomes will be. However, in returning our attention to the focused preparation of potential missionaries, it feels as though we are returning to the role that God intends the local church to play in his mission. Paul, after all, reminds us that the work of the local church is that of *equipping* the saints for the work of ministry (Eph 4:12). How we all wish that our work was simply *rubber-stamping finished projects* for the work of ministry! That would be much easier! Perhaps, in time, if we maintain our focused commitment to "present everone mature in Christ" (Col 1:28), we will come to the day that simply affirming the missionary calling of one of our members is all that will be necessary. So until that day, we must continue to embrace the work of preparation.

Ryan Harmon is the global outreach pastor at Lincoln Berean Church (www.lincolnberean.org) in Lincoln, NE.

Notes

[1] Zach Bradley, *The Sending Church Defined* (The Upstream Collective, 2015).

[2] Avant Ministries, www.avantministries.org.

[3] Elane O'Rourke, *A Dallas Willard Dictionary* (Kindle Locations 460–61). Kindle Edition.

[4] Dallas Willard, *Renovation of the Heart*, iBooks.

CHAPTER 16

Sardis Church

The Antioch Model

Jon Luesink

The blueprint our church settled on for building a pipeline of servants for the kingdom of God has turned out even better than we imagined. There we were, a medium-sized church in western Canada, launching another missionary couple in less than ten months. That brought us to a total of nine homegrown missionaries from our neighborhood church. During this most recent commissioning service, our lead pastor reminded us that eight years ago we sent out two missionary families while completing our Community Life Center. Now, two more couples were heading out as we moved into our Worship Center expansion. With joyful laughter we heard his challenge that if we ever wanted to complete the proposed gym, we'd better find four more missionaries to send out!

> Now there were in the church at Antioch prophets and teachers, Barnabas, Simeon who was called Niger, Lucius of Cyrene, Manaen a lifelong friend of Herod the tetrarch, and Saul. While they were worshiping the Lord and fasting, the Holy Spirit said, "Set apart for me Barnabas and Saul for the work to which I have called them." Then after fasting and praying they laid their hands on them and sent them off. (Acts 13:1–3)

It feels pretty special to realize we're kind of like an Antioch church, sending out our Paul and Barnabas to make an impact on the world for Jesus. For a church[1] that has been steadily growing toward 400 at an average Sunday meeting, it has been worth pondering, "How did this come about?" How does a church launch nine homegrown missionaries while also conducting multiple building programs?"

I had the privilege of being on staff for twelve years and then becoming one of those nine missionaries. From this perspective I interviewed two of our long-time pastors to explore those questions. As we ruminated over the long history of how this came to be, as we applied our heart to what we observed, we realized that while we weren't following a completely intentional recipe, we have been doing a lot of wise things, on purpose. Perhaps a saying might be thus rendered:

> The recipe for becoming an Antioch church that sends out homegrown missionaries requires many diligent ingredients marinated in purpose and time.

As we examine these ingredients, I hope you'll notice how these blend together, the one influencing the other, improving the whole. While reading about our experiences, I invite you to reflect on your own, hoping that you might find your way even faster than we did.

Fostering a Global Heritage vs. Village Mindset

Fortunately, we have a rich natural heritage. Our church was started by faithful pioneers who had previously been church planting missionaries in Columbia, South America. That helped embed a DNA of welcoming the missionaries who were returning from around the world, which in turn infused us with a consistent global mindset. Our current lead pastor for the past fourteen years, David Lee, has sought to make sure this spirit doesn't die, lest we become "a village church with a village God."[2] John Stott's warning tells us that an inward looking church devolves toward a tribal view of their god, while a globally minded church will understand God's great reign and concern over heaven and earth.

Our leaders have pioneered this approach themselves by spending time in mission fields both near and far. We've made sure to send our pastors out to minister in places like Armenia, Haiti, and inner-city Vancouver. As leaders, they return passionate for a needy world because they have seen it with their own eyes. They *know* what we are praying for, and believe in sacrificing to meet the need. This is a key infecting kernel to make sure that we remain focused on taking the Great Commission seriously.

Rod Heppell, who served five years in Bolivia with his family before joining our pastoral staff, says, "Our mission at home is the same as for the world, to all nations to the end of time . . . If there is no sending, where's the going? If we don't talk about it, it won't happen." With a sincere grin forming, he continued, "We started praying, 'Lord of the harvest, raise up workers.' Now we're praying, 'Lord of the cattle on a thousand hills, provide the means to support them!'"

A long-term goal of the church is to give 10 percent of its annual donations to global mission. Combining the special projects, such as our long-term development partnership in Haiti, it's closer to 20 percent of our annual budget. Next, consider what it takes to fully support nine adult missionaries. Beyond the budgeted amount from the church, households add personal gifts such that our missionaries have been supported between 20–60 percent from their home church alone! That's why we can keep engaging in building projects. When church leaders model giving away resources beyond our village, they teach individuals the joy of giving sacrificially beyond the desires of their personal kingdoms.

Stewarding Our Inheritance

Heidi was the first homegrown missionary who went out from our church. She's a great example of how we simply needed to steward our inheritance. Heidi grew up in a family that loved serving Jesus wherever Dad's job took them. When she was nine years old, the Lord gave her a life vision, "You came from a great family. Many children don't have that. I want you to go and care for them." As her youth pastor, I had the privilege of watching Heidi grow up through high school and then join my volunteer staff in the youth ministry while she got her training in early childhood education. Through two internships abroad, she found her niche in Bolivia at a ministry called El Jordan. She works with a team focused on the salvation, discipleship, and rehabilitation of the poor in the city of Santa Cruz.

Heidi came from an amazing family; her parents were leaders and mentors in our church. When she started showing an interest in ministry, we just encouraged her in her gifts, provided opportunities to practice service and ministry, and then helped launch her as she left our "village" and our continent. In retrospect, it seems we were simply stewarding the inheritance we'd been entrusted with for a season. Illustratively, Pastor Dave describes parenting in a way that can be applied to the work of the church in raising up children: "Be the best parents you can be, don't try to control your child's outcomes. They need to choose, but give them the best environment possible." Heidi was a good example of this process, not only because her parents lived this wisdom, but also because our church family did this for her as well.

Discipling a Servant Pipeline

Over the years, our church has had growing clarity that we need to start challenging believers to serve from a young age. This starts in Sunday school, where 100 percent of the money given goes from our children to "Heidi's Kids" in Bolivia. While these children invite their friends to soccer camp, those that have graduated from being campers find opportunities to serve in this summer outreach program. As those youth move up into senior high, they are challenged to serve the junior youth and so on, with young adults staying on for years as volunteer leaders for the senior youth program. To encourage further discipleship and training, the church gives earned scholarships to go to summer camps, and even supports students to prepare for ministry by studying at Bible colleges.

We are blessed to have our denominational seminary an hour down the highway. This allows us to further engage in this development pipeline through sponsored internships with students. Two of these interns eventually became missionaries in Africa and Italy respectively. Like much of what has already been described, this has reciprocating benefit. While we invest in the next generation by equipping them while they are with us, we get to know them, see their heart, and *know* who we are standing behind when we send them out.

Another example of this servant pipeline was a short-term mission trip we organized to Bolivia. While a recent study shows that the majority of churches in Canada see the main goal of these short-term trips as the discipleship and evangelism of team members,[3] we chose to use it as a vehicle to bring potential future full-time missionaries to the surface. Chantelle is a beautiful example of how this servant pipeline worked. She grew up hearing about the ministry of El Jordan in Sunday school. She joined our trip as a teenager and was inspired to return as a young adult. There she met her future husband, Tim, and they are the most recent couple we have sent out from among us, joining Heidi down in Bolivia. Ironically, it was on this trip that I first heard God asking me and my family to consider becoming missionaries. We launched two years later, but instead of Bolivia, we felt drawn to the mission field of Europe.

Our church has chosen a blended focus when it comes to our investment in foreign missions. We engage in temporal social justice for the poor, while still sharing the eternal message of the gospel. You could say we're engaged in saving lives now, and for eternity. An exciting example of this is the providential connection that surfaced through members of our congregation in Haiti. We're getting ready to send out a third short-term team. Working in this notorious "black hole" of foreign aid, it is essential to make repeat visits with credible local ministry partners.[4] Our consistent connection there awakens our local church to the needy world beyond our doorsteps. When our team witnessed a demon-possessed woman actually walking up a wall, but then set free, and then the next day they saw her in the market, transformed . . . we asked "What isn't God able to do?"

At a bare minimum our teams return home as strong supporters of missions, providing the broad foundation for being an Antioch church.

Unselfish De-nesting by the Leadership

Nelson Henderson, a second-generation farmer from Manitoba, Canada, once said, "The true meaning of life is to plant trees, under whose shade you do not expect to sit."[5] Our lead pastor has been living this out for decades. I remember so clearly, ten years ago, telling Dave that we were getting cold feet toward becoming missionaries. We worked well together, and it would have been a perfect opportunity for him to nudge us toward staying on. I had been on staff for nearly twelve years overseeing youth and worship, and my family and I had become integral to the life of the church. He quietly listened to my reasons for staying, then went away to pray. Two weeks later he pulled me aside and said these memorable words, "It doesn't make sense for me, and it doesn't make sense for the church, but I think the kingdom of God needs you out there, now. I can't encourage you to delay." This proved to be a turning point for us in removing any doubts we had, and we began our focused launch to become missionaries in Prague, Czech Republic.

This unselfish attitude proved even more personally costly for Dave when his son and daughter-in-law were ready to launch into missions. Karin was one of our seminary interns in whom our church had invested, while Dave's son Rob was one of those faithful leaders who had taken on more and more responsibility in the church since his youth. Now they were ready to leave to Italy with their young children to respond to God's call to plant churches there. Not only would a pastor be losing these key producers that he had mentored, as a father and grandfather he would also feel the loss of not having these members of his family nearby. I guess

> ❚❚ Just like parents who provide freedom and the best possible environment, we tend our soil to produce the fruit of faithful missionaries and the unselfishness to de-nest those we have cultivated. ❚❚

that's the effect of living out our mission statement: *"Centered in Christ, Visible in Community, Transforming our World."* Our church, especially our pastors, has been consistently ready to unselfishly de-nest our key leaders.

For decades, in a series of three churches, Dave has mentored, trained up, and sent off leaders who went on to be a blessing beyond his sphere of influence, either as pastors of other churches or missionaries in other countries. I appreciate that he considers these personal losses a labor of love for the greater good of the kingdom of God.

Andre and his wife, Alex, are further examples of this sacrificial belief infused by our lead pastor. During the years that Dave mentored Andre, this gifted young man struggled to enjoy traditional pastoral pulpit work. Andre also wondered how his calling to go to seminary could harmonize with his undergraduate degree in agriculture and resource management. It was through deep times of prayer, as is Dave's custom, that a viable convergence presented itself. Andre and Alex explored Dave's suggestion and are now engaged in their second assignment with Emmanuel International, a relief and development agency that includes agricultural development and natural resource management. Their current work in Tanzania focuses on holistic community transformation through the local church. One component is teaching local farmers not to simply tend crops, but to start with tending the soil that produces the crops.

This concept brings us full circle. Just like parents who provide freedom and the best possible environment, we tend our soil to produce the fruit of faithful missionaries and the unselfishness to de-nest those we have cultivated.

As you read through the book of Acts up to chapter 13, you will see that the preparatory journey of Barnabas and Saul began long before their service in Antioch. You could say that this young church already practiced a servant pipeline, stewarded their inheritance, and from the list of leaders in verse 1, they were already blessed with a global mindset. F. F. Bruce remarks, "It is perhaps worth noticing that the two men who were to be released for what would nowadays be called missionary service overseas were the two most eminent and gifted leaders in the church."[6]

Reflection for Change

It appears to be true that the recipe for becoming an Antioch church that sends out homegrown missionaries requires many diligent ingredients, marinated in purpose and time. Take a moment to live Proverbs 24:32: "Then I saw and considered it; I looked and received instruction." By looking through the window of the church we've become and by hearing about the things that we've done, what are you already doing well and what might you need to change or add to your current attitudes or practice?

- Describe how you are fostering a global heritage over a village mindset
- Examine how you are stewarding the inheritance with which you've been entrusted
- Lay out the ways you are discipling a servant pipeline
- List key leaders that you have unselfishly de-nested

May we all enjoy producing fruit like that young church in Antioch such that Paul's vision could be our reality: "Those who have never been told of him will see, and those who have never heard will understand" (Rom 15:21).

Jon Luesink and his wife, Jill, served with Avant Ministries (www.avantministries. org) for eight years leading a church planting team to Prague, Czech Republic. Jon is presently serving with Avant's Canadian office as director of mobilization.

Notes

[1] Sardis Fellowship Baptist Church, Chilliwack, BC, Canada.

[2] John Stott, "A Village Church with a Village God," Ten Great Preachers: Messages and Interviews, Ed. Bill Turpie (Grand Rapids, MI: Baker, 2000), 117. https://tollelege.wordpress. com/2016/05/03/a-village-church-with-a-village-god-by-john-stott/

[3] Canadian Evangelical Missions Engagement Study, Report 1: Canadian Evangelicals and Short-Term Missions, February 23, 2017. https://www.evangelicalfellowship.ca/Communications/ Research/Canadian-Evangelical-Missions-Engagement-Study/Report-1-Canadian-Evangelicals-and-Short-Term-Mis

[4] Steve Corbett and Brian Fikkert, *When Helping Hurts: How to Alleviate Poverty without Hurting the Poor* (Chicago: Moody, 2009)—Provides Vital Guidance for Churches Wishing to "Alleviate Poverty without Hurting the Poor and Yourself."

[5] Nelson Henderson, https://en.wikiquote.org/wiki/Nelson_Henderson, as quoted from *Under Whose Shade* (1982), by Wesley Henderson.

[6] *The New International Commentary on the New Testament—The Book of Acts, Revised Edition* (Wm B Eerdmans, 1988), 246.

Connecting to the Pipeline

1. What are some things you learned from these church leaders that you can apply to your church?

2. What are some things you read that may work for other churches but may not work in yours?

3. Are there any "rites of passage" that already happen in your church that you can adapt and use for missionary mobilization?

4. On a scale of importance, do you have resistance from your leaders to move forward with a mobilization strategy; do you have permission from them; or do you have a mandate from them?

5. Many of these church leaders have published books or offered printed materials that are available to you. See **www.MissionaryPipeline. org** for up-to-date links to books, lists of resources, and downloadable versions of materials to help you along your journey.

Part 4

The Local Church: Preparing to Become a Sending Church

This section of *Pipeline* is intended to help your mobilization team prepare for a successful deployment. If the hypothesis is true that "when you build it, they will come," then you should know that building the infrastructure to accommodate missionary candidates will take some time. Thankfully, there are consultants, coaches, and training organizations which have already developed some resources for you to benefit and glean from their experience.

Just like the church needs to prepare to be a sending church, your team needs to prepare to become a mobilization team. Take the time necessary to read, study, attend live and online conferences, and network with other churches, agencies, and consultants so that you are well equipped for this ministry.

The writers in the following chapters come from a variety of backgrounds: mission pastors, field missionaries, agency recruiters, life coaches, etc., so they are available to help you begin this journey.

CHAPTER 17

Perspectives on the World Christian Movement

Awakened to God's Global Purpose

Brett Clemens

"The body of Christ awakened to pursue the fulfillment of God's global purpose within every people for his glory."—Perspectives US Vision

During my high shool years, I was involved in a variety of athletics, organizations, and extracurricular activities that often precluded me from beginning my homework until late in the evening. Consequently, I would often find myself up until the late hours finishing schoolwork. Before going to bed, I would regularly set the alarm clock.

At 6:00 AM, the alarm would go off, but I typically continued sleeping right through the alarm, which ironically was branded as "extra loud." With the extra-loud beeping blaring through the entire house, my dad would say in a forceful but still loving way, "It's time to get up, your alarm is going off." Those words would wake me up enough to reply, "I *am* awake." Then I would stumble across the room to silence the beeping alarm. However, after declaring that I *was* awake and shutting off the alarm, I routinely would get back into bed and fall fast asleep. My "awake-ness" was in words only—I was not truly awake.

How many in the body of Christ are not truly awakened to Jesus' promise that the " . . . gospel of the kingdom will be proclaimed throughout the whole world as a testimony to all nations [*ethne*, peoples] . . ." and his command to all believers to " . . . make disciples of all nations . . ." (Matt 24:14 and 28:19). How many hear these words in the church and fall back asleep? How many in your church are asleep today?

" Perspectives is a discipleship course
for every Christian, not a missions class just
for some. It is about moving closer to God
and his heart for the nations,
and challenges Christians to discover
their role in God's great plan. "

I am a millennial who was asleep in the church. Due to the work that God is doing through the Perspectives on the World Christian Movement course, I have been " . . . awakened to pursue the fulfillment of God's global purpose within every people for his glory." My wife and I took Perspectives in 2014 when our church hosted the course. The Lord then used others to reveal his plan for my life to serve as a volunteer coordinator for the 2016 KCNorth Perspectives course. During the course, God made it clear that I was to use my gifts for his glory mobilizing others through Perspectives full-time. I left the business world in 2016 and began transitioning into the role I have today—mobilizing the church as the Perspectives regional director for the Central Region (Kansas, Missouri, Nebraska, and Iowa).

Perspectives on the World Christian Movement is a ministry of Frontier Ventures (formerly called the US Center for World Mission), a nondenominational ministry based out of Pasadena, CA. The late Dr. Ralph Winter founded the Perspectives course in 1974, eventually stating, "*Perspectives* joined a movement of God that was already in progress."[1] Today, forty plus years later, Perspectives has educated more than 250,000 students worldwide.

Perspectives is a fifteen-lesson course that focuses on taking students beyond their current realities—where the Lord currently has them—and into the passions of God and his heart to redeem all the nations. From Genesis to Revelation, God clearly reveals his purpose for his glory to spread to all peoples; everyone has a part to play in the story of God's glory. The fifteen lessons are designed around four vantage points (biblical, historical, cultural, and strategic), with each perspective highlighting a different aspect of God's global purpose. "The biblical and historical sections reveal why our confidence is based on the historic fact of God's relentless work from the dawn of history until this day. The cultural and strategic sections underscore that we are in the midst of a costly, but very 'doable' task, confirming the biblical and historical hope."[2]

Perspectives is a discipleship course for every Christian, not a missions class just for some. It is about moving closer to God and his heart for the nations, and challenges Christians to discover their role in God's great plan. Our prayer is that all believers would be transformed and live devoted to a purpose that is larger than their life—a life that is devoted to God's ultimate purpose, to spread his glory, his blessing, his name, his church, and his salvation to ALL peoples. "After this I looked, and there before me was a great multitude that no one could count, from every nation, tribe, people and language, standing before the throne and before the Lamb" (Rev 7:9, NIV).

Mobilizing Through Educating

"To mobilize by educating the body of Christ to strategic engagement in God's global purpose."—Perspectives US Mission

John Piper states, "Knowing comes before doing and shapes doing."[3] Perspectives, as a mobilization-through-education course, aims to shape the doing of the church by first educating the body of Christ. When you see the word *course*, you likely *hear* the academic meaning and think to yourself, "not another course!" Walk into any Christian bookstore and you will find a plethora of books and resources to "help" with almost anything. Even this book that you are reading right now is filled with great content on engaging the church in mobilizing the next generation of missionaries. However, if the content is only contained in the head and does not make its way into the heart, the impact of the hands will be temporary at best, but often nonexistent. The transformation in the head quickly grows cobwebs as it lives among the other great head knowledge pieces in the library of the mind. But how do you transform the head, the heart, and then the hands?

Think back to a time when you experienced that "summer church-camp high." You or someone you knew came home on fire and filled up only to have the world flood in and extinguish the flame. A real struggle was maintaining the mountaintop moment when life was waiting on the other side. Coming down the mountain and returning to life in the forest eventually eclipsed the mountaintop. How could the fire burn out so quickly?

Compassion, and its ability to pull on the heartstrings, is sometimes responsible for starting the fire or taking one to the top of the mountain. It can start through stories of those with no access to the gospel, statistics of disproportionate resources, or real-life encounters with unreached peoples. However, this emotional response alone is not enough to sustain the ups and downs of living in a fallen world. If compassion for the peoples that are lost is the only fuel, the fire will burn out. Compassion alone will quickly fade without the passion of God.

Developing God's passion in our heart, not just compassion, is essential for long-term awakening within the body of Christ. God has used Perspectives in powerful ways to clearly reveal his passion and his heart for the nations. Spending nine lessons looking from both a biblical and historical perspective helps students clearly see God's passion. Results show that before taking Perspectives, 36 percent of the students have a strong understanding of God's heart for the nations; after taking Perspectives, those with a strong understanding jumped to 94 percent.[4] Here is an excerpt from a student's personal response when reflecting on the biblical section of the course:

> The lessons of the first five weeks have been a fascinating journey. This course is so aptly named since it truly brings a whole new "perspective" on the way history has played out according to the plan of God and his Great Commission. Throughout the readings and teachings, I am simultaneously fascinated, enlightened, and just a bit frustrated. The fascination and enlightenment have to do with the consistency of the Lord's presence and working throughout the course of time. The frustration is, as a Christ-follower for thirty years and at the age of fifty-two, having never been taught the whole of these truths and not having concluded these things from my own study of Scripture. However, I am ultimately blessed by the redeeming power of our Lord and Savior, Jesus Christ! Praise the Lord for his perfect timing within his perfect will.

Kingdom Impact

While Perspectives is a mobilization-through-education course and has much to do with transforming the head and the heart, we are deeply concerned with the impact of the hands. The course, as the title states, is about the World Christian Movement and invites all believers to participate in the movement. "World Christians are day-to-day disciples for whom Christ's global cause has become their integrating, overriding priority. God's mission is the unifying focus of all they are and do."[5] After lesson 15, students are launched out to find their part in God's story. The practices of a World Christian include going, sending, welcoming, mobilizing, and praying. The following quantitative results come from *The Church Unleashed* publication of Perspectives, and shows the kingdom impact of Perspectives. Before the Perspectives course, 25 percent of the students responded as having a strong understanding of the five practices of a World Christian, whereas after Perspectives, 91 percent had a strong understanding. Furthermore, after Perspectives, 85 percent responded as understanding their personal role in the Great Commission, a 52-point increase over those with an understanding before Perspectives. Here are the statistics that paint the picture of the kingdom impact Perspectives is having in the church:

- Going: 19 percent of Perspectives alumni have served long-term (defined as more than six months) in the mission field
- Sending: 27 percent of Perspectives alumni increased giving to the local church; 61 percent increased giving to mission agencies
- Welcoming: 23 percent of Perspectives alumni increased involvement with the international community at home
- Mobilizing: 21 percent increase in recruiting others to enter the mission field
- Praying: 66 percent increase in frequent prayer for missionaries

All praise and glory be to God for the work that he is doing in and through Perspectives. He has made this resource available, and it is through him the kingdom is being impacted in such a significant way. Our prayer is that more of the body would be awakened, but a challenge is finding kingdom partners to open their doors. When perceived outsiders come knocking, those entrusted to shepherd and protect the flock are on high alert. Know that Perspectives wants to collaborate with you on ways to leverage, integrate, and utilize this training and mobilization resource that complements the ministry efforts already being done.

J. D. Greear, pastor of The Summit Church of Raleigh-Durham, states: "Perspectives is, in my experience, the single best discipleship course to mobilize churches to God's mission. Perspectives gives people their first crucial steps, opening their eyes to God's work in the world and God's call on their lives."

How many in your church are asleep today? Open your doors and partner with God through Perspectives on the World Christian Movement to awaken the body of Christ.

Brett Clemens and his wife, Colette, serve as missionaries with Avant Ministries in Kansas City, MO. Brett is assigned from Avant to Perspectives (www.Perspectives.org), mobilizing full-time as the Perspectives regional director for the Central Region.

Notes

[1] Dr. Ralph Winter, Perspectives History, https://vimeo.com/12776762.

[2] Perspectives History and Ministry Vision, http://www.perspectives.org/About#/HTML/our_history_and_ministry_vision.htm.

[3] John Piper, *Training the Next Generation of Evangelical Pastors and Missionaries* http://www.desiringgod.org/messages/training-the-next-generation-of-evangelical-pastors-and-missionaries, The Evangelical Theological Society (ETS) Annual Meeting, Orlando, FL, November 20, 1998.

[4] Perspectives on the World Christian Movement, *The Church Unleashed* booklet, based on research from online survey conducted by CORE4 Research, www.c4research.com.

[5] Perspectives Lesson 15—Instructor Guidelines.

CHAPTER 18

Mobilization Ideation

Shop Talk

Mark Stebbins

Mobilization Ideation began officially in 2008, as mission mobilization practitioners in the greater Chicago area wanted to take their informal "shop talk" into a more focused and formalized setting. Three mobilizers from Global Partners, the mission sending arm of the Wesleyan Church, were the prime movers in bringing together the first critical mass for a guided twenty-four hours together. The primary goal was to have mobilization enthusiasts "ideate" together on how to improve mission mobilization and identify best practices. A clear objective was relational connections, practical content, and dynamic collaboration.

But this group was different than the traditional summit gathering around a topic in a surprising way. They wanted to have a formal meeting that tapped into and showcased the individual issues and ideas of each participant. The agenda was built around a survey that each attendee completed before coming. The questions uncovered the current and real frustrations, obstacles, ideas, tools, breakthroughs, experiments, and dreams of those in the mission mobilization domain. Answers were built into a twenty-four-hour agenda, curated by a small group of facilitators. The relevance was high, and the atmosphere was electric!

By May 2009, word had spread about the annual event, and some attended from other parts of the country, driving and flying to Chicago. Churches, denominations, and mission agencies sent mobilization leaders and practitioners. A key ingredient to success for Mobilization Ideation was not broadening the invitation list beyond those who were hands-on mission mobilizers. Because of the niche audience, the number attending was

Mobilization Ideation is experienced by
those who attend as highly practical, giving
them new ideas, tools, skills, and solutions
to take back into their mobilization arena.

normally less than fifty. This size added to the vibrant, in-depth exchanges and a sense of family camaraderie around a common purpose—sending more qualified workers into the global harvest. Interactions at the Ideations were more individualized, in-depth, and consequently more helpful to those who came than at larger conferences. Highly stimulating, personalized cross-pollination always occurs.

As the market for Ideations has grown, new ones have been added in Colorado Springs, Atlanta, and Pasadena, CA, since 2014. In 2017, Seattle and Dallas hosted their own Ideations for their regions. Deep, cross-missional friendships and collaborations have resulted regionally and nationally to keep motivation and momentum high. Denominational and organizational affiliations have taken a back seat to the strong sense of being workers together in the broader kingdom and church under Jesus Christ.

Mobilization Ideation is experienced by those who attend as highly practical, giving them new ideas, tools, skills, and solutions to take back into their mobilization arena. A frequent testimony is "I can't wait to try this!" and "This has been a blast of fresh wind in my sails!" At a typical Ideation, there are opportunities for one-on-one interactions, topical skills workshops, large group popcorn sessions, and many small affinity group discussions. And the pleasure of being with those who truly understand each other's work is of great added value! These groups "get" each other, being very much of like heart and mind. Facilitators volunteer from a wide variety of missions traditions, and help lead, present, and facilitate the multifaceted agenda.

No one group "owns" Mobilization Ideation. Several individuals from a variety of organizations contribute to an informal leadership network. MissioNexus has embraced the value for these events and helps to sponsor them on their website. Currently, the events all take place in May, which seems to be a quieter time in the missions mobilization calendar for most participants. The events typically start after lunch on a Thursday and end with lunch (or just before) on Friday, allowing generous travel time to come and go. Most often, the Thursday schedule includes meeting into the evening.

One story to highlight the value of Ideation for the local church occurred in 2012. A layperson from a church's mission committee in Michigan attended the Chicago Ideation. She caught a vision for mobilizing her entire congregation toward missions, even though their Evangelical Free church had a mission sending history and practice, along with a robust mission committee. Through those she met at Ideation and ensuing teleconferencing, an innovative plan for mobilizing the church was agreed upon. It included a type of "points and reward" system for congregants to engage in a broad spectrum of church-sponsored mission activities. It created a buzz of excitement for the entire church to enthusiastically and creatively reconnect with established mission initiatives and opportunities. Countless follow-up collaborations like this one have grown out of Mobilization Ideation.

Another major component of Mobilization Ideation is the developmental benefit it offers to attendees. There is not very much in circulation in the missions community to offer to mobilizers for their training and professional development. These events offer a premier opportunity for sharpening the mission mobilizer's axe in a networking context.

To paraphrase a biblical principle, when God's people come together around his purposes, good things happen. Those involved with Mobilization Ideation have strong convictions that God has authored and orchestrated these events for such a time as this in the North American mission movement. These nimble, practical, and highly relational gatherings produce a high-octane boost to the mobilization efforts of those fellowships represented.

To find out more about Mobilization Ideation, and when the next ones are offered, check under the events tab at www.MissioNexus.org for a blessing near you!

Mark Stebbins is on collegiate staff with The Navigators (www.navigators.org) in Colorado Springs, CO, and is also a missions mobilization consultant with MissioNexus (www.MissioNexus.org).

CHAPTER 19

Influencing Youth

How to Teach for Transformation

Daniel T. Haase

Are You Filling Pails or Lighting Fires?

Ancient wisdom attributed to Plutarch suggests, "Education is not the filling of a pail, but the lighting of a fire." Too often in our missionary preparation and training we are taught to fill pails when we could be lighting fires. How often do we talk at and tell the learners in our midst the truth they need to hear when we could be casting a vision that ignites a response? Truth in a pail is a heavy weight and often a burden to carry. Truth as a fire draws forth an image of the Holy Spirit that refines as well as lights our path. So, in your church, are you filling pails or lighting fires?

This metaphor of the fire is a helpful image to consider when thinking about how teaching for transformation takes place in our churches. Fire brings light and warmth. Good things happen around a fire; relationships are deepened and stories are shared. A caution also comes forth, however, as fires need to be tended so as not to grow wild and out of control. Being a good steward of the fire is a serious responsibility for church leaders who are seeking to mobilize the next generation of missionaries. At the heart of this responsibility are the best principles and practices of teaching and learning. Not surprisingly, it begins with decreasing that Christ might increase.

Rest in Peace Through Dialogue

Not every death is a defeat. In fact, some of the most profound and inspiring stories of life are born out of a story of death. One such story is "the death of the professor." My personal experience has shown that this metaphorical death does indeed bring life. When I enter my classroom as

> **"** Truth in a pail is a heavy weight and often a burden to carry. Truth as a fire draws forth an image of the Holy Spirit that refines as well as lights our path. So, in your church, are you filling pails or lighting fires? **"**

a learner among my students, I challenge the power structure within the traditional student-teacher relationship. What I value as a teacher shifts; this, in turn, affects the posture of the students. I am not lecturing at them; I am listening with them. I design for dialogue. Herein, my content matters to me deeply, but my learners matter to me even more. The "death of the professor" ushers me into a role wherein the opportunity to link content with students' lives expands. Together we commit to a learning-centered approach of education. I welcome this "death" because it breeds safety, respect, sound relationships, and a willingness to engage in dialogue.

Jane Vella, a global educator who was a colleague of Paulo Freire (the Brazilian educator and author of *Pedagogy of the Oppressed*), recalls this interaction with him on the topic:

> Another vital principle of adult learning is recognition of the impact of clear roles in the communication between learner and teacher. As Paulo Freire put it in conversation with us one evening: "Only the student can name the moment of the death of the professor." That is, a teacher can be intent upon a dialogue with an adult learner, but if the learner sees the teacher as "the professor" with whom there is no possibility of disagreement, no questioning, no challenge, the dialogue is dead in the water. Adult students need reinforcement of the human equity between teacher and student and among students. It takes time for adults to see themselves and the teacher in a new role.[1]

It is through this "new role" that students and teachers alike can enter into transformational learning. As Vella suggests, this new understanding of roles takes time, and death can be a painful process. Due to our traditional learning structures, these ideas are easily questioned: Is such a "death" really necessary? What about all the information my students must possess? I know more than my students, why would I waste time with dialogue? How will the students learn what they need to know if lecture is diminished or removed? As valid as these questions may be, they are born out of an understanding of teaching and learning that is limited to the lectern or the pulpit.

When a teacher moves away from a hierarchical relationship with students into one of collaboration and participation, the result is a learning environment framed by active dialogue. Herein, the lecturing teacher experiences a death, as lecture is no longer utilized as the only way to teach. The teacher will have to talk less and is required to facilitate participation. This takes serious preparation and knowledge of content, as well as skillful use of open questions while facilitating conversations around topics of relevance. The teacher welcomes and designs for student engagement. The teacher's role is not simply to tell, but rather to invite others to talk. The teacher becomes another learner in the classroom. They start fires.

As a teacher creates a safe space wherein students are invited to dialogue and practice the truths they are exploring, an opportunity for transformation arises.[2] This application of learning through dialogue is a desperately needed practice in all our venues of teaching, from church ministry to higher education. Through dialogue, as opposed to monologue, the teacher and student enter into the possibility of disagreement, questioning, and challenge. This dialogue (or *dia* + *logos*: "the word between us") turns the chairs of the classroom away from the lectern and toward one another. In this pedagogical shift, the teacher, as lecturer alone, dies; yet the classroom is not a funeral parlor but transforms into a living room of celebrated learning. No longer does content matter more than the people in the room. The complexity of learners and their multiple intelligences and learning styles are identified and engaged. The teacher and student are together and meaningful human relationship is fostered. The "death of the professor" does not end with a lifeless corpse in the classroom. Rather, the "death" that Freire suggests is one wherein the teacher and the student are led to a new relationship.

Burden of Proof

It is important to note that lecture can be an effective way to bring new content before a learner.

At times, it can even be the best way. In fact, this essay represents a form of lecture and I believe learning can come from it. However, lecture is but one methodological approach and therein geared toward a limited frame of learning styles; this is all the more true if new content is not engaged physically, emotionally, and mentally. For the use of lecture to be effective, one must consider how the learners are actively connecting with the material. I am not suggesting we remove preaching from our ministries. I am asking how our ministries provide points of engagement and interaction within the lecture-style teaching so prevalent in our ministry settings.

The point: knowledge is more than content and information. For learning to matter, there must be real-life transfer and impact. Simply sitting and listening to a message does not lead to transformation. It can be a helpful point of contact, but the whole person must be invested for deeper learning to take place. As we seek to mobilize the next generation in our churches to surrender their lives to Christ and serve him overseas, learning needs to go beyond the intellect to be established deeply into their heart and soul.

How we understand what we know is also a crucial factor. Too often the design for learning defaults to lecture with the assumption that if the teacher speaks it, it is known. Freire questions this approach when he refers to turning students into "containers" or "receptacles to be filled by the teacher." One recalls Plutarch and the filling of pails. He continues,

> Education thus becomes an act of depositing, in which the students are the depositories and the teacher is the depositor. Instead of communicating, the teacher issues communiqués and makes deposits which the students patiently receive, memorize, and repeat. This is the "banking" concept of education, in which the scope of action allowed to the students extends only as far as receiving, filing, and storing the deposits.[3]

Freire reminds us how quickly an educator can create a space wherein creativity and curiosity are devalued, all the while damaging the opportunity for exploration and inquiry.

Consider Henri Nouwen's chapter title on teaching in his book *Creative Ministry:* "Beyond the Transference of Knowledge." Herein he warns against the dangers of "teaching as a violent process" marked by competitive, unilateral, and alienating characteristics. He concludes by stating, "The core idea of this chapter has been that ultimately we can only come from a violent form of teaching to a redemptive form of teaching through a conversation that pervades our total personality and breaks the power of our resistance against learning."[4] In essence, we need dialogue. And this dialogue is not merely conversation for conversation sake. It is rigorous and thoughtful engagement built around structured tasks designed for learning. Content matters for sure, but the learner matters first; for our interaction with information is a relational endeavor. We are invited to come and gather around the fire of God's truth.

Kurt Lewin, a founder of social psychology, draws attention to the fact that sustained learning is more effective when it is an active process.[5] Unfortunately, the traditional lecture format of learning found in most educational settings (from churches to schools to businesses) is more informed by the passive tendencies within a monologue approach. The invitation is for the teacher to bring their expertise to bear on the lives of those in their midst and therein design for interaction. For deep and impactful learning to take place, the environment must be one where the cognitive, affective, and behavioral aspects of being human are engaged. Educators must pay attention to the learners in their midst and always ask, "What will enhance the learning?" The answer needs to include the whole person as well as the multifaceted variables involved in any system of learning.

After Death Comes Resurrection

The foundation that teachers build is crucial, as it determines the support offered to their students; or, to use an axiom of Jane Vella's, "The design bears the burden." Ironically enough, when one designs for "the death of the professor," one offers life to the student. The teacher's knowledge and expertise, as important as it is, is not of utmost importance. The learners and the learning take precedence over the lecture. In fact, use of lecture, if it is to be used at all, is to propel learning. The teacher is identified not by the accumulation of knowledge but by the opportunity to invite others on an adventure of learning. The teacher is a wise guide and a trusted friend. Parker Palmer provides a helpful orienting posture when he asserts that good teaching cannot be reduced to technique but comes from the identity and integrity of the teacher.[6] Again we find that teaching is more than information. The teacher finds an enlarged identity as she leaves the lectern and takes a seat in the circle of learners. In the end, the death of the professor leads to the resurrection of an educator. The fire is lit and people begin to come and gather.

Dialogue Heals

Dialogue Education, Jane Vella's learning-centered system of teaching and learning, offers the principles and practices to employ as the teacher moves away from monologue and into dialogue.[7] The lecturer takes a seat and listens, for dialogue requires attention. As the teacher becomes a learner among learners, safety and sound relationships guide the teacher-student interaction. This does not negate the needs for expertise in the teacher's field of instruction. Educators grow as students of their content areas, as well as students of their students; and herein the power divide, too often separating teachers from students, diminishes. Respect is fostered within these relationships, as well as a love of learning. One becomes a shepherd who guides and cares. Voices of both critique and encouragement, met through challenge and support, are welcomed; and issues of relevance are addressed with immediacy and engagement. Learners are invited to be decision-makers in their learning, and accountability is offered as learning happens through practice and reflection. Ideas, feelings, and actions all come together so that the whole person is taught. Learners flourish in such environments where these principles and practices are reinforced; teachers flourish as well. The learning is sequenced in a way wherein these above characteristics continually mark the experiences inside and outside the classroom. These qualities, once embodied, invite the learner into a transformed consciousness wherein peace is made manifest.

The brilliance of Vella's approach to teaching and learning is that it is a structured and yet open system. The teacher is called to design with great intentionality wherein definition leads to direction. Attention to sequence and reinforcement of learning is key. The steps of design within dialogue education focus on eight questions. My own brief summary is listed below, but it is crucial to note that the execution of what looks like a simplistic list of steps requires great diligence and intentionality to master.[8]

1. Who: understanding the learners, of which the teacher is one
2. Why: the situation in light of the needs of the learners
3. So That: the desired indicators of change in the learners
4. When: time frame and its influence on depth of learning
5. Where: location and factors that will enhance or distract learning
6. What: content (knowledge, skills, and attitudes)
7. What For: achievement-based objectives addressing what the learners will do
8. How: the design and facilitation of learning tasks

One of Vella's greatest offerings to the field of education is in the linkage of content (step 6) and the construction of "achievement-based objectives" (step 7). This approach to design requires the teacher to identify specific content (as nouns) and the corollary achievement-based objectives (as verbs in the future perfect tense, i.e., "At the end of our time, learners WILL HAVE . . ."). This tense forces a strong verb and allows for accountability in the learning as well as clear objectives that can be evaluated because they lend themselves to a specific "achieved" product or behavior. For the purposes of this book, we want to see students develop a knowledge of God's call to the nations as well as a heart of compassion for the lost.

Students are then given all the resources they need to respond within the learning environment (step 8). To establish these resources, the teacher commits to the rigorous preparation of design and development of tasks that will enhance learning. This leads to a trust of the design with a focus on the learning. As Vella is apt to say, "The means is dialogue, the end is learning, and the purpose is peace." Herein the teacher is offered a vision and construct for transformational and healing encounters. With this focus on learning through dialogue, the teacher is released from an arrogant approach to the educational endeavor. Death humiliates. Peace is restored. The fire is ablaze.

When the educator puts to death the traditional model of lecture wherein content is king, a new order is established. For the church-based educator this invitation "to lead out" (i.e., to educate) is an opening of oneself to a new kind of rule. A rule established within humility wherein the Holy Spirit is the ultimate guide. The teacher is no longer alone. The Helper has arrived and his arrival is within a community of believers. The teacher, the students, and their Maker all meet together and the classroom becomes a sanctuary. Light enters the world and the darkness flees.

Dialogue Education: Believe It, or Not?

My invitation is for you to engage the content within this essay. In that vein, I offer the following learning tasks to move from monologue into dialogue:

IDENTIFY a learning experience (in a traditional or nontraditional setting) wherein you learned through dialogue. **NAME** how this differs from an experience wherein you learned through lecture.

LIST two phrases from the essay that strike you as valuable in your setting. Next to each selected phrase, **WRITE** down one practical way you will implement it with your learners.

CHOOSE one tip (from the list below) to apply in your context. **CREATE** a detailed design of how you will engage your learners though dialogue:

1. Facilitate five minutes of dialogue for every twelve minutes of lecture.
2. Discern what content is most valuable to the learners and guard yourself from trying to "cover" material: tell through dialogue.
3. Invite immediate engagement when new content is brought before the learner and ensure holistic learning and teaching by paying attention to the cognitive, affective, and psychomotor needs.
4. Engage multiple intelligences and learning styles as you teach.
5. Guide learners from simple to complex content and interaction.
6. Ask open questions that lead to meaningful and relevant interaction.
7. Restructure the learning space set up for easier engagement and dialogue.
8. Break into small groups or pairs to stimulate interaction with posed open questions.

   READ one of the books in the resource list or search the Global Learning Partner's website for more on Dialogue Education. **SHARE** your learning with me or other ministry partners.

Daniel T. Haase is an instructor of Christian formation and ministry at Wheaton College (IL) (www.wheaton.edu), where he also serves in the Center for Global and Experiential Learning (www.about.me/dthaase).

Notes

[1] Jane Vella, *Learning To Listen, Learning To Teach: The Power of Dialogue in Educating Adults* (San Francisco: Jossey Bass, 2002), 20.

[2] Parker Palmer, *To Know as We Are Known: Education as a Spiritual Journey* (San Francisco: HarperCollins, 1993).

[3] Paulo Feire, *Pedagogy of the Oppressed* (New York: Continuum, 1990), 58.

[4] Henri J. M. Nouwen, *Creative Ministry* (New York: Image Books, 1971), 3–20.

[5] Kurt Lewin, *Field Theories in Social Science* (New York: Harper Collins, 1951).

[6] Parker Palmer, *The Courage to Teach: Exploring an Inner Landscape of a Teacher's Life* (San Francisco: John Wiley & Sons, 2007), 10.

[7] Global Learning Partners, "About Dialogue Education," Accessed January 25, 2014. http://www.globallearningpartners.com/about/about-dialogue-education.

[8] Jane Vella, *Taking Learning to Task: Creative Strategies for Teaching Adults* (San Francisco: Jossey Bass, 2001) & Jane Vella, *On Teaching and Learning: Putting the Principles and Practices of Dialogue Education into Action* (San Francisco: Jossey Bass, 2008)—for further exploration of the structure and design of Dialogue Education.

CHAPTER 20

Women's Issues

Helping Women Thrive

Lorrie Lindgren

Thrive Ministry was founded in 1997 to provide support and encouragement to help missionary women thrive on the field, lower attrition, and expand God's kingdom. The ministry is interdenominational and serves almost 700 evangelical mission agencies sending approximately 75,000 North American women serving as career missionaries.

Thrive is the only member care ministry ministering exclusively to missionary women. For the past twenty years, and by God's gracious provision, we have joyfully ministered to thousands of faithful sisters in Christ who share the good news around the world. We believe providing spiritual, emotional, and physical refreshment is a critical investment for the effectiveness of expanding God's kingdom. Because of a woman's God-given design, she has a deep need to relationally connect with other women who "get her life" as a missionary.

There is tremendous energy and momentum to get workers on the field but a lack of intentional effort to provide spiritual, physical, and emotional support once serving overseas.

Many global (missionary) women feel alone and are barely surviving. It has been estimated that the average length of a cross-cultural worker's career has dropped to only eight years. In the book *Too Valuable to Lose*, William Taylor states that one missionary in six never completes the first term.[1]

Imagine, just when they become proficient in the language and begin to understand the culture, they tragically leave the field! Thrive's goal is to bring change to that reality by caring for, connecting, and creating community for global women.

" There is tremendous energy and momentum to get workers on the field but a lack of intentional effort to provide spiritual, physical, and emotional support once serving overseas. **"**

"Small (mission) agencies have an alarming attrition rate of 33% each year," according to Rob Hay in his book *Worth Keeping*.[2] One of the top five reasons a family leaves the field is because the woman is struggling emotionally. Ruth Ann Graybill of the Rosemead School of Psychology notes, "Too many of our missionary women become casualties in battle, and the whole world suffers for it. Their loss becomes our loss."[3]

Attrition is a silent enemy of God's calling to effective long-term kingdom building. It affects every sphere of relationship that God calls each worker to influence, whether it be their national, team, or cultural relationships or their family and friends. As the body of Christ, we need to support and encourage the women who by faith are serving the Lord cross-culturally. Thrive exists for this very reason: to help global women thrive on the field, lower attrition, and expand God's kingdom.

Our Primary Strategies to Help Missionary Women Thrive on the Field

Community/Connection Through Our Online Magazine (Thriveconnection.com)

The founding focus of Thrive (formerly Women of the Harvest) was to publish a bimonthly magazine written by missionary women for missionary women—providing a place to be transparent about the joys and struggles of missionary life. The online magazine, *Connection*, transitioned to a weekly publication in 2014 and provides an interactive forum for women to connect through magazine articles, Bible studies, forums, etc.

Community/Connection Through the Retreat Ministry (Thriveministry.org/Retreats)

In 1998, we began hosting retreats in various regions around the world and invited North American women to a four-day "gift" to get away from their demanding work for a time of rest, renewal, and refreshment. As of

July 2017, we have been in thirty-eight different international locations and hosted fifteen retreats in the US for women on home assignment. More than 4,500 women have attended a life-changing retreat as our guest. A prayer team of over nine hundred people join us to pray for each attendee and their country of service through our 30 Days of Prayer guide.

Our retreat objective is to provide spiritual refreshment through worship, Bible study, prayer, and rest. It is a place where they can be nurtured, encouraged, and meet other women serving in tough places. We facilitate connection in the context of their small group, multiagency interactions, and time with others who "get their life." The retreat setting provides a safe place for women to be themselves and share their unique challenges outside of their church and agency. Many of our attendees work in remote locations where running water and electricity are not available or dependable. By hosting our retreats at a Western hotel, we provide an environment for physical, spiritual, and emotional renewal. Each retreat hosts approximately one hundred missionary women who represent an average of forty different mission agencies.

We bring twenty-five to thirty volunteers with us to each retreat to serve our missionary guests. Our speaker is a missionary woman herself and strong Bible teacher. The attendees participate in small groups to dialogue about the Bible teaching and to pray for one another. We are intentional to make sure no two women from the same agency are in a small group together to provide an environment to share openly. The attendees enjoy five hours of free time each afternoon to allow them to spend significant time alone with the Lord and to participate in soul-care activities. Each attendee is prayed for individually and specifically seven to eight times over the course of the retreat. Worshiping in English (their heart language) is always a highlight!

Two responses from previous participants are encouraging to us:

When I came, I was just looking for connections with other global women. What I found was a holy space to meet the Father surrounded by others on the same journey. Thank you for hearing and obeying the Father because I'm leaving feeling refreshed, affirmed, encouraged, and renewed. Truly. Thank you!

I came in deep need of healing, and after one of my greatest seasons of burnout. Thank you for making me feel cherished, delighted in, and lavished over by my Father. It's helped spiritual truths and vision penetrate an exhausted, bewildered heart. Grateful.

What We Have Learned

The Top Five Needs of Missionary Women
(as identified in our 2013 survey of more than ten thousand missionary women)
- To be spiritually mentored
- To feel connected
- To be known, understood, and prayed for
- To have a close friend
- To have time away from ministry / life responsibilities

Common Themes Heard by our Counseling Team
- Team Conflict Issues
- Women in Leadership
- Workaholism
- Fatigue
- Loss of Ministry Passion
- Need for Self-Care
- Grief and Loss (Tangible and Intangible)
- Transition
- Marital Stressors: Sexual Abuse, Moral Failure, Communication, Cross-Cultural Marriage
- Addictions
- Loneliness
- Isolation
- Depression
- Singleness
- MK Issues: Schooling Choices, Adult Children Struggling in the US

An Advocate for Global (Missionary) Women

In addition to providing care, resources, and community to encourage and empower global women to thrive, we are called to be their advocate.

After twenty years of ministry, we discovered that many churches, agencies, and individuals are unaware of the critical needs of global women. Therefore, there is a significant need to engage and educate Christian communities to be equipped and empowered to proactively meet the needs of global women.

Retreat attendees in the Middle East said:

If possible, keep teaching churches back home that they can always do more (prayer, emails, notes) to let us know they haven't forgotten about us. That was a recurring theme in our small group. Women felt forgotten and neglected by friends, churches, and at times, family. We need much more than a check once a month!

Please train our church mission committees to have a deeper understanding of caring for global workers.

A strategic opportunity to be an advocate is actually a by-product of training our retreat volunteers. Each year, approximately seventy-five to one hundred volunteers travel with us from all across the US (and representing all denominations) to serve at our retreats. From this experience, they learn more about the lives, ministries, and challenges of missionary women. We train them how to ask intentional questions to allow the missionary woman to share from a deeper place in her life. We model and train effective member care. We have the privilege of being a catalyst to increase awareness of missionary needs as the volunteers share the retreat experience with their local churches.

We want to invite *your* church to consider regularly sending women to serve with us at a retreat. We provide pretrip training, postretreat debriefing, and process all support funds. It's a short-term mission trip "in a box" that will strengthen your strategy for missionary care!

We also provide a sixteen-question member care quiz for church mission leaders. A few sample questions are:

- How do you encourage them to cultivate their walks with the Lord?
- How do you verbalize that they are valued for "being" vs. "doing"?
- How do you model and teach them the disciplines of rhythm and rest?
- Do you provide opportunities to refuel and rest?
- How does your church value and protect your single missionary women?
- The full member care quiz can be requested at info@thriveministry.org.

Our vision is to be global leaders, providing expertise and setting excellent standards of care for global women. We believe women will thrive, in part because individuals, churches, and mission agencies provide holistic, proactive care. What will you do to better care for your female workers?

Lorrie Lindgren has been the executive director of Thrive Ministry (thriveministry.org) since 2005.

Notes

[1] William D. Taylor, *Too Valuable to Lose: Exploring the Causes and Cures of Missionary Attrition* (Pasadena, CA: William Carey Library, 1997).

[2] Rob Hay, *Worth Keeping: Global Perspectives on Best Practice in Missionary Retention* (Pasadena, CA: William Carey Library, 2007).

[3] Ruth Ann Graybill, *The Emotional Needs of Women on the Mission Field*, Biola Counseling Center, La Mirada, CA.

CHAPTER 21

Men's Issues

A City of Refuge for Men

Stan De La Cour and Brandon Boyd

The old Bob Dylan song goes "The times, they are a-changin." This is true with ministry today. At one time, moral issues were a small part of the screening process. The marital status box was checked either with single, married, divorced, or widowed. Now we need to consider the morality of our missionary candidates. Even the Apostle Paul worked with an elder board with a past. The list preceding 1 Corinthians 6:11, "And such were some of you," covered all sorts of sexual immorality. However, there was a reckoning—a dealing with the past, a halt to the pattern of sins: "But you were washed, you were sanctified, you were justified in the name of the Lord Jesus Christ and by the Spirit of our God."

While serving in Japan, I was in an accountability group when I asked an expatriate if he was having any problems with pornography. He quickly responded, "Nope . . . I rather enjoy it." He foolishly thought this conduct did not harm him or anyone else, nor detract from his ministry. He was dead wrong. It was the crack in his spiritual armor that allowed more and more impurity into his life. I wondered how many others would answer the same way, ignorant of or blatantly ignoring the damage moral sin inficts on their life.

SIM, originally the Sudan Interior Mission, expects the men and women who enter ministry to live in a manner that is worthy of the gospel—pure and above reproach. Biblical morality is a priority for our personnel, regardless of location or role; it is one of our core values. Our missionary candidates have been nurtured and discipled in a local church. Men and women coming from a sordid past have baggage to deal with.

In fact, we all do. Some consequences of sin are harder to deal with than others, but there is hope through God's work on the Cross—help can be found and lives restored.

Pornography is not only a problem in our society; it is a problem in our churches. Sadly, statistics show that 80 percent of men in the pews look at some form of porn many times each month.[1] Does that percentage change when it comes to missionary candidates? Because of this question, SIM USA is committed to dealing with men's moral issues with a goal of healing and restoration for the individual and couple, if married.

SIM has been launching Christian workers into ministry since 1893, bringing good news to people who are living and dying without the gospel. The initials have now become our name, tethering us to our founders' vision but encompassing our work around the world. Today SIM has over four thousand workers from sixty-five nations serving on six continents in more than seventy countries . . . and our heart remains the same.

When SIM USA's member care department is made aware that a male missionary is involved in pornography or other forms of sexual immorality, the man is referred to one of the member care counselors (the same protocols apply to women as well). The counselor meets with the man and his wife (if applicable and possible) to assess needs and develop a healing and restoration plan. Each situation is handled individually, as each man's situation is unique. The plan includes getting the couple into counseling, ensuring proper filtering software with accountability, while getting him involved with personal accountability and into a support group. This plan also addresses the needs of the wife, since the goal is healing and restoration of the man and his wife. The SIM USA counselor tracks with them throughout this process and is part of the support team for them.

We are committed to addressing this issue of pornography. We will walk with willing people down the road toward freedom and redemption through Christ's grace. We want to see people experience the power of God's forgiveness and be restored to a proper relationship with Jesus. We want to assist people with finding and accessing the resources necessary to overcome obstacles to their purity and spiritual health. We also want to reassure people that viewing pornography does not mean they are immediately going to be dismissed. Each situation is handled individually, carefully, lovingly, and with dignity.

▐▐ There needs to be a safe place for men to find help, a "city of refuge" in which to be honest about struggles and failures without fear of being judged or attacked. . . . Church leaders and mission agencies need to be ready when one of their own confides in them with openness and honesty. We must address the struggles and addictions in our own lives as well. **▐▐**

Much prayer and study of best practices were given to developing appropriate SIM policies and keeping them current. Once a situation is reported, a counselor is assigned to determine the depth of addiction and level of offense. A support system is suggested and established, typically including the sending church. The couple or single works toward restoration throughout the process with the aid of various support people. A term of treatment is encouraged, which sometimes means a later return to the field, if returning is possible.

An excerpt from the SIM internal document entitled "Human Sexuality and Sexual Conduct" states:

In Scripture, maintaining sexual purity includes abstaining from certain sexual behaviors. These behaviors fall under the broad designation of "sexual immorality" (Greek "porneia," e.g., 1 Thess 4:3; Eph 5:3) and include, but are not limited to: Premarital sexual relations (1 Cor 7:2,9; 1 Tim 5:2); Adultery (Ex 20:14; Heb13:4); Homosexual relations (Lev 20:13; Rom 1:24–27); Intentional viewing of pornography (Job 31:3; Matt 5:28).

The list of affirmations found in SIM's code of conduct agreement is reviewed and signed by our missionaries every three years. The code says:

I understand that any sexual misconduct, including but not limited to premarital and extramarital sexual relationships, homosexual acts, use of pornography, child abuse, and sexual harassment, is unacceptable in those who serve as part of SIM or any entity to which I may be seconded by SIM.

The sending church's role is to cultivate and nurture sexually healthy men and women who maintain that godly attitude throughout their lives and ministries. The local church must persistently model and teach holiness and purity. There needs to be a safe place for men to find help, a "city of refuge" in which to be honest about struggles and failures without fear of being judged or attacked. SIM seeks to provide these as well, and we trust that churches will help to encourage missionaries throughout their career. Church leaders and mission agencies need to be ready when one of their own confides in them with openness and honesty. We must address the struggles and addictions in our own lives as well.

Two of the biggest barriers to being freed from the bondage of pornography are shame and secrecy. We need to break the silence and foster an atmosphere in which people who are dealing with any type of sin can approach us openly and find acceptance, God-honoring care, and healing. Through us the Holy Spirit can remind hurting brothers and sisters who they are in Christ and restore them to a growing, vital relationship with Jesus.

In his book *In the Shadows of the Net,* Dr. Patrick Carnes explains that compulsive viewing of cyber-pornography, a subgroup of sexual addiction, has a recognizable behavior pattern similar to other addictions. Internet sex addiction has a progressive nature like other addictions, and sex addicts will take ever greater risks to engage in sexual activity online as their addiction progresses.[2]

Today, over 70 percent of sex addicts report having problematic online sexual behavior. Two-thirds of those engaged in these behaviors have such despair over their internet activities that they have had suicidal thoughts. Sexual acting out online has been shown to manifest in similar off-line behavior. People who already were sex addicts find the internet accelerates their problem. Those who start in the online behavior quickly start to act out in new ways off-line.

Fortunately, Dr. Carnes also found a high rate of recovery success with those sex addicts whose recovery plan included:

- Three- to five-year recovery journey
- Minimum of two years of individual counseling
- Two years of group therapy, including psychoeducation
- Two years of twelve step groups

These battles for the mind can be won through the power of God, and the believer's submission to the Holy Spirit's control. God is using counseling, small groups, retreats, 12-step programs, Celebrate Recovery and other similar programs, treatment centers, and most importantly, the nurture of a vibrant Christian community to bring restoration back to many couples. The church and the mission agency must work together to foster this godly atmosphere of Christian discipleship and grace. There are strategies for defeating the private secrets that threaten men's lives and ministries, so you do not have to bear this burden alone.

Rev. Stan De La Cour serves as director of church partnership, SIM USA, with his wife, Faith, who is the vice president and chief people officer, SIM USA (www.sim.org). They served in Japan for over thirty-four years with Asian Access (A2).

Brandon Boyd is a licensed professional counselor associate with SIM USA, with his wife, Cheri, who provides education support. They served in Chiang Mai, Thailand, for five and a half years.

Notes

[1] Jay Dennis, *Christians & Pornography; Pastor & Church Leadership Resource Guide,* 2015, Pink Elephant Resources, PO Box 118, Lakeland, FL 33802 page 7, ISBN: 978–0–9904907–2–2.

[2] Patrick Carnes PhD, *In the Shadows of the Net: Breaking Free of Compulsive Online Sexual Behavior* (Center City, MN: Hazelden, 2007).

Resources

Gentle Path at The Meadows, 1655 N. Tegner St., Wickenburg, AZ 85390, www.GentlePathMeadows.com

Jim Cress, M.A., LPC, CSAT www.JimCress.com

Pure Desires Ministries, Ted Roberts, 719 NE Roberts Avenue, Gresham. OR 97030, www.PureDesire.org

The Porn Phenomenon: *The Impact of Pornography in the Digital Age* by A Barna Report, Produced in partnership with Josh McDowell Ministry (a Cru Ministry), Barna Group, Ventura, CA, 2016. ISBN 978–0–9965842–6–4

CHAPTER 22

MK/TCK Issues

Tension Between Calling and Craving

Michèle Phoenix

Julianne is an MK from Italy. Growing up on the Old Continent, she trained for ten years as a classical dancer, eventually earning scholarships to elite academies across Europe. Poised on the brink of adulthood, with ballet companies vying to recruit her, she began to feel guilty about dancing for a living. After all, she'd been raised by parents whose passion was church planting. She understood the crucial role that type of ministry plays in reaching the world for Christ. She'd been prayed over by pastors and congregations who referred in hushed voices to the sacrifices the whole family had made to serve overseas, lauding them for the sacred calling that set them apart from "ordinary" believers.

Though she was uniquely gifted and qualified for the dancing contracts being offered to her, Julianne opted not to accept them. She applied to a Bible college instead, studied theology, and returned to Europe to plant churches in Italy. She knew the language and culture, after all. And it was the family trade—noble work God was pleased with.

After three years in the messy trenches of missionary work, Julianne had nothing left to give. Depleted from forcing herself to participate in a ministry for which she was neither gifted nor truly passionate, she returned to her passport culture defeated and disillusioned. She'd chosen significance over gifting, as so many do, and her misguided quest had ended in personal and spiritual burnout.

Julianne's is not a unique story. The pressure on MKs to become missionaries is undeniable. It comes at them from so many different sources that it's hard, as they grow up, to envision a future in which they do something other than traditional ministry.

Their parents, for obvious reasons, see missionary work as the most important career they could have chosen. The church celebrates missionaries as superior players in the battle for global souls. The broader Christian world as a whole elevates mission work as the most significant calling a person can possibly receive.

Is it any wonder that so many MKs, like Julianne, feel that there are no career options as validating and meaningful as ministry?

Don't get me wrong. There are countless MKs who have returned to the field for all the right reasons. Because of their upbringing, they can apply linguistic aptitude, cultural fluidity, and ministry know-how to the task. They can be valuable members of the missionary world *when it is truly what God has called them to do.*

That's where it gets a bit murky. How do MKs differentiate between wanting to "go home" (back to a place and job that are familiar to them) and a genuine divine urging to use their God-given abilities in a context for which they are uniquely equipped?

The good news is that those same voices that unwittingly promote the false "MKs must become missionaries" narrative can play a part in intentionally refuting it and preparing the missionaries' kids in their sphere for the life decisions they'll have to make.

Four Crucial Steps to Help MKs

1. Redefine Significance

There have been numerous articles written encouraging churches to celebrate all work as God's work. These articles question why pastors give ten minutes in a service to missionaries, but seldom yield the stage to teachers, lawyers, tradesmen, and Uber drivers. They ask why we're so quick to praise those engaged in ministry while overlooking those who shine God's light in factories, boardrooms, and nail salons.

In his insightful book *Futureville,* Skye Jethani makes the case that every individual is created to influence the world for good. He finds in Genesis three major categories for which each of us was uniquely designed: to cultivate beauty, to cultivate order, and to cultivate abundance.[1] So when someone like Julianne, who was divinely equipped to cultivate beauty through dance, chooses traditional church planting as a career, she is working outside the realm of her natural gifting, a state that is harmful and not sustainable over long periods of time. The same would be true of an electrician attempting a career in botany or a business-minded woman pressured into working full-time in a daycare.

Too many MKs are gathering from the unspoken pressure of the Christian world that traditional ministry is the only means to a significant life—that sharing the gospel is a higher calling than any other. This actually runs contrary to current trends, which recognize that the most effective way of sharing Jesus with others is for him to be visible in us wherever we are—in the way we engage with our work, our colleagues, our neighbors, strangers, and society at large.

In giving in to the expectation that they become missionaries, some MKs might extinguish their potential to draw people to their Savior simply by reflecting his heart in the sphere for which they were divinely designed.

There is nothing more beautiful or influential than a cashier, a police officer, a doctor, or a chef who radiates Christ. They are just as important to God's influence on culture as the missionaries who are sent out by churches every year. We need to help MKs to understand that truth.

2. Self-Evaluate

While we're reframing the meaning of significance, we can also be helping MKs to identify the strengths we see in them. Churches rightfully validate spiritual traits like faith, honesty, selflessness, and helpfulness. It would be wonderful if they were equally eager to affirm creativity, problem-solving, inquisitiveness, enterprise, and mechanical skills, in order to steer all young people (not just MKs) toward a career that reflects their God-given skill set.

We need to adapt our conversations too. When MKs visit churches, the primary questions we ask are about their family's work and the country in which they live. Once relationship has been established, it may be helpful to expand the subject matter, to ask them about what they enjoy and to engage them on those topics. When we know more about them, we can pair MKs with adults working in a field that's of interest to them. If they're musicians, we can invite them to play with the youth worship team. If they're contemplating a career in the sciences, we can introduce them to activities (museums, contests) that will expand their abilities and knowledge.

3. Distinguish Craving from Calling

I've mentioned it before: just like Dorothy wanted to go back to Kansas in *The Wizard of Oz*, it is natural for MKs to crave a return to the foreign

"" *How do MKs differentiate between wanting to "go home" (back to a place and job that are familiar to them) and a genuine divine urging to use their God-given abilities in a context for which they are uniquely equipped?* ""

country and culture they call home. Having grown up between worlds, they love multiple places, and those places will continue to hold a piece of their hearts long after they've left them.

As you can imagine, this can be a confusing factor when it comes to identifying the urge they have to engage in foreign mission work as adults. Is the chief motivation a desire to go home? Is it God whispering to them that this might be a good use of their skills? Or is it a combination of both?

Don't get me wrong: wanting to go home is good and healthy. I would never advocate that we dismiss that urge. That said, removing it at least for a time from the rational, skills-based and prayer-infused decision-making process might allow for a less emotional conclusion to be reached.

4. Grow in Their Faith

The notion that MKs are spiritual superstars is not only misguided—it's harmful. My own upbringing in a Christian home, steeped in Christian ministry, did not seal my faith. By the time I was twenty, I had serious doubts as to whether God existed at all and even graver doubts about the authenticity of the believers I knew.

Though growing up on the mission field instills a deep, abiding love for God in a large number of MKs, for some it has the opposite effect.

That's one of the reasons I'm so careful to refer to MKs as "missionaries' kids," not "missionary kids." It's a small but important distinction. As children, they are not missionaries—their parents are. They may participate in the work their mom and dad do, but it's their parents who sensed the call to missionary work, who chose their foreign or local field, who found an organization to send them and recruited an army of donors to support them. Not the children.

The unspoken expectation, when we refer to MKs as missionary kids, is that they are doing the work. More dangerously, it might also communicate to them that they should have the same deep, committed passion for Christ as their parents do. That's simply unreasonable.

Churches can help. The first step they might take to foster a healthy and genuine faith in MKs is to stop assuming. Just because they may know more answers to Sunday school questions does not necessarily indicate a thriving faith. Just because they can quote John 3:16 in four languages does not mean they have a personal relationship with Jesus.

Engaging MKs in a spiritual way, *without pressuring them to be more knowledgeable and invested than others,* is crucial to offering them a safe place to grow in their faith. We need to invite them into our programs in the same way we'd invite anyone else, drawing them in gradually and authentically, so they build up the confidence to be vulnerable and honest.

In some cases, we may need to help them find clarity, as so many MKs have developed a distorted view of God because they grew up in a family that "worked for him." Others might have suffered trauma or neglect on the field and might view him as the inflictor of that pain, because he called the family, he demanded everything of them, and, in the worst cases, didn't seem to step in to prevent the harm they endured.

Some missionaries' kids, rather than being peer leaders in churches, might need to be given the space to process the hard part of their lives with trusted adults who understand that despite all their experiences and knowledge, they're still just kids trying to figure out their relationship with God. Only when they've found stability in their faith will they be able to clearly contemplate pursuing a life in traditional ministry.

Another book by Skye Jethani that I've found to be extremely helpful in addressing some of the faulty conclusions MKs reach about God's heart for them is *With,* and I hand it out like party favors to any MK who crosses my threshold![2]

If the church is to help MKs to navigate crucial crossroads in their lives, we must first be fully engaged in fostering in them a realistic definition of significance, an honest assessment of themselves, a guiding understanding of calling vs. craving, and a genuine faith that will inform their decision making.

None of this is possible without relationship. Truly knowing MKs will require that we refocus our attention from their parents to them—that we invest in building trust, that we ask meaningful questions, cultivate their interests, and walk alongside them in the process of discernment.

Michèle Phoenix is a mentor, writer, and speaker with a heart for MKs. She taught for twenty years at Black Forest Academy (Germany) before launching her own ministry advocating for third culture kids (www. michelephoenix.com).

Notes

[1] Skye Jethani, *Futureville* (Nashville: Thomas Nelson, 2014).

[2] Skye Jethani, *With* (Nashville: Thomas Nelson, 2011).

CHAPTER 23

Church-based Candidate Orientation

Skills, Knowledge, and Character

Greg Carter

While it may be attractive for a wannabe missionary to begin his foray into the preparation process by forging ahead on his own, the proper order is to start with church leadership. A preferred approach has the local church proactive in its role by providing an encouraging environment and supportive experiences.

This chapter will address the role of the local church in this partnership. As the local church engages in world evangelization, it is working in cooperation with three other groups: (1) the missionary sending agency, (2) the formal school, and (3) the specialized training organization. Each has a realm of expertise that provides specific training along with the necessary environment for the preparation, sending, and supervision of the missionary candidate.

The reader is encouraged to understand how these four entities complement one another.[1] Understanding the help that comes from the others allows us to look specifically at the role of the local church in the preparation of missionary candidates.

The church is especially suited and called to disciple its members. When this is pursued with intentionality, the sending agency will be the recipient of healthy individuals and families who are spiritually mature, emotionally and physically healthy, and relationally secure. We are not talking perfection, but maturity is essential.

The material in this chapter is primarily excerpted from *Skills, Knowledge, Character: A Church-Based Approach to Missionary Candidate Preparation*, Greg Carter, 2010, Turtle River Press.

> *The church is especially suited and called to disciple its members. When this is pursued with intentionality, the sending agency will be the recipient of healthy individuals and families who are spiritually mature, emotionally and physically healthy, and relationally secure.*

The church, both through relationships as well as systematic programs (for example, youth ministries, women's Bible studies, and men's accountability groups), prepares its members to be effective witnesses in their respective spheres of influence. Accordingly, as it teaches a global view of evangelism and discipleship, some in the body will be called to service outside of the context of their local community.

Missionary sending agencies don't grow their own missionaries (apart from children of missionaries who choose to become missionaries). They ought to be the natural by-product of local churches: men and women committed to the expansion of the kingdom of God through the planting of churches that reflect normative cultural aspects. The local church, acting within the above-noted partnership, develops, empowers, and releases its members in cross-cultural service. What they do will hopefully be aligned with the direction and ministry emphasis the local church has within its own community. The missionaries work out of an area of skill, commitment, and conviction in which they have been well schooled by their local church.

The local church is an excellent environment for learning interpersonal skills and how to relate to all kinds of people of all ages. The servant of God can be given opportunities to serve others who are less than appreciative, manipulative, cantankerous, domineering, spiritually unmotivated, often offensive in attitude, and generally a pain in the posterior. All this is good experience for the development of interpersonal skills.

The local church affirms appropriate behavior, measures out forgiveness in generous doses, rallies behind those who are flagging in their Christian walk, cares for those in crisis, rejoices with those who laugh, bears with the recalcitrant, mourns with those who weep, encourages the restoration of broken relationships, and counts others as more important. From within this context will come healthy people who will be healthy missionaries.

The church will teach me to like who I am and why I am significant. I can learn why I have every reason to be humble before God, but that at the same time I can be completely confident that God can do marvelous things through me. It creates in me godly contentment when I understand that it is he who sovereignly distributes the gifts. When I do well in a particular area, pride is not the result because I know that the ability to function capably is directly from his hand. And on the other hand, where I am insufficient, I don't shrink in embarrassment. My security and sense of well-being then is not dependent upon performing well. I recognize that who I am is from the Father; successes and failures neither swell my head nor make me reach for Valium.

The end product of a planned approach to missionary candidate preparation should be healthy individuals and families. Health is a many-faceted jewel that can be measured in different lights and from different angles. Church leadership will observe from high and low to be well convinced that holistic and balanced health exists. It will consider emotional, financial, physical, spiritual, relational, and cultural benchmarks. These do not exist simply as vague hopes; they can be measured. The astute church sets standards, examines, and measures.

In the same manner, potential missionaries place themselves under the leadership of the local church, believing that the body of Christ will direct and care for them in the best way humanly possible. Fallibilities aside, having church leadership actively engaged with the cross-cultural discipleship of a missionary candidate is a beautiful thing.

Living and serving in another culture as a missionary is filled with significant challenges that will test both the capacity and the calling of the wide-eyed servant. Even those with a cross-cultural preparation course certificate under their belt will be uncomfortably surprised. Preparation and attitude are vital components of this change. The latter can always be adjusted and fine-tuned along the way. The former, by its nature, must be accomplished prior to entering the new culture. If we can correctly anticipate the challenges, we can help the missionary candidate to employ activities, acquire skills, and gain understanding that will help him arrive on site with a better likelihood of success.

Because we know this to be the case, the local church should work hard to fulfill its role in the development of the requisite skills, knowledge, and character in the individuals and families whom it sends cross-culturally as kingdom workers. Preventable departure is expensive both emotionally and financially.

A word of caution here is very appropriate: Life can never be fully anticipated. The cultural value of control, so important for Americans, lurks behind the concept of preparedness. Health issues, political unrest, traffic accidents, economic meltdowns, mission politics, and terrorism are potentialities. Stuff happens, and you have to live with it. Preparation is necessary, but it is not our savior. Prepare for life and then live with what happens.

A recommended approach is to appoint a mentor to coach the potential missionary toward the requisite proficiencies. Securing the mentor early will be one of the critical elements of this process. Church leadership should maintain frequent and open communication with the mentor. He or she is the most important element in the success of this process.

Nearly every church can provide ministry experience that is cross-cultural in nature.[2] A love for people who are different can't come from a distance; face-to-face interaction is requisite for God, through the church, to affirm a person's gifting as a missionary. The ability to live comfortably outside of his normative culture and with "differentness" is absolutely critical. This would be shown in food, communication patterns, personal schedule, social interaction, etc. The person who wants to be a missionary must be comfortable living in these situations in order to adapt well to his adopted country.

Generally speaking, the foundational premise is that the missionary candidate will be developed in a broad area with attention to skills, knowledge, and character, each of which interfaces with the other. Knowledge of observation, interpretation, and application principles allows the candidate to teach. The skill to exegete accurately I Thessalonians 4:1–8 builds into the person's character the desire for sexual purity. Looking out for the interests of others will cause the person to develop the skills of affirming others and asking good questions in order to engage them in conversation.

Skills, Knowledge, and Character

Knowledge is probably the easiest of the three areas to address and evaluate. Skills can also be taught and measured, though not with the same ease as knowledge. Perhaps the most critical of the three and the hardest to evaluate objectively is character,[3] yet that is the very one that anchors the other two. A buffoon with character will be humored. He may not do much that is worthwhile, but he will also likely do little damage.

The skilled missionary without character can wreak havoc and leave in his wake destruction that will take years from which to recover.

The development of character, as described in the Scriptures, seems to stem from difficulty. Ruth was called "a woman of noble character" (Ruth 3:11, NIV) a trait no doubt acquired from the godly response to the hardship she had experienced. Romans 5:3,4 instructs us that " . . . we also glory in our sufferings, because we know that suffering produces perseverance; perseverance, character; and character, hope" (NIV).

Additionally we see that choice of friends is a crucial component, for "Bad company corrupts good character" (1 Cor 15:33, NIV). The Bereans are described as being "of more noble character than those in Thessalonica . . ." (Acts 17:11, NIV) in their receiving the message with great eagerness and examining the Scriptures daily. It is not clearly noted which is the causative agent. Whichever, character was foundational and they were thus portrayed very positively.

All three are needed and ought to be addressed by the local church as part of a thorough missionary candidate preparation process. A worthy but certainly not exhaustive list of skills, knowledge, and character includes:

Skills
- social: active listener, reads body language, resolves conflict, adaptive, observant, learner
- financial: lives within means, plans for the future
- emotional: understands how he responds in various situations, knows how to regenerate
- ministry: does evangelism and discipleship, works comfortably in a team setting, can teach, shows personal initiative, sets goals
- cross-cultural: navigates the unfamiliar, knows how to limit vocabulary appropriately, employs observation skills, embraces the awkward
- language learning
- spiritual: can do inductive Bible study, can use spiritual gifts appropriately

Knowledge
- biblical: theology, ecclesiology, missiology, missions history, spiritual warfare
- sociology/anthropology
- country specific: history, culture, politics, and Christian history of anticipated country of service

- spiritual gifts
- personal and corporate health issues (emotional and physical)
- self-awareness: aware of oneself, including traits, feelings, attitudes, behaviors, and how this colors who he is and how he is perceived by others; exhibits strong mental health
- identity in Christ as center of self-worth

Character

- uses appropriate language
- has high standards of conduct with the opposite sex
- practices personal hygiene
- has high standards of honesty and integrity
- follows through with projects assigned, exhibits tenacity and perseverance
- is resilient in the face of opposition and difficulty
- handles criticism well, both valid and unjust
- has experienced suffering
- exhibits humility
- is teachable
- shows an ability to forgive
- is compassionate
- shows discernment in behavior, life choices, activities
- has a servant attitude
- is submissive to authority
- applies scriptural truth to thoughts and behavior
- displays contentedness, is generous
- is patient
- shows tolerance and deference, yields personal preferences
- defers immediate gratification, understanding the long-term benefits
- is known as wanting the best for others

The combination of the three components of skills, knowledge, and character produces confidence, competence, and credibility.[4]

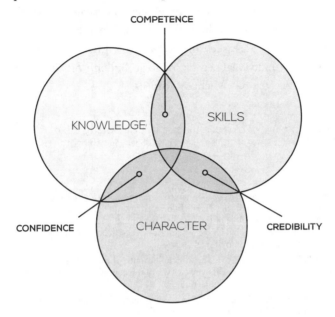

The candidate preparation process consists of successive phases or steps that represent a graduated process for progressing from an initial interest in mission work to ultimate commissioning as a long-term missionary. While each phase includes specific requirements and objectives, they are intended to be a framework within which the potential missionary and his mentor establish a pace and goals that are appropriate. Every situation is unique; tailor what follows to the need.

One caution to be offered is the recognition that we each gravitate to that which is preferable. We are naturally drawn to what we do well and enjoy, but tend to resist those things and activities that make us uncomfortable, where we have less confidence or will be stretched. Remember a good truism in all of life: do the hard thing.

A wise man has said that "discipleship is getting people to do what they don't want to do in order to become who they want to be."[5] Further, Hebrews 12:11 tells us, "No discipline seems pleasant at the time, but painful. Later on, however, it produces a harvest of righteousness and peace for those who have been trained by it" (NIV). The team assisting the potential missionary will enter into his life in such a way as to guide him but also to observe and reward personal initiative. Don't prod. Hold the standard high, reward, commend, affirm, praise, compliment.

> Both the Bible and common sense therefore suggest that the best method is not to call for volunteers but to set up a draft! The most that an individual can do is express his *willingness*. Others must determine his *worthiness*. The individual may be *free* to go, but only his church knows if he is really *fitted* to go.—Michael Griffiths[6]

Greg Carter is pastor of global engagement at Liberty Bible Church (www. findliberty.net) in Chesterton, IN. He is also founder/director of Future Missionaries (www.futuremissionaries.com).

Notes

[1] David Mays, *Stuff You Need to Know about Doing Missions in Your Church* vol. 3 (Brownsburg, IN: David Mays, 2008), 56. Crediting Terry Hulbert. Adapted from: Discipling Leaders with a Vision for the World: The Role of the Local Church in Missionary Preparation, Terry Hulbert, Th. D., Columbia International University. Source: ACMC National Conference address by Dr. Terry Hulbert, Columbia International University.

[2] Even Blackduck, MN, population 696, about 80 miles south of the Canadian border, has a significant Hispanic population. They are drawn to the community by jobs at Anderson Fabric Workroom, a custom drapery manufacturer.

[3] Steve Hoke, "Cross-Cultural Ministry as a Crucible of Spiritual Formation and Character Development, Part 1," Webinar, April 22, 2010, The MissionExchange.

[4] Diagram from 360 Degree Preaching: Hearing, Speaking and Living the Word, 2003, Michael Quicke. Used by permission of Baker Academic, a division of Baker Publishing Group, Grand Rapids, MI.

[5] I have loved this quote from the time I first heard it (or something very similar) used by Bill Hull many years ago when he was teaching T-Net, a discipleship training approach for a local church context. It was only recently when I met him and commented that I had been using his quote that I discovered he had adapted it from Tom Landry, the legendary former coach of the Dallas Cowboys, who made this reference in regard to coaching.

[6] Michael Griffiths, *Get Your Church Involved in Missions!* (Singapore: OMF Books, 1987), 14.

CHAPTER 24

Building Cultural Adaptation and Language Acquisition

Seven Essentials in Ministry Training

Brian Gibson

John and Mary hope to move to a village north of Dushanbe, Tajikistan, and share the gospel with Tajiks. What must they learn as they prepare for this transition into cross-cultural ministry? What must you as a church leader involved in sending them ensure that they gain and internalize? In the period of prefield selection, preparation and training, it is vital that candidates identify certain paths and begin taking steps down them. This will orient them toward enculturating well, growing in principles of ministry effectiveness, and gaining skills to thrive physically, emotionally, mentally, and spiritually. We want to see people become equipped and prepared to serve with *effectiveness* coupled with *longevity*. Without the first, their ministry is unlikely to bear fruit; without the second, they are unlikely to last long enough on the field to bear fruit.

Some candidates will have already journeyed down harmful paths that may wreck them on the field, and those paths are not always so easily discerned. In part this is because the Christian context within which we live in the US can allow for a greater degree of personal inattentiveness, even laziness, toward those elements of health. These elements become absolutely essential in the more isolated context of life and ministry overseas. It is imperative that they be exposed to and challenged with truths that can move them to the healthier paths we will explore below. This is for their own sake, as well as the people whom they serve, the church that sends them, and our Lord who calls them. Needless to say, there is much at stake! So just how will John and Mary become effective cross-culturally, and what do they need to know?

The list of essentials can quickly become quite long. Reverse engineering the process, however, we can ask ourselves, "What are among the most costly things for them *not* to know?" With recent research indicating that approximately eight thousand missionaries leave the field every year, and with 71 percent of those departures deemed as "preventable losses," we have plenty to draw from.[1] Others would compose a somewhat different list, but there is consensus around the essential nature of a key set of issues.

It is easy at this point to become exclusively focused on getting John and Mary equipped with skills for maximum productivity in ministry. Such skills are helpful, and yet they prove to be insufficient. This has always been so, but has become all the more evident in recent decades. Long is the list of those who have gone out with a litany of ministry skills and education, and yet have detonated due to being inadequately equipped with tools and skills for longevity due to areas neglected or unexplored in their preparatory phase. If you are not familiar with the expedition to the South Pole and the stories of Captain Scott and Roald Amundsen,[2] a brief read will underscore the significant impact that adequate equipping and longevity principles have on a strenuous undertaking.

The adventurous expedition is worth the gripping read, but for our purposes here it is enough to say Amundsen planned far more wisely, bringing energy-sustaining food and relying on lessons he had learned from Inuit Indians. After the grueling eight hundred-mile journey across ice and snow (one way!) to the South Pole, Amundsen's men had actually gained weight. This was due to a combination of good planning, excellent self-care, and wise selection of tools.

Scott and his men, on the other hand, saw significant deterioration to their health by the time they arrived at the South Pole, and sadly, all the members of his team would fail to complete the return trip, perishing along the way. Scott had packed inadequate sustenance for his team, communicated poorly regarding resupply expectations and locations, and ignored important findings.

Both leaders and their respective teams were hardy and well trained in the skills for success. What led one to success and the other to failure had much less to do with professional skill levels and much more to do with principles for longevity on the mission. A key takeaway: ministry skills won't go very far if you're dead!

You might be surprised that some of the seven elements outlined in the pages to follow may not seem immediately connected with equipping candidates to be successful in their mastery of language and culture for the sake of cross-cultural effectiveness. Please know that in our experience these elements are not at all tangential to the task of ministry effectiveness but are parts of an integrated whole. What follows is the result of years of trainings, feedback, evaluation, on-field experience, and collaboration with other trainers.

The seven essentials in ministry training are: maintaining spiritual vitality, building interpersonal and conflict resolution skills, learning cultural adaptation, learning language acquisition skills, building trust, knowing themselves and self-discovery and communicating clear, realistic expectations.

Maintaining Spiritual Vitality

For John and Mary, and many in a typical North American church, the spiritual atmosphere is generally one of richness, an environment in which a number of others assume responsibility for their spiritual growth and well-being. It is often surprising to count just how many other individuals cater to their spiritual sustenance, their experience of community, and general well-being. This includes men's groups, women's groups, prayer gatherings, small groups, morning church gatherings, evening church gatherings, discipleship groups, growth groups, home groups, and so on. Many candidates transition from this experience to the very opposite end of the spectrum: from spiritual richness to spiritual scarcity. Once on the field, it often becomes evident how little the candidate had previously been called upon to exercise his or her own spiritual muscles, as others had done so much of the heavy lifting.

Are those you hope to send out tested and proven as being able to nourish themselves spiritually? Individually? As husband-wife? As parents to children? The assumption can be quite deadly and the appearance of spiritual maturity in a place of plenty will be equally so in places of want.

In our own training at TRAIN International, where I serve as director, we address the critical importance of and need for maintaining one's spiritual vitality and an intimate connection with the Lord. Have your candidates experienced seasons of spiritual dryness? If so, how have they handled and recovered from them, and if not, how would they? Are you able to detect what your candidates are building their identity upon? A house built on sand with scattered stones mixed in, though it offers the appearance of some solidity, proves equally unreliable as one built solely on sand.

Few things are as poisonous or harmful as sending out workers who are more attached (and even addicted) to achievement, approval, and success as their source of worthiness and value than the steady and certain declaration of approval and value we enjoy in Christ. How do you imagine these dear sons and daughters of the Lord will fare when sent from fields in which their ability to "produce" is high, to fields in which they may labor years with little to no detectable fruit? This is challenging for anyone, but all the more in those whose identity in Christ and whose spiritual vitality is not cemented.

We have candidates consider their often extensive sources of spiritual input, and how they will prepare for the reality that their spiritual supply sources will decrease, while demand remains steady and even increases in transition into cross-cultural ministry. Also, extensive interactions and teaching regarding identity feature prominently. It has been our observation that no amount of missiological training will compensate for a candidate's lack of spiritual vitality or an inability to replenish spiritually.

Building Interpersonal and Conflict Resolution Skills

John and Mary must understand how to cultivate and maintain healthy relationships and resolve the conflicts that will inevitably arise, often without others around to buffer against those conflicts or facilitate their resolution. These skills will be put to the test on their teams, in their marriages, with their leaders, with those whom they lead, with the broader missionary community, and in other areas. In time, those skills will be tested in their relationships with nationals.

John and Mary will find themselves much less able to escape those conflicts in the tiny context of Christian relationships they will encounter in Tajikistan. Perhaps in the States, in a sizeable fellowship of hundreds or even thousands, when one relationship is strained or begins to sour, rather than engage that reality, other relationships can be brought to the front burner while the challenging ones are pushed to the back burner. In cross-cultural ministry, this is often no longer an option; to whom shall they go when fellow believers are countable on two hands at most, maybe one?

These interpersonal skills and the ability to identify and resolve conflict are essential, as we are not talking about "if" but "when." Conflict will arise, and when it does, it must be resolved or else become the kind of powder keg that has decimated many a team and otherwise fruitful ministry. Do your candidates have a history of broken relationships? A tendency to cut ties with those who anger or confront them? Do you notice a string of "We don't talk anymore" dotting the landscape of their relationships? Ensure that your candidates have a healthy dose of reality that these kinds of habits are precisely the kind of relational gasoline that the enemy hunts for. He is happy to set fires and watch families and teams go up in flames that will prevent their meddling in cultures and peoples in desperate need of the gospel of grace.

Ensure also that whatever their skill level is in this area, proper attention is given to its primacy. Courses like Sharpening Your Interpersonal Skills (SYIS) can be destiny-altering. In our own prefield trainings, this subject and these skills are given serious attention. On the field, you can be sure that beyond the occasional bouts of culture shock and the steady hum of ministry stress, a continual stream of relational stress will ensue. This is quite normal, but only emphasizes the need and value of having the skill to engage and deescalate these stressors and conflicts, rather than seeking to run from or conceal them.

Learning Cultural Adaptation and Language Acquisition Skills
These two are distinct enough to each warrant their own subject, but sufficiently intertwined enough so as to be addressed here together.

How will John and Mary substantively engage the Tajik culture at its core, asking incisive, perceptive questions that lead to meaningful discovery? It is one thing for them to adapt well enough to certain cultural differences and annoyances so things don't drive them crazy. It is another thing entirely to unlock key cultural insights that can shift annoyance to understanding, empathy, even respect.

In what places within a given culture can missionary candidates position themselves so as to glean deep cultural insights? How does one go beyond simply asking questions such as "What are these strange things these very different people do?" and "Why don't they just wait in single-file lines, or make future plans, or behave more wisely with their money?" Cultural insight will not be unlocked by the judgmental questions that condescendingly compare their "inferior" culture to ours. And yet, without intentionality, it is precisely here that missionary candidates can become stuck, asking the lawyer's depositional line of inquiries rather than the ethnographer's questions of exploration, which unlock not only cultural insight but the very hearts of those with whom the missionary hopes to build genuine, trusting relationships.

Also, John and Mary will need to understand realities of culture stress and culture shock. While it is immensely helpful to know what physiological and emotional responses to expect in the midst of culture shock, this alone is insufficient. Those in our trainings do learn about cultural value differences, culture shock, and its typical phases, but also about stress management and resiliency. Resiliency includes both the strength to bear the weight of a load and the ability to manage and reduce that load when needed. In the midst of intense, prolonged stress, what habits, activities, and practices, both general and unique to the individual, will lower these levels of stress? It may be common knowledge, but it is far from common practice that high and prolonged levels of stress will land a person in the sickbed or hospital and must be mitigated. Cultural adaptation lessens the load and impact of cultural stress, as an individual learns to decode the culture and better understand the "why" behind the "what" among their people.

When we speak of the essential nature of cultural adaptation, we must also realize it has great bearing upon John and Mary's ability to share the gospel with their new Tajik friends. Here in the United States, John and Mary may be quite gifted evangelists, able to articulate the gospel in compelling ways that bear fruit in the hearts and lives of those with whom they share. Now put John and Mary in a Tajik village. Are these new friends most directly impacted by the guilt-innocence dimension of the gospel John and Mary are so familiar with? Do they even have any frame of reference for such terms as sin and guilt? Or are they more attuned to the needs met by the gospel through the power-fear or honor-shame dimension?[3] Without a doubt, the ways John and Mary are accustomed to effectively sharing the gospel in their home culture must shift. But how? And toward what? By becoming students of their culture, global workers are better able to understand and unlock the hearts of their people, which has significant implications not only for building meaningful relationships but also for the level of effectiveness in sharing the gospel.

The combined undertakings of cultural learning and language acquisition in a given culture are among the most potent builders of credibility that a missionary can engage. Asking the right questions, in culturally appropriate ways, in the right settings, and of the right people, will be of massive importance.

When it comes to language acquisition, the importance and impact cannot be overstated. Taking on the humility Christ displayed, the missionary candidate's willingness and commitment to stoop down to the level of a child once again and aspire to speak the language (one day, after much effort!)[4] like a five-year old, conveys a depth of interest, care, and concernand a desire to form friendships. Such willingness and commitment are often incomparably convincing and quite disarming to the people to whom the missionary goes. Some benefits are easily predicted, but others less so.

Culture and Language Fluency Outcomes

Predictable Outcomes	Nuanced Outcomes
1. Better able to engage in spiritual conversations	1. Decreased experience of loneliness and isolation
2. More effective in communicating the gospel	2. Increased confidence in all ministry areas
3. Better able to make disciples	3. Guard against paranoia and negativity toward nationals and host culture
4. More effective in leading a team through challenges and onboarding new teammates	4. Higher level of empathy and support for fellow missionaries and expats
5. Deeper sense of trust between missionary and nationals	5. Deeper levels of understanding of culture, behavior, values, and worldview

However, we must not reduce this language learning to merely utilitarian terms, asking, "What's the payoff?" Certainly, language fluency will help missionaries to thrive, to stave off the loneliness and isolation that often result from an inability or very minimal ability to speak into or connect deeply with the world around them. And certainly, this fluency paves the way for more potent gospel declaration, sets the stage for disciplemaking acumen, and can speed the missionary along toward ministry fruitfulness. Yes, language is a tool, and learning it will prove to be of great value and usefulness. And yet, the very process of language learning itself is not merely preparation for ministry, but is *itself* part of the ministry, not to be hastily discontinued once some measure of language has been learned. For further reading on this, see Brewster and Brewster's excellent and very readable book on the subject: *Language Learning IS Communication—IS Ministry!*[5]

In our trainings, we provide candidates with strategies for success in language acquisition and have them immediately begin to implement them. With the variety of learning styles and multiple intelligences, it is inevitable that some strategies will work very well for a given individual, while others will run counter to their giftings, personalities, and learning styles. They will leave our trainings having identified some of their "sweet spots," having tested them out, and having positioned themselves for a more successful and less frustrating launch into the wild waters of learning a new language.

We can sum up these intertwined elements of missionary preparation with two generalized overstatements: First, the candidate who will not intentionally pursue cultural and language acquisition in his ministry efforts to be an ambassador of Christ among the perishing is either pursuing something other than the advancement of Christ's kingdom or is poorly informed as to what constitutes missionary effectiveness. Second, the candidate who has a willingness to pursue these dual components but who does not have the tools and roadmap for success is like one launching her boat into the waters of cross-cultural ministry without paddle, rudder, or motor. Her forward movement will be more at the mercy of the capricious currents of circumstance than that of the intentional and skillful navigator equipped with necessary tools.

It will be critical to ensure that John, Mary, and your future missionary candidates have a grasp of the gravity of these critical elements along with the training and tools to be successful in learning language and culture.

Building Trust

Most missionary candidates who have the United States as their dominant frame of reference may know how to cultivate trust in the context at home, but these tactics don't necessarily translate well into the context of other cultures and countries. In fact, some of the ways they are accustomed to building trust may be the very things that erode trust, create suspicion, or characterize downright villainous behavior in other cultures. A pat on the back, a thumbs up, the A-OK sign, a smile, looking someone in the eye to communicate attention, assuming a welcoming posture, being honest and direct in communication: all these gestures, tactics, and means of interaction within our cultural context often convey quite the opposite of their intended meanings in other cultures.

By helping John and Mary to formulate plans that involve building trust in culturally appropriate and effective ways, and by orienting their expectations toward the prime importance of building this trust, hopefully they will overcome hurdles, solid walls, and deep pitfalls. More missionaries than you can count journey off to the field with the blissful idea that behaviors labeled as kind back in the US and the gospel preaching that works back there will serve them as they always have. In truth, it is not merely language and cultural norms that must be relearned; virtually everything must be. And as you prepare your global workers for these realities, you help instill in them the attitudes of a learner which may disarm the doubting and skeptical people to whom they go to serve. In short, you help them grow into people who can earn trust.

Adopting the posture of a learner, will go a long way in helping John and Mary learn how to build trust with their Tajik friends. Attentiveness to the ways by which people of a given culture establish and strengthen trust among one another is a surprisingly nuanced skill, but one in which people can be trained. In our trainings, we offer both general principles and specific cultural insights regarding the cross-cultural formation of trust.

Knowing Themselves and Self-Discovery

Self-discovery at deep levels is critical. Who do these candidates become under long periods of intense stress, and when the needs and demands of ministry seem to dwarf their resources? That is missionary life in a nutshell. A considerable portion of our own prefield training puts missionary candidates outdoors, in the wilderness, sleeping on the ground beneath shelters that we teach them to build mere hours before they must sleep under them. They literally lie in the beds they have made. Some build their shelters poorly, of proverbial straw, leaving much to be desired when the rain comes and a poorly constructed shelter robs one of warmth, a dry bed, and much needed sleep. During this time in the wilderness, and in extensive periods of reflection upon our return from it, participants are confronted with truths about themselves they may have been able to dodge, deny, or conceal for much of their lives. We have seen missionaries change course and delay their departure in order to address issues they have been confronted with during the training. Others have even gone so far in their course correction as to remain at home and reconsider their calling.

Though by no means an overt goal, it should be celebrated with both relief and joy when such issues are brought to light. It's especially helpful that they can be addressed and overcome in the relative safety, expertise, and care of one's home culture rather than being discovered on-field in the heat of battle, often with dire consequence.

Readiness assessment tools can be helpful as well, particularly those that involve multiple sets of eyes. Missionary preparation should be, in many respects, uncomfortably rigorous, and the shakedown cruise will ideally take place in settings in which alterations, suggestions, and corrections can be made and then evaluated. We aren't merely putting people on planes for adventures abroad during which we are hopeful to see a few come to Christ. We are thrusting people out who are called by the Master to be ambassadors and agents of his reclamation of the earth and its inhabitants. They are his rightful possessions, purchased by the blood of his crucified Son, revived by the striking of the death blow to death itself, sin, and the powers of hell. They are wresting from Satan's grasp those so far beyond the help of any power save that of the Almighty God that without his intervention, certain and inevitable doom and distance from God would be their only destiny.

Opposition will be fierce enough without missionary candidates having themselves as their own worst enemies. Thus, self-discovery is essential, and all the better when conducted within an observable context in which unpleasant discoveries cannot be minimized, edited out of a report, or concealed from view.

Communicating Clear, Realistic Expectations

Our unspoken expectations are like buried landmines; we realize that we have discovered one only after it has blown off a leg. On the other hand, communicated expectations are like guardrails and road signs, helping to establish boundaries and to provide helpful direction in navigating relationships.

Are candidates able to identify expectations, evaluate whether they are realistic, and communicate them to relevant parties? Simple exploratory exercises to concretely identify the following sets of expectations will help a great deal to enable everyone involved to journey forward with minimal loss of limbs due to explosion of unspoken expectations.

Expectations Identification Exercise

	God	Church	Agency	Candidate
God	X			
Church		X		
Agency			X	
Candidate				X

In our trainings, we work through a series of questions for each involved party:
What does **God** expect of the missionary candidate, and vice-versa?
What does the **church** expect of the missionary candidate, and vice-versa?
What does the **agency** expect of the missionary candidate, and vice-versa?
What does the **candidate** expect of him or herself?

The church is much better able to maintain strong and positive relationships with those whom it sends out when there is clarity *before deployment* between the missionary, any involved agencies, and the sending church as to what is offered and expected of each party. Much disappointment, frustration, and tension can be avoided through these explorations.

Conclusion

In helping John and Mary prepare for long-term ministry fruitfulness, these critical factors must be considered and care taken to ensure they are adequately trained and supplied with tools and resources necessary for their health and success. For their success is not merely their own. Bound up with them are the sending church, those additional supporting churches cheering them on, future missionaries, the people to whom they go, the believers who will come to Christ through their ministry, and a host of other witnesses and fellow workers. Excellence in the preparation of missionary candidates is as much a matter of stewardship as anything else.

How will you and your church steward the opportunity and responsibility to send well-equipped workers into the harvest field? Hopefully the critical elements described in the preceding pages, as well as the pages that follow, will help you to answer that question in ways that will please our Father, the Shepherd of our souls and the Lord of the harvest.

Brian Gibson is executive director of TRAIN International (www.traininternational.org) in Joplin, MO.

Notes

[1] William D. Taylor, *Too Valuable to Lose: Exploring the Causes and Cures of Missionary Attrition* (Pasadena, CA: William Carey Library, 1997).

[2] Captain Scott and Roald Amundsen, https://en.wikipedia.org/wiki/Comparison_of_the_Amundsen_and_Scott_Expeditions.

[3] Jayson Georges, *The 3-D Gospel: Ministry in Guilt, Shame, and Fear Cultures.* (Time Press, 2016).

[4] Patrick Johnstone, *The Future of the Global Church: History, Trends and Possibilities* (Downers Grove, IL: IVP, 2014), 227. Johnstone's insights are worth noting here. He shares that the period of greatest missionary fruitfulness is in years 7–17. Much of this is born out of the missionary's accumulated cultural understanding and language fluency.

[5] Tom & Betty Brewster, *Language Learning IS Communication—IS Ministry!* (Lingua House, 1982). This work is often coupled in a single book with another of their works, *Bonding and the Missionary Task*, both invaluable.

CHAPTER 25

Building Resiliency

The Value of Coaching

Sherri Dodd

Resiliency is defined in the dictionary as "the capacity to recover quickly from difficulties; toughness." Resiliency is needed in every season of life, but with the many challenges and losses of the missionary life, it is crucial to survival.

In terms of the global mission force, many career missionaries prematurely leave the field every year to return home. "Of those who leave, 71% leave for preventable reasons." This is a sobering statistic from the book *Too Valuable to Lose.*[1] In response to this great challenge, how can churches build resiliency into their missionaries? One of Advance Global Coaching (AGC)'s partner churches, North Point Community Church, pastored by Andy Stanley, has decided to promote the health of their missionaries by providing a season of coaching for each of their new missionaries as they transition to the field. By doing so they are saying, "You are important. What you do is important. We care about you. We want to invest in you."

Here are some of the ways coaching helps missionaries develop resiliency:

1. **Celebrating wins**

   We celebrate victories. One of the first things in each coaching call is to invite the coaching client to share praises and wins. In a realm where there is always more work that could be done, it is important to honestly celebrate accomplishments, even small ones. Whether the report is, "This week I had three fundraising appointments," or "Today, I went to the market by myself for the first time," or "I said what was really on my heart in the team meeting," good news is worth acknowledging. When we celebrate the "wins" with our missionary clients, it empowers them to take the next step forward.

2. **Providing accountability**

   When my clients know I am going to ask how things went with their action items from the previous coaching call, there is accountability. It is not a tough "Did you get it done?" but a soft, supportive approach that lets them know their decisions are important and their actions matter. Accumulative small steps make a giant step forward. All of us know we accomplish more when there is someone who is going to ask about our actions. When a coach asks, "What obstacles got in the way?" and then really listens, the client hears himself and evaluates his own efforts. When a coach asks, "How would you like to move forward with this?" or "What is another small step you could take within the next couple of weeks that would keep you moving toward your goal?" he is basically modeling how we overcome hurdles. We try again by looking at our values, rethinking our strategy and our motives. All of this creates tenacity.

3. **Offering emotional and spiritual support**

   We pray out loud for each client on each call. Many workers are touched emotionally and feel spiritually supported just by hearing their name lifted up to the Lord. We share our belief in our client's ability to grow, to achieve, to do the good works God has prepared in advance for them to do. We come alongside our clients, meeting with them on a regular basis. This shoulder to shoulder approach provides unbelievable support. We serve as a safe place to "dump," unload, or vent, if necessary. Getting something safely out into the open helps clear the air, freeing up emotional and mental energy. A coach approach is a supportive one that builds resiliency as the relationship develops.

4. **Validating and normalizing feelings**

   The challenges missionaries face are normal. What a privilege to tell them, "No, you are not crazy. You are right on track; this is a normal part of transition." Often stressful feelings arise from partnership development, team dynamics, and language learning. We know what the adjustment curve in cross-cultural ministries looks like and have ridden that "roller coaster ride" ourselves. We provide validation and encouragement that though life may be hard, this is doable.

5. **Brainstorming ideas**

   When we brainstorm with our clients, we help them get "unstuck." Resiliency is fostered when missionaries know they have options and can see there is more than one possible way forward. The mission field often helps workers "unlearn" things that need to be let go. Their perspectives will change; they will grow in ways they had not anticipated. We help the client find new ways to strategize when faced with a problem.

6. **Deepening trust in God**

   As Christian coaches, we are always leading our clients back to God and his Word as the basis for their lives and decisions. As missionaries grow in their trust of God, they develop a greater ability to lean into him when times are hard and they cannot see him at work. Sometimes we are helping missionaries clarify their calling, and other times we are helping them realign with their calling. Knowing they are where they are supposed to be gives a fresh measure of tenacity. Sometimes we are reminding our clients of what they already know to be true about God's character, in order for them to grow in their faith.

7. **Adding a fresh perspective**

   Since the coach is outside the client's everyday world, the coach provides a different look at the circumstances. Having a coach who is not part of the client's sending church or sending agency provides the safest place for the missionary to process their challenges objectively.

8. **Developing life balance**

   Any area of life can be brought to the table in a conversation with a life coach. The coach seeks to help missionaries look for ways to maintain their emotional, spiritual, relational, and physical health. Conversations about stress, rest, Sabbath, exercise, etc., are pertinent and valuable.

   All of these factors go into building a "bounce-back attitude" in our clients. Many times clients have expressed, "If it weren't for the support I have received through coaching, I wouldn't still be here." Just knowing there is someone you can call in a time of need is therapeutic. Our clients have email and phone access with their coaches in between sessions, as needed.

   Coaching provides accountability that is supportive but not directive. Coaches do not tell clients what to do, but instead help them discover their own steps forward. All of us know that we accomplish more and are more successful when we have the proper support.

Missionaries thrive when someone takes the time to listen to them, to encourage them, and to help them think in ways they might not otherwise have thought. Resiliency is built through coaching missionaries at each stage of their journey—from their initial interest in mission work until they are entering a new season of life upon their return.

Sherri Dodd is founder, chief executive officer, and Christian life coach with Advance Global Coaching (www.AdvanceGlobalCoaching.com), which helps churches build resiliency in their missionaries. You can email her at Sherri@AdvanceGlobalCoaching.com.

Notes

[1] William D. Taylor, *Too Valuable to Lose: Exploring the Causes and Cures of Missionary Attrition* (Pasadena, CA: William Carey Library, 2013).

CHAPTER 26

What Missionaries Wish They Knew Before They Left

Disequilibrating the Bravado

Jon Luesink

Finally, you're launching out to be a missionary. You've been a faithful servant at home. Many have affirmed that you have the gift of crossing cultures. You've responded to the challenge and, having been commissioned by your church, you've boarded the plane. Mixed with your feelings of excitement over the adventure ahead, a worried voice is sincerely asking, "What have I gotten myself into?" Listen to that voice. Beyond the hint of warning, this is what I wish I had known before boarding that plane.

Disequilibrating the Bravado: Upsetting the Bravery of the Foolhardy

To bring the realism to life, let's begin with a fable of contrast. Imagine you are a Canadian who has just volunteered for the army during the Second World War. You've been informed that there is a 4 percent chance of your dying within the next six years.[1] That's roughly a one in twenty chance you'll become a permanent casualty. Sobering, but there's still a fairly good chance of making it. Even though you participate in the invasion of Sicily and then in the harrowing D-Day landings at Juno Beach in 1944, somehow you survive, going on to liberate Holland and finally returning home safely to Canada.

Next, because of the spiritual needs you've seen in Europe, you decide you want to become a missionary. During the training, you're told that

---

This chapter is adapted from Eugene L. Lowry. *The Homiletical Plot: The Sermon as Narrative Art Form* (Atlanta GA: John Knox, 1980).

" 71% leave for preventable reasons. . . . In response to this great challenge, how can churches build resiliency into their missionaries? **"**

the chances of finding yourself unexpectedly returning home before you planned, mission incomplete, are about one in two. Really?

Stepping fully out of imagination, a series of worldwide studies (the Reducing Missionary Attrition Project [ReMAP], 1996 and 2003, examining reasons for missionary attrition) found that, depending on your sending agency, up to 52 percent of missionaries return home sooner than they planned to (in the first 5–10 years).[2] Furthermore, up to 71 percent of those returned for *preventable reasons*.[3] If you were a World War II veteran now becoming a missionary, hearing those statistics for the first time, how would you feel? What would you do?

With a casualty rate drastically higher than during my war service, I'd want to find out the top reasons missionaries leave before they intended to! I'd want to find out what those preventable reasons are and how I could counter them.

Here are some of the discernable reasons missionaries return home before they planned to:
- Unpreventable reasons include:
  o death in service
  o loss of visa, expulsion from the country
  o disability due to illness
  o promotion, completion of project
  o caring for aging parents / schooling for children
- Preventable reasons include:
  o failure to deal with culture shock
  o failure to deal with job shock
  o disunity with fellow missionaries
  o moral failure
  o lack of finances

Of these preventable reasons, do you know what the top reasons that missionaries leave the field early are? According to the attrition research of the ReMAP studies, "The prime causes of preventable early return of missionaries cluster in areas of character and spirituality, relationships and interpersonal conflict."[4]

Exploring the Depths of the Problem

Angie Washington,[5] a missionary to Bolivia, confirms this in her refreshingly honest blog:

> When we were in missions school one of the teachers told us that the top three reasons missionaries leave the field are: money matters, sickness, and relationship problems. He went on to expound on the difficulties missionaries tend to have getting along with others. The famous quote we took away from that class made me laugh.
>
> "Missionaries are like manure. Spread them out and they do some good. In a group they are just a stinking pile of . . . crap.".
>
> I didn't believe it. Until I saw it with my own eyes. Missionaries fighting against missionaries. Mission organizations undermining other mission organizations. The saddest? People who had given up everything they once knew to help the people of a foreign land, leaving earlier than planned because they couldn't get along with their team.

In our European field within Avant Ministries, we recognized a similar problem. Our regional director[6] at that time examined our region's attrition, between 2008–16, to find the reasons for our losses. Though not everyone might have admitted it on the surface, digging to the next layer revealed they were indeed leaving due to conflict with fellow missionaries. However, this was more of a trigger issue that provoked their departure. The real issue was something deeper still.

Peeling back another layer, we could see that we had not selected people for our teams with enough care. Our regional director expressed it simply, "We were way too optimistic about who we thought could fit on a team. We had people who lacked the interpersonal skills to manage conflict in a healthy way." Behind this we could further perceive that the people who left "did not have a clear sense of call to plant a church. They had a call to be in ministry largely for personal development/growth reasons. When it got hard, they left."[7]

That seems to be a sad irony, but the revelation of this weak motive leads us to clues for resolution. They probably actually felt drawn to mission work out of a quest for personal fulfillment and happiness based on becoming a heroic, self-sacrificing church planter . . . and when that effort didn't feel nice, they left. To make sure that we do not end up as one of those unfortunate casualties, we need to consider what felt so terrible. To do so, take a moment for personal reflection here:

- Think about a time in your life when you quit something sooner than originally planned—a job, a team, a relationship, a church.
- Ask yourself if that situation revealed a character flaw in your life.
- Next, imagine going next door to recount this discovery with your new neighbor or coworker. What would it be like to have that discussion with them?

If you're like our average missionary, you probably just came to grips with the difficulty of being transparent about your faults in front of your peers. Who likes having their manure exposed?

Still, you might be having trouble believing this could create enough pressure to drive a missionary to abandon the field early. To expand your empathy, allow me to paint a picture for you of what the first two years of life are like for many new missionaries.

- You receive a hero's send off, and land in your new country with a sense of adventure and excitement. Within months the honeymoon is over, and reality sets in. Culture shock comes just as they predicted—but from an unexpected angle. So, you follow your training and learn to hold loosely the core cultural values that were so much a part of your foundational identity. You push yourself to explore the beauty of a new place and find ways to allow them to become a part of your new self.
- A complicating surprise is that you have found language learning not just a difficult task, but an actual assault on your personal identity. You are daily frustrated that you can't fully express yourself with the locals you hoped would become your new friends. Some days you despair of ever being able to feel like your full self in this new language.
- While you persevere in this work to facilitate your calling, something you never learned about hits you. "Job Shock" is what you end up calling it.[8] You never realized how much sense of significance and identity security you derived from your job and role in North America. Missionary life in an unreached country has you swimming in so much ambiguity that you're not even sure of what to do to be competent, let alone successful. All your normal sources of pats on the back are gone. The ego you didn't know you had is starving for affirmation. The fearful voice of failure and shame whispers ominously.

> **"** The prime causes of preventable early return of missionaries cluster in areas of character and spirituality, relationships and interpersonal conflict. **"**

- As though timed with diabolical precision, the forgivable quirks in your fellow missionaries are now becoming intolerably irritating, and these are growing into a twisted threat. On the surface, your expectations have been disappointed. You thought you were joining a team so that you could each function like a body—one part making up for the weaknesses of the other. Instead, a subconscious fear now fights to remain undisclosed: "What if my faults are also becoming apparent to them? What if the real me is surfacing, the one I had managed to keep hidden below the surface for years?" Your home-culture coping mechanisms are eroding; your manure is beginning to show.

This is the subconscious straw breaking the camel's back. This job of being a missionary has required so much personal change . . . and now you're being hit with the deepest destabilizing challenge of all: You next need to change your deficient character. The fearful voice speaks louder, offering a way out of the shameful need to be transparent, a way out of the discomfort that will be required for deep personal change. It seems the crisis allows only a binary solution: Either I can't accomplish my mission with them, or I need to seek to accomplish my mission without them. The manure philosophy beckons, "Spread them out so they can do some good!" This will allow you to avoid the painfully deep personal change, the spiritual transformation of your weaknesses. You begin to compose acceptable phrases for your newsletter that will be required to explain your choice to your supporters.

Disclosing the Clues to Resolution

In *Too Valuable to Lose* (based on the ReMAP study in 1996), William Taylor presents a marvelous alternative. He relates the discoveries of a young missionary couple:

These last three years on the field have been crushing ones. Our outward circumstances were tough to begin with, actually a matter of survival with the combination of stifling heat with suffocating humidity, little water, no electricity. We simply could not get away from it! When suffering comes from unbelievers or Muslims, it's understandable, but the worst crushing came from other missionaries within the body of Christ, even from leadership. We simply wanted to get out! But during the third year, we saw God opening our own eyes to let us know why He was orchestrating these things in our lives.

We saw the worst of ourselves; we saw evil in our own lives. We had failed the spirituality test miserably. But then we began to discern God's purposes, even as our lives fell into the ground as the seed, to die, and then to come back to life. God was crushing us to knock our shell off, in order that Christ would be revealed in us, and thus our people group would see Him and not us. Three years in the grinder. Then the power of Christ speaking to us. We are on a lifetime plan with God. God brought brokenness to our own lives during this last term, but it was to teach us and to equip us for the long-term task. And we will return to our assignment early next year.[9]

An old saying goes, "You're full of whatever spills out when you get bumped." And nothing bumps you deeper than trying to be a gospel-sharing missionary among an unreached people. In the book *How People Change*, the authors describe how these difficult situations in life elicit a reaction. If we find ourselves responding with love, this good fruit demonstrates a good root, anchored in the gospel of Christ.[10] Like the couple in Taylor's reflection above, perhaps the crushing awakens awareness of blind spots in our gospel comprehension. We see them because our thorny reactions expose a bad root that needs to change in our heart. The question switches from "Should I escape my circumstances?" to "Shall I continue in my transformation toward Christ?"[11]

My friend and colleague Steve Cochrane has spent most of his life in West Africa as a missionary kid and then with his own family as a missionary. To describe what he's seen happen time and again, he uses this analogy:

At home we built a very nice tree house to live in, around a tree that was not quite sufficient to hold it up. So we built stilts to support our tree house. When we moved to our host country, all the stilts got kicked out from under us, causing the tree house to wobble and collapse dangerously.

In such moments we are tempted to retreat from this disaster that is threatening us—perhaps away from fellow missionaries, maybe even away from that foreign hell. Or, despite the difficulty, we can choose to rebuild around a tree that has grown to become strong enough to support us like never before.

While enduring this serious challenge as a missionary team leader in Prague, I was rescued from a disastrous retreat when God showed me these thoughts from Paul's letter to the Philippians. A core message of the book runs like this:

- I am God's work in progress, until I die or Christ returns. (Phil 1:6; 3:10–16)
  - o Progress is marked by change in my character.
  - o Change in character will be proved by how I relate to others.
  - o How I relate to others is inspired by and modeled on Christ's way of relating to us (Phil 2:1–13).
- What needs to be changed gets exposed in rocky relationships.
  - o The closing case study shows how Euodia, Syntyche, and their church need to apply this theology in order to get along with each other (Phil 4:1–9).

Paul emphasizes, in Philippians 3:12–16, that this journey into Christ-likeness is a lifelong work in progress. He uses this pointed turn of phrase: "I press on toward the goal for the prize of the upward call of God in Christ Jesus. Let those of us who are mature think this way, and if in anything you think otherwise, God will reveal that also to you." My meditating further on this book led me to question whether "manure theory" was in any way aligned with God's calling for believers. These questions cascaded as I worked through the Scriptures:

- Did God invent the idea of church on purpose?
- Is the purpose of church so that we can learn to get along with others in the same way that God chooses to get along with us, with patient grace and mercy?
- If our church planting team is going to try to start a church, isn't the way we get along with each other going to be like the DNA we insert into the new church we hope to start in Prague?
- But if missionaries are like manure, only causing a stink when they're together, then how on earth can they plant a healthy church, since they can't seem to be a healthy church *together*?

Experiencing the Gospel in Us First

The book of Ephesians unveils the answers to these questions. Combined with the message of Philippians, these books rescued me from my blindness and fear. Incorporating Lane and Tripp's language, we might say that the opening chapters of Ephesians give us our gospel identity.[12] We are overwhelmed with how much God loves us and are enabled to experience unfathomable contentment and joy by grasping that God views us as his special masterpiece, his work of art.[13] The security and freedom of our identity and position in Christ is joyfully staggering!

Then, through Ephesians 2:11–4:3, Paul draws us into what he aptly called a mystery. He tells these Ephesians that not only have they been given peace with God as individuals, but something much broader has occurred: radically different individuals are brought into peace *with each other* through Jesus. Specifically, in the context of this letter, Jews and Gentiles are no longer racial and social enemies, but in Christ, these two hostile people groups are united into one new body. To picture how revolutionary this is, just reflect on what you might consider to be strong examples of racism . . . and add to that racism fueled by religion.

Our diverse missionary team in Prague wasn't quite that bad, but close enough. We came from very distinct evangelical cultures from all across the spectrum in North America, from KJV[14]-only Baptists to West Coast fans of *The Message*.[15] When culture shock, job shock, and language incompetencies stripped away the self-confident North American versions of ourselves, our irritating warts and thorns were all on display. A palpable tension rose to the point of our becoming shaking mad at each other.

The tension that existed in Paul's day between Jews and Gentiles was deeper and more divisive. This, then, is the mystery that Paul says he was commissioned by God to unfold: Christ's "purpose was to create in himself one new humanity out of the two, thus making peace, and in one body to reconcile both of them to God through the Cross, by which he put to death their hostility" (Eph 2:15,16, NIV). What is the mystery? The unfathomable purpose of Christ to make peace and create one body out of two of the most diverse people groups on the planet: Jews and Gentiles. As this finally dawned on me, I needed to read closely, because in 3:10,11 we get to the linchpin: God's "intent was that now, through the church, the manifold wisdom of God should be made known to the rulers and authorities in the heavenly realms, according to his eternal purpose that he accomplished in Christ Jesus our Lord" (NIV).

It's as though God is saying, "Hey, angels, my enemies, and my loyal servants—all of you! If you want to understand my wisdom, look at my new creation. It's called church! You've seen how humans normally live: hostile and segregated, arguing, fighting, despising, and even going to war against each other. You already know that I've made a way for these humans to live in peace with me again. Well now, when they get united with me in Christ, they get united with each other in Christ's body, and a whole new paradigm for humanity has begun!" This new philosophy of living is that Christ's church is a place where spiritually revived people learn to get along with each other—to love like they've been loved! This isn't plan B, this isn't an afterthought. This is God's core plan, his eternal purpose.

The passage continues to unfold God's provision for making this science fiction a reality. Paul prays that we will soak ourselves in the height, width, length, and depth of Christ's love for us, "that you may be filled to the measure of all the fullness of God" (Eph 3:14–20, NIV). Furthermore, the same power that raised Christ from the dead (1:19) is the very power at work *in us* to do "immeasurably more than all we ask or imagine" (3:20, NIV). Ephesians 4:1–3 then slams it home in no uncertain terms:

As a prisoner for the Lord, then, I urge you *to live a life worthy of the calling you have received.* Be completely humble and gentle; be patient, bearing with one another in love. *Make every effort to keep the unity of the Spirit* through the bond of peace. (NIV, emphasis added)

If you continue reading through the rest of Ephesians, you'll see how much courageous transformation this is going to require, and you'll see how almost all of it is focused around relationships, one believer with another. So, if God's intent for the church was to show off his wisdom by putting normally hostile people groups together in one body so they can live out the grace they've been given, why should it surprise us that he puts missionaries on the same team who have trouble getting along with each other? To continue with that logic, what if getting along with our brothers and sisters in Christ on a missionary team might actually have the same beautiful effect of displaying God's wisdom to an unreached people group we are there to serve?

With these foundations in mind, our team in Prague began a life-changing process. After we realized how badly things needed to change on our team, we took a week off to read the Bible and pray, asking God to reveal "what I am doing to irritate the others on my team." We came back together to confess what we had been shown, to seek confirmation and deeper understanding of how it affected them. Do you know what happened? The more we engaged in this vulnerable but loving conversation,[16] listening and talking in turn, the more I realized that this brokenness of mine wasn't surfacing on just this team (as though it was a new phenomenon and *their* fault). Suddenly I realized this was probably the reason why a good family left the church where I had been a pastor. Further back, I saw that this was the weakness my mentor in seminary had been trying to alert me to.

Deeper still, it dawned on me why I was kind of a social outcast in high school. It was something that went back even to my childhood. It was not my current teammates I needed to get away from, because "wherever I go, there I am." My circumstances didn't need to change . . . it was something in me that needed transformation. Then these same teammates who helped reveal my faults helped me understand the steps I could take to discipline myself to change, to become a more pleasant person to be around. It was like the manure was yielding to the potential of becoming an enjoyable flower.

It was a similar journey for everyone else on our team. The Spirit brought them to exactly the key thing they needed to change next. Remarkably, they all discovered it went way back to who they were long before they were missionaries on this team. We were transparent with each other, and we helped each other to take steps of transformation. After that, God began to plant a church through our team.

Anticipating the Results

Several years later we were floored to hear the core of new believers in Prague reflecting on what first attracted them to read the Bible. They had seen a love between us as missionaries that they had never experienced among their friends, not even in their family. They felt us extending this love to them. This convinced them, "Now I need to find out who this Jesus is, this one who they say has inspired them." We went from being missionary manure . . . to a flower patch, smelling better in bunches. We were pleased to discover that we had ended up living out what Jesus describes as the strongest apologetic for his divinity:

> I do not ask for these only, but also for those who will believe in me through their word, that they may all be one, just as you, Father, are in me, and I in you, that they also may be in us, *so that the world may believe that you have sent me.* The glory that you have given me I have given to them, that they may be one even as we are one, I in them and you in me, that they may become perfectly one, *so that the world may know that you sent me* and loved them even as you loved me. (John 17:20–23, emphasis added)

Thankfully the effects of our vulnerable transformations didn't stop there. They were infectious among the new Czech believers. At one point, a young believer was a walking contradiction—showing gifts of leadership while being so arrogant that he was repelling seekers. As we told him our transformation stories, lovingly challenging him and supporting him, he changed. Months later, after one of those irritated seekers had also become a follower of Jesus, a most wonderful scenario played out in front of my eyes. This young leader had gone through such a transformation that a lady, who had once found him repulsively obnoxious, personally asked him to help her and her husband start an evangelistic meeting in their home for their skeptical friends.

It turns out that the predominant cause of missionary attrition is actually part of a divine recipe to cure what ails us. "The prime causes of preventable early return of missionaries cluster in areas of character and spirituality, relationships and interpersonal conflict."[17] On the mission field, God provides the crucible for deep, inward change. We can choose to walk with God through these defining moments, or we can retreat to what feels safer for us. We can choose to embrace God's calling for us, to live in transforming unity, or we can make our excuses and escape from the initial reek of the manure. As Kenn Oke observed, "When it got hard, they left." He went on to say, "When we got the right people, with a sense of call that was bigger than themselves, they weathered the inevitable conflict." [18] Their calling was full-fledged—they were called to bring the love of Jesus to a foreign land, and they were called to be a church while doing it. They embraced being that church, which would require ongoing deep spiritual changes in character.

If this is God's design for church, for believers, even for missionaries, then take a moment to consider:

- What are you already doing well to be used by God in a team setting (as a missionary, in a church, as a spouse, child, friend, or employee)?
- What do you need to begin to change, and how could you start in the next forty-eight hours?

With these practices of vulnerable transformation embedding themselves into your life now, you're setting yourself up to avoid being one of those unfortunate casualties from the mission field. Better than that, you'll be part of shifting the paradigm from stinky manure piles to fragrant, contagious flowers in foreign lands that so badly need to catch the scent of the beautiful gospel.

Jon Luesink and his wife, Jill, served with Avant Ministries (www.avantministries.org) for eight years leading a church planting team to Prague, Czech Republic. Jon is presently serving with Avant's Canadian office as director of mobilization.

Notes

[1] Military history in Canada, https://en.wikipedia.org/wiki/Military_history_of_Canada_during_ World_War_II.

[2] World Evangelical Alliance, ReMAP II: Worldwide Missionary Retention, Study and Best Practices, Missions Commission, February 24, 2010, http://www.worldevangelicals.org/ resources/rfiles/res3_96_link_1292358945.pdf.

[3] William D. Taylor, *Too Valuable to Lose: Exploring the Causes and Cures of Missionary Attrition* (Pasadena, CA: William Carey Library, 1997), 13.

[4] Ibid., 351

[5] Angie Washington, "*Friend of Missionaries,*" November 15, 2012, http://www.alifeoverseas.com/ friend-of-missionaries/.

[6] Ken Oke, now vice president of Avant Field Ministries West.

[7] Taylor, op cit.

[8] Timothy S. Lane and Paul David Tripp, *How People Change* (Greensboro, NC: New Growth Press, 2008), Loc 193 of 332. Authors Lane and Tripp describe this as one of our "gospel gaps," a blindness to our gospel identity: "For too many of us, our sense of identity is more rooted in our performance than it is in God's grace. It is wonderful to be successful at what God has called you to do, but when you use your success to define who you are, you will always have a distorted perspective."

[9] Taylor, *Too Valuable to Lose,* 341.

[10] Lane and Tripp, *How People Change.* For more, see the context around Figure 6.1 (page 96 of 256).

[11] Janet O. Hagberg and Robert A. Guelich. *The Critical Journey—Stages in the Life of Faith,* Second Edition (Salem, WI: Sheffield, 2005). The authors explore why this is especially hard for those who are moving from "the productive" stage of life (see pages 83–89), into the very difficult "inward journey" (pp 91ff) and why we often retreat and get caged, because we frantically resist going through the terrifying "wall" (pp113ff) that would enable our deep transformation.

[12] Lane and Tripp, op cit. (loc 181 of 332).

[13] Articulated by Pastor Jeff Peterson of Lincoln Berean Church, NE, at Avant Europe Conference, June, 2014.

[14] King James Version of the Bible, completed in 1611, public domain.

[15] A modern paraphrase-translation of the Bible by Eugene H. Peterson, completed in 2002.

[16] We were guided by the training of Brady G. Wilson and Alex Somos as introduced in the *Juice: The Power of Conversation* (Toronto: BPS, 2009).

[17] Taylor, *Too Valuable to Lose,* 351.

[18] Kenn Oke, during his investigation into Avant Europe's missionary attrition.

Connecting to the Pipeline

1. Go to the Perspectives website (www.perspectives.org) to see if there are any courses being planned near you. You do not have to organize a special class just for your church since it is best to join with other churches/organizations in your area. Have your entire team sign up for the next one available—it is that important!

2. Find the next Mobilization Ideation (www.missionexus.org) happening near you. Take the whole team. Also, check into mission conferences as well as denominational events.

3. Make a list of all the leaders and volunteers in your children's ministry and youth ministry. Pray for them by name and ask the Lord to begin working in their hearts so that they will catch a vision for being missionary mobilizers every week.

4. Seek creative ways to introduce missions education and history into the men's and women's ministry events. There are many books, videos, guest speakers, and other tools that will meet the needs of these ministries in the church as well as expose people in the church to the Great Commission.

5. By building up resiliency in missionary candidates, can you think about ways that may help your church members in their own personal resiliency?

6. How can being a sending church be beneficial to your local community of believers? See www.MissionaryPipeline.org for a list of training organizations, coaches, and ministries that are willing to help your church prepare candidates.

7. Can you see that the intentional investment in your future missionaries will bring reciprocal growth to those tasked with directing and implementing the process?

Part 5

Partners: Serving Along Side the Sending Church

"Pay, Pray, and Stay Out of the Way!"

This is the blunt way of saying what many missionary sending agencies subtly believe is the role of the church in sending missionaries. A Bible-based and Christ-centered agency should see that their mission is assisting the local church in the Great Commission, while a poorly organized agency will seek to take the Lord's mandate away from the church in order to do it for them. As a sending church, it would be wise to thoughtfully consider partnering with only a few select missionary sending organizations. Out of more than a thousand agencies to choose from in North America, your church will find that compatibility is a very desirable asset as you help move missionary candidates along their journey through the pipeline.

Remember that you are not outsourcing your mandate for the Great Commission, but you are seeking a partner to fulfill the needs that your church is unable meet like, administration, on-field accountability and oversight, payroll, international medical insurance, retirement, contingency planning, hostage negotiations (yes—it happens), and a variety of other areas of expertise that should only be handled by experienced and highly trained experts. You have already heard from Doug Lucas at Team Expansion, Larry W. Sharp at Crossworld, and Stan De La Cour at SIM. Highlighted in these chapters are leaders from other recommended sending agencies whom you will find to be faithful partners to consider for your pipeline.

CHAPTER 27
Avant Ministries

Mobilizing Among Millennials
Russ

Three Generations

There are three groups of people whose ideas illustrate the challenge of mobilization in these shifting times as I've been able to observe so far. John, the Beloved, wrote to children, fathers, and young men. It seems that mobilization has something to do with knowing God and embracing these three generations. In the following paragraphs, I'll share three pictures that contribute to the perplexity of mobilizing in our era and three different ways that we're trying to respond faithfully so that Jesus will be joyfully worshiped in nationally led churches among the unreached areas of the world.

Here's a synthesis of how John addresses each generation:

> I am writing to you, little children, because your sins are forgiven for his name's sake. I am writing to you, fathers, because you know him who is from the beginning . . . . I write to you, young men, because you are strong, and the word of God abides in you, and you have overcome the evil one. (1 John 2:12–14)

Fathers

I stood next to another John, waiting for what was sure to be not only a profound answer but the solution to all of my mobilization problems. I had only been focused on mobilization for a few months, just long enough to get to that first of many clearings between the dense thickets of calendared mayhem. But John was the premier veteran, having begun his missionary career in the 1940s while GIs were still on their way back from the Old World. It was meant to be the classic moment where the young man finally asks the right question of the elder statesman after struggling against the grain for so long, and suddenly the journey falls into wisdom's way and the well-worn path of faithfulness is united with the wheels of youth. But, there I was still waiting. After what seemed too long to be settling, John answered that he would think about it and get back with me. I supposed it made sense. After all, it took John much longer to cross the Atlantic by ship as he first sailed to Maroc in the '40s than it had taken me to fly to touristy Tangier. So it's no surprise that, forty-eight hours later, John stopped me in the hallway saying he had his answer. It must have been a riddle, but I was only disappointed when John told me that he simply didn't have an answer. He said that times were too different. "No one had ever heard of *short-term*," he said with the candor of lightly veiled disdain and a raised brow. "We went out for life." It took me a while to discern, but it wasn't his lack of an answer, it was the reason behind his nonanswer that brought focus. I'm not bold enough to lasso down the fiery tin tubes of our shrinking world, and if I can't slow globalization, it's obvious that this is the elephant on the landscape we'll have to nurse. But (most) mission agencies *hate* short-term deployments—I mean, it's our mark of authenticity.

Young Men

Steve is too passionate to be a recruiter. That's why he's not actually a recruiter. The reason he's on our mobilization team is a long story, and for a long time I didn't really care to figure it all out. I wanted to figure out how to make Steve a recruiter. But, like I said, Steve is too passionate. Paul is too empathizing. And Doug is too discerning. How are we supposed to onboard missionaries when the only people who can match Steve's passion are college students—who aren't usually ready for the rigors that wrought his seasoned zeal? Steve's knowledge of the Word and experience of God's faithfulness in trial is enough to draw in small hordes of my generation for stories, but we aren't sure we have what it takes to get there. Paul has known the pain and the joy of missionary life since he was a boy in the Amazon River Basin, and he'll sooner comfort and counsel than challenge and call. Young men will flock to Paul for advice, but it's hard to think of being like him when we've never even built a fire without a Bic or hiked off the sidewalk. Then Doug is the systems man who dissects cultures and fits parts with wholes to make sense of ideas—he doesn't do elevator pitches. He has a PhD, but our most intellectual thoughts come from *Radio Lab* and Vice News. These men long to see the next generation go to win the nations to whom they gave the formative years of their lives, but they're leery to release this task to people so paranoid of commitment and often don't know how hungry we are to be told we can.

Children

I love and hate barely being a millennial. Mostly, we're just so full of contradictions. I love Julia Woodward because she must not have heard of the word *furlough* when she left home before the turn of the century. She went for the unreached and she beckoned our young parents to become pioneers while the getting was good. Maude Cary seems not to have heard of the word *furlough* either, because she planted herself faithfully through both world wars while fascists and Nazis waged war against a purer America and her allies. We millennials long for the vintage days where even the dogmatism was pure, maybe credible, and everyone must have sung with conviction "We Belong to the Land" so much that we'll hardly shop at Walmart, unless we're in a huge hurry. We'll spend hours making our own soap and sauerkraut, but then we'll stand in a weak hotspot for seventeen minutes just to make sure our apps are updated. As contradictory as we are, the craving for authenticity defies programmatic approaches and we can sniff out the marketing we didn't make. What we crave is the proud localization and the belonging, but it's also the far-reaching and the embracing. We still want to change the world, but we want people to acknowledge our problems and brokenness and affirm us in the midst of it all.

Ways Forward

Those are the three characters on stage; these three distinct generations know the same God and bear the same task to glorify his Son in all the world. We'll be synthesizing observations and ideas into efforts as learners as long as Avant exists, but for now here are three ways we're responding to these pieces on the board.

Mentorship Over Marketing

So, short-term mission trips weren't around in the middle of the twentieth century. And short-term mission trips aren't Avant; we send lifelong missionaries, who may move dozens of times, to plant churches

"
> Our mobilizers want to see those from the next generation, whom the Lord is calling into missionary service, hear the call and understand that the fields are white for harvest. Jesus is the ultimate mobilizer, for the fields are his.
"

among the unreached. Meanwhile, short-term mission trips are often what millennials need—the freedom to explore possibilities by stringing together several smaller commitments. What's the answer? We're not big enough to just divide and conquer.

It's not that our church planters don't care about the next generation of missionaries, but they are focused on reaching the unreached—not college students who may or may not have the calling to invest long-term. It's not even that our field missionaries don't have time to mentor college students on the ground, it's that there is so much investment that has to be made before the student ever arrives on the ground in preparing them even for a couple of months in a new place. This is where our regional mobilizers begin to fill the need and operate in their strengths. We're working to release regional mobilizers to do just that—invite young men and women to come alongside them and intentionally take steps to develop their cross-cultural awareness, their practice of evangelism, and their ability to use a foreign language. Our mobilizers want to see those from the next generation, whom the Lord is calling into missionary service, hear the call and understand that the fields are white for harvest. Jesus is the ultimate mobilizer, for the fields are his. Do you remember when he took the disciples into Samaria? He took them right into the heart of a Samaritan town and straight into the life of one of that town's most broken citizens. From there, deep into cross-cultural ministry and deep into the lives of the disciples he is mentoring, Jesus beckons the disciples to look up and recognize what he is inviting them into.

Hearing His Voice In Their Stories

Assessment is one of the most important tasks that our mobilizers have. It's already challenging to hear God's voice about how to move forward in our own lives. If trying to discern God's voice in someone else's life isn't harder, we may just be hearing what we expect to hear. On the one hand, we could always say that there are so many people who have yet to hear the gospel that we can't exclude anyone with a willingness to go to the nations and preach Christ. On the other hand, missionary life brings about one of the most complex sets of challenges to a person's (let alone a family's) physical, psychological, and emotional health that we ought not appoint anyone!

It's crucial that we discern God's voice in someone's understanding of their call to move forward. This is where our mobilizers shine when they are able to mentor and where they would burn out if they were merely marketing. We've divided the task of assessment into two essential blocks, fitness and readiness (Fit and Ready Assessment), and we've divided this assessment among our team so that anyone seeking to join Avant will have a minimum of four in-depth conversations with different members of our mobilization team dealing with these two ideas. Oftentimes, people want to talk about what they are going to do or where they are going to go, but these questions are far from our primary concern. Our mobilizers are listening first for who this person is in Christ and how they function in his body.

Second, we're listening for what God is doing in the person's life now to bring about these steps toward cross-cultural missionary service and what barriers need to be overcome. A missionary candidate's identity in Christ and that lived out within the local church is far more important than skills and passions. Further, God's work in the candidate's life—cultivating faith through trial and love for the nations—is much more indicative of future health in a hard field than their personality.

It's not that we don't care about what the candidate wants to do or where they are burdened to go. It's that we care more about the long-term health of a lifelong missionary. Within the Avant family, we're careful about how we define missionary health. Since we're seeking to multiply and sustain healthy cross-cultural church planting missionaries, and since people and circumstances are always in motion, our definition of health is fundamentally relationship driven. What that means is that a healthy missionary is going to be constantly growing in the missionary's relationship to God, to the Avant family, to the support team, and to those the missionary is reaching. These four relationships are at the core of missionary health. Every training we do for every missionary is always going to have growth in at least one of these relationships as its primary end.

Trusting Him and Trusting Them
It couldn't have been Wednesday, because I think we each ordered tacos. Then again, maybe we were just nervous about the other thing on the table.

Why would Evan and Jessie join Avant? Obviously they were going to the unreached, but we didn't even have much momentum in the part of the world on their hearts yet, and they weren't the kind to make decisions on personal ambition. Evan and Jessie had just graduated and gotten married. It was clear to them that the Lord had called them to a hard soil and they bore it with bright resolve. They had both spent at least two semesters of their college time among unreached people groups and could already sustain simple conversations in the target language. The real question for them was about team, belonging, and locality, and the idea on the table was not as tried and true as taco Tuesday.

Since that day we've prayed, planned, and dreamed; we've failed our way forward, adjusted, regrouped, and prayed more. We've watched this couple grow exponentially more than they would have on a traditional path. They've cast vision and recruited young men and women to live with them as they prepare for the field. They brought those just a step below them on the ladder not only to live with them, but to train with them as they grow in cultural awareness and language usage, even to struggle with them through the dynamics of team communication and life together. All of this was in a more controlled environment, until they all took off together to live among the unreached for a couple of months. Ultimately, they're mentoring the next generation even before they've become tested missionary leaders. They're the millennials that we believe in, and we back it up by being willing to entrust big responsibilities to them and coach them through failure and unmet expectations. We believe in them because we've heard God's voice in their life and we've learned to trust him by entrusting them with the task of mobilizing their way to the foreign field. And so, this is the way of mobilizing millennials.

Russ serves as director of recruitment with Avant Ministries (www.avantministries.org) in Kansas City, MO.

CHAPTER 28

Frontiers

Starting Churches among Muslims
Bob Blincoe

Frontiers began in 1992 when Greg Livingstone walked the beach at Ventura for two weeks. He was burdened to hear the Lord speak clearly about doing a new thing. He knew the vision God was giving him meant a costly discipleship for himself and those who would join him. "Lord, why another mission agency?" he asked as he wrestled with God. "There are already so many good ones." But there was none devoted totally to making disciples in the *Muslim* world. And there was none planning to *start churches* among Muslims. There was none sending *teams* to live in Muslim countries.

There was no mission agency authorizing the team leaders to make final decisions on the principle that they are closest to the action (back in America, the Frontiers office would be a *sending base,* not a command and control center). The leaders on the field would hold one another accountable for godly character and best mission practices.

Greg believed that young and relatively inexperienced Christians could go, provided they had a sending church and were eager for coaching and upgrading along the way.

And finally, Frontiers teams would be "grace-oriented" toward one another, relying on the Bible in all matters, but respecting differing, valid interpretations.

These are the Frontiers differences. We minimize rules and regulations, and maximize a go-for-it attitude. Our passion is glorifying God by attempting to plant churches and catalyze disciplemaking movements among all Muslim peoples, in partnership with others who share this vision.

For me, the thrill of joining Frontiers was like breaking out of jail. It was like finding one's lost relatives. I remember Greg cheering us onward, as our

> " Our passion is glorifying God
> by attempting to plant churches
> and catalyze disciplemaking movements
> among all Muslim peoples, in partnership
> with others who share this vision. "

day of departure drew near. Nothing compared to selling our possessions, closing a chapter on all that was familiar, and opening another chapter on the "frontier." For my family and my team, in the 1990s, that frontier was northern Iraq. We lived among the Kurds, "between Iraq and a hard place." One week a US television crew came to film our story. I remember admiring my wife for saying on television, "Iraq is a great place to raise a family." These days reninded me of Paul's words in 1 Corinthians 16:9: "A wide door for effective work has opened to me, and there are many adversaries."

Today dozens of missionaries live in Kurdistan. That is so great! But the frontiers have moved. I help church leaders discover hundreds of locations in the Muslim world where there are no pushpins in any missionary maps. Planting churches in the farther, final places is the task remaining. Mission agencies and church leaders have mapped the locations of where the missionaries live in the Muslim world. But mapping the entire missionary presence has revealed great swaths of humanity in Asia and Africa where there are no missionaries and no followers of Jesus. These are the unengaged peoples and places. But the laborers are few. What if this generation were to "give up their smaller ambitions," as Francis Xavier said, and "Go East to preach the gospel?" Our part is turning "what if" into "what is."

We have gathered in some firstfruits of our labors. But many more Muslims "will come from east and the west, and will take their places at the feast with Abraham, Isaac and Jacob" (Matt 8:11, NIV). Many is many, and we have not seen it yet. Call me crazy, but nothing is impossible with God. If you love the glory of the impossible, then have faith that the hundreds of Muslim peoples that are unengaged today may have missionaries among them by the year 2025. With the love of God compelling, and the Holy Spirit empowering, and the witness of the martyrs looking down on us, and the promises of God in play, we are going to "attempt great things for God" and "expect great things from God," as William Carey once said.[1]

At this eleventh hour of history, we are in a great countdown toward zero remaining unengaged Muslim peoples. If you can think of anything more exciting than that, you will have to tell me, because I can't. No wonder Jordan Grooms said, "If God calls you to be a missionary, do not stoop to be a king."

An increasing number of church leaders are realizing that it is life-giving for their own congregations to send long-term mission teams from their own membership. In his remarkable book, *Gaining by Losing*, J. D. Greear of Summit Church in North Carolina explains why the future belongs to churches that send many, many missionaries. Pastor Greear says that Jesus Christ's teaching in John 12 has changed him into a pastor who is passionate to send out many missionaries. In verse 24 Jesus said, "Very truly I tell you, unless a kernel of wheat falls to the ground and dies, it remains only a single seed. But if it dies, it produces many seeds." Because of this principle, Summit began sending in great numbers. Greear says, "Let's be honest: too often we church leaders measure the success of our ministries by one criteria alone: how large is it? So, we tend to spend all our money on things to increase attendance and capacity." "But," Greear adds, "If John 12:24 is true, then Jesus measures the success of our ministries not by how large we grow the storehouse, but by *how widely we distribute* its seeds."[2]

The number of churches that send their own long-term teams is increasing. You may be asking, "What is the incentive for a church leader to send his own people to plant churches in Muslim countries, where it's harder even than in America to plant churches?" Incentive is very important. For those who obey Jesus' command to go and make disciples, he promises great rewards. It doesn't matter whether your missionaries live or die, they will be rewarded, as will those who sacrificed to send them. In 2012 I heard of a church that pledged to send a hundred missionaries. Such an audacious goal had never entered my imagination. Who has ever heard of a church that would send a hundred missionaries? But in fact, this church has achieved their goal. And instead of resting on their laurels, the church leaders have pledged to send a hundred more. Now, I know of three more churches that have made this hundred-missionary pledge.

Church-based teams are life-giving to the church, to Muslims, and to themselves. For example, a church in Oregon has sent a long-term church planting team to Muslims in India; another team from a church in Kentucky is pledging to move to Southeast Asia; and a team from a church in Texas is making plans to sell everything and move to Turkey. Now, more than ever, churches are sending their own teams, in partnership with Frontiers: church-based teams. And we're just getting started.

We have had some early victories in our quest to plant churches and make disciples among all Muslim peoples. But there are no shortcuts; it is a costly discipleship. Consider the cost borne by John and Cassandra. After eighteen years residing among a Muslim people in Central Africa, this persevering couple is rejoicing that the chiefs of the tribes have at last opened their villages to the message of the gospel. New life has come to many. The repair of people's relationship with God has led to a hundred social repairs: marriages, parents with children, neighborhoods, tribal relationships—after eighteen years.

Or this remarkable story from Iraq. Layla and her family left their city, Fallujah, when ISIS rolled in. Layla could taste the falling ash and smell the smoke of war. She and her husband and kids could not outrun the rapidly approaching black-flagged convoy. But just when things were looking hopeless, a white pickup truck pulled up; the driver said, "Get in the back." They did, and off they zoomed to the city of refuge. There, in a refugee tent, Layla had a dream; she saw a man who would show her the way to God. Her dream came true. Through a Discovery Bible Study, she and her husband accepted Jesus Christ as their Lord and Savior. And just as importantly, Layla and her husband began to invite other families to start their own Bible studies. They have started twenty! "It's as though God has given us a pickup truck," Layla says, "to save others who were like us before we believed."

We have learned a lot from making mistakes. Failure has been our teacher. That is why we are always reviewing our training program, examining our methods, sharing the latest research. With more than 240 teams on the field, Frontiers is a network of laboratories, dedicated to solving one of the great problems of our day: how shall it be that *many Muslims* shall come from east and west and take their places at the feast?

On a future day Frontiers missionaries will say they paid a great price. Some will give the last full measure of devotion to go everywhere in the Muslim world and preach the gospel. The price they paid is worth it. "Your steadfast love is better than life, my lips will praise you" (Ps 63:3). Frontiers missionaries are neither heroes nor victims. Faithful church members may be shocked to realize there are twenty-four churches for every McDonald's in America. For Frontier missionaries, there must be a greater purpose than increasing it to twenty-five.

Going to the farthest final frontiers is who we are. Our fathers went to the moon, but they saved exploration of the galaxies for this generation to explore. As Greg Livingstone says, "It's still too soon to celebrate, too soon to quit." Let's go there together.

Bob Blincoe is president of US Frontiers (www.frontiersusa.org), coaching new team leaders to go and preparing new churches to send.

Notes

[1] Originally spoken by William Carey in his sermon to the Baptist Association meeting in Nottingham, England, May 30, 1792, at the Friar Lane Baptist Chapel.

[2] J. D. Greear, *Gaining by Losing: Why the Future Belongs to Churches that Send* (Grand Rapids, MI: Zondervan, 2015).

CHAPTER 29

The Navigators

Multiplying One-to-One Discipleship

Mark Stebbins

The Navigators is an international, interdenominational ministry begun by Dawson Trotman, a visionary layman, among naval service members in 1933 in San Diego. A trademark for The Navigators over the years has been the utilization of practical tools to accomplish and multiply one-to-one discipleship. Today The Navigators is established in roughly one hundred countries, and decentralized into a worldwide partnership led by an international executive team. Each country has an autonomous leadership structure affiliated in a global network of ministries.

The mission statement of The Navigators, known as our "Core," serves as a shared banner across our work representing our calling, core values, and vision. Our mission calling statement is: "To advance the Gospel of Jesus and his Kingdom into the nations through spiritual generations of laborers, living and discipling among the lost."

Each national ministry is envisioning a growth process that moves through four stages over time. The first stage, *Initiating*, occurs when a pioneer team begins intentional ministry in a new location. The second stage, *Developing*, occurs when local leaders and laborers begin to emerge, and the foundations for generational ministry are evident. The third stage, *Maturing*, occurs when national leadership becomes the primary leadership, shaping strategy and direction for movement of the gospel. The fourth stage, *Partnering*, occurs when new generations of local leaders and laborers are being produced and interdependence is functioning within the worldwide partnership. The sending of cross-cultural workers has begun in the Partnering stage.

The United States is the most senior Partnering country within The Navigators. Missionary sending from the US began in 1949 and has continued essentially without interruption since then. Frequent requests for US workers come from all across the Navigator world. Currently, over 300 workers from the US are living and serving internationally.

The primary sending base for US international workers is The Navigators US Collegiate Mission. This department hosts nearly 800 staff working on almost 200 campuses across the country, touching the lives of more than 50,000 students each year. The campus ministry structure is divided into thirteen US regions. Each region is tasked with developing their own mission strategy and explicit sending goals. National collegiate mission goals and supporting initiatives help weave together a national collaboration in support of these programs.

The primary campus missions platform across the country is the cultivation of International Campus Partnerships (or ICP's). There are currently between forty and fifty of these regionally sponsored partnership cooperatives with international locations, in various stages of development. The ultimate goal for each is to become reciprocal, reflecting the biblical beauty of such partnerships evidenced especially in Paul's intercity forays and linkages in the ministry of the gospel. In particular, Paul's letter to believers in Philippi from the church in Rome highlights such mutuality, as well as the narrative of collaboration between the church in Jerusalem with the nascent church in Antioch (Acts 11 through 15). Oneness in heart, mind, resources, struggle, prayer, and strategy can be traced throughout.

ICPs have become an experiential immersion for our campus constituents, leavening God's heart for the nations throughout US Navigator campus ministries. Partnering staff and students are moving toward reciprocity with testimonies of the ensuing blessings that come from these alliances. Frequent benefits reported include learning to live and think like a missionary and exhilarating, long-term kingdom friendships forged from the cross-cultural practice of biblical one-anothering.

These partnerships have proven to be a catalyst and an engine for further missions engagement and sending. Partners are helping and praying for each other, thinking gospel movement strategy together, and increasingly sending emissaries both ways. Mid-term and long-term missionaries are emerging out of these missional relationships.

At times ICPs hit significant roadblocks or seem to have run their course. Sending or receiving capacities change and significant adjustments are made through dialogue. Lavish communications characterize mitigation of such challenges and ongoing success. On occasion, partners agree to a temporary hiatus or to an ending. Understanding these potential eventualities helps to calibrate partner expectations from the beginning.

Since 2011, another formal collegiate missions program called "International EDGE Corps" has gained significant momentum. EDGE is an acronym for Evangelism, Discipleship, Growth, and Experience. Recent grads join teams of two men and two women to deploy to help primarily on international campuses for two years. Each year, three teams on average are sent.

Long-term workers are also sent annually from the US campus work into increasingly diverse global roles. Other US departments such as our Military Mission also endeavor to send long-term workers every year. Business as mission, community development, NGO positions, and jobs in education are perennial needs, along with positions serving alongside our national works worldwide. A look at The Navigators worldwide website will give you a peek into our world and what the Lord is doing with us globally (www.navigatorsworldwide.org).

The US Navigators missions department, NavMissions, lists many of our current openings for Americans at www.navmissions.org. A tremendous advantage that The Navigators has in recruiting missionaries is the strength of our local US ministries, where candidates most often originate. Local fellowships provide our best recruiting pools for mission positions. However, this reality also presents The Navigators with a sometimes unintended denominational dynamic, which can feel insular to those coming in from outside. Increasingly, our local US ministries are working to provide inroads for greater recruitment and inclusion. Our missions department is also seeking to establish more orientation and training centers for those coming to us from outside our local US ministries to take on international assignments with us.

Mark Stebbins is on collegiate staff with The Navigators (www.navigators.org) in Colorado Springs, CO, and is also a missions mobilization consultant with MissioNexus (www.MissioNexus.org).

CHAPTER 30

Pioneers

The Forgotten Lord's Prayer

Steve Richardson

Mobilization for world evangelization has not always been a high priority over the last 2000 years since the Great Commission was given. What might have happened if, for example, in addition to reciting the "Lord's Prayer" (Matt 6:9–13) each Sunday thousands of churches had also recited the "forgotten" Lord's Prayer of Matthew 9:38: "Ask the Lord of the harvest, therefore, to send out workers into his harvest field" (NIV)? We can only imagine how different the course of church history might have been.

Every generation of believers must be mobilized anew for the church's God-given mission. This requires tremendous intentionality in the face of significant environmental headwinds. Are missionaries still needed? What is their role? Are our candidates qualified? What about the risks and the costs? Questions like these force us to constantly reevaluate our approach to the unfinished task. The clearer we are on the answers, the more impactful our harvesting efforts will be.

When believers and churches do catch the fire of God's heart for mobilization, amazing things happen. One important outcome is that they begin to form cooperative structures to carry out the mission. We call these *agencies,* better known in past generations as mission "societies." An agency like Pioneers, the one I have served with for many years, answers the question, "What could it look like if thousands of local churches in many different countries partnered together—crossing national, cultural, and denominational boundaries—to place church planters among the least reached peoples of the world?" An agency, then, is simply a collaborative nexus for Great Commission obedience.

Virtually every church movement around the world can be traced to the pioneering efforts of one or more mission agencies. The concern is sometimes expressed, "Agencies exist only when the church isn't doing its job." Personally, I think the opposite is true. Mission agencies are not a reflection of the church's inadequacy or negligence, but a visible sign of their missionary vitality. When God's people are self-absorbed and lose sight of the bigger picture, the perceived need for mission agencies diminishes.

The task faced by sending churches and their agency partners is complex, the opposition immense, and the human element profound. Collaboration in the global harvest is not for the faint of heart. As one of my mentors sometimes commented in my early days on the field, "Putting a man on the moon is simple compared to reaching a Muslim people group." Yet, sobering as the terrain may be, effective church-agency partnership is a foundational aspect of the mobilization process.

Finding the Right Agency Match

Identifying one or more agency partners will be an important goal for most sending churches. I would suggest that the inner circle of your primary relationships should ideally include no more than three or four partners. Beyond this, it will be a challenge to maintain the level of familiarity and communication required to foster higher levels of collaboration.

A church leader may want to include the following considerations in their search for a partner agency:

1. **What is the mission and focus of the agency?** Is their goal and approach to ministry compatible with your church's objectives and mission philosophy? Do they serve in the locations where you want to go and in the ways you want to work?

2. **What is the overall reputation of the agency?** No agency is perfect. Each will have strengths and weaknesses. Cross-cultural work is tough, yet you will need to reach an acceptable level of trust and confidence based on the track record of your partner. What are the observations of other experienced mission practitioners? If possible, seek several opinions and include the views of more than one missionary who currently serves with the agency, not just one that has had a difficult experience. What is the enthusiasm and loyalty quotient for those who serve with this agency? Are their processes and protocols clear? Do you sense excitement, passion, and professionalism? Are younger generations being attracted to the vision?

3. **What are the agency's core values?** This gets to the question of organizational culture. Most candidates coming to Pioneers site our core values as the primary rationale. They are particularly attracted by our emphasis on the least reached, teams, and flexible ministry approaches. Are the publically stated values truly fleshed out in practice? What might be the unstated values of the organization (these are sometimes just as important as the stated ones)? How are decisions made, accountability provided, and differences resolved, for example?

4. **How does the agency view the role of the sending church in the sending process?** Not only in the early stages, but how does the agency view the sending church in the long-term ministry development and care of the worker? How is this priority expressed in practical terms? Is the participation of the church welcomed, formalized and facilitated? Do they have written guidelines for sending church involvement?

5. **Is there good personal chemistry?** The kingdom of God rides on relationships. Get to know the agency and its leaders as much as you can. You will be making a big investment over coming years, so it will be worth the time and effort. Are your missionaries attracted to work with this particular agency? This may take time to discern. Don't force your workers to work with a group that doesn't feel right to them.

Pioneers: A Case Study in Mobilization

Every church and agency has their own unique story. The Pioneers story may yield some helpful reference points for anyone seeking to mobilize a significant number of workers for the harvest.

Pioneers started in a local church in 1979. Founder Ted Fletcher, a Wall Street executive, stepped out by faith to help an initial core group of Bible school graduates to serve in difficult and least-reached areas. The mission grew rapidly. Present membership, thirty-eight years later, includes about 1,800 US staff and appointees, and an equivalent number from other nations. In the United States we process more than 200 new applicants for long-term service each year. In the process, we have been blessed to partner with thousands of churches.

I was personally drawn to this small, untested group of people and their embryonic vision as a college student in 1983. There were only a handful of people involved at the time. Over the years I've watched the vision grow. I have concluded there is no single silver bullet for successful mobilization, particularly if our aim is to generate sustained, healthy growth over an extended period of time. Like any good recipe, effective mobilization requires a thoughtful blend of complementary ingredients.

Very briefly, here are just a few of the elements that I believe have contributed to the mobilization momentum of Pioneers over the years.

Vision: Pioneers' vision crystallized early. The goal is to catalyze church multiplication in cultures that have little church presence or access to the gospel. The name *Pioneers* was specifically chosen to reinforce the mission. Today it remains synonymous with ministry to unreached or "least access" peoples. *Is your agency partner synonymous with a particular expertise or ministry niche?*

Values: Pioneers emphasizes values more than policies or specific methods. Together, these values form an attractive organizational culture. Within the framework of our mission and eight core values, missionaries and their teams are free to engage in a broad range of ministry activities. Values are strongly reflected in the core documents, training process, team meetings, decision making, and promotional media. Missionaries throughout the movement can articulate the values and frequently discuss their implications. *Are the values of your partner agency embraced by all?*

Worship: We sometimes underappreciate the supernatural dimension of God's work. God reserves glory for himself by routinely reducing us to knee-bending reliance on him. "Soli Deo" (God alone) is a deliberately cultivated spiritual environment that permeates our movement. A global, virtual team known as the Soli Deo team leads the organization in prioritizing its first and most important core value, "passion for God." *Is the spirit of prayer and worship alive and well in your mission community?*

Multiplication: Agencies tend to inherit the DNA of their founders. Ted Fletcher was a visionary mobilizer. As national sales manager for the Wall Street Journal he was highly relational and goal oriented. Pioneers developed a similarly positive and proactive organizational outlook. Everyone has a part to play in the harvest. Nothing is impossible. Trust God for the next step.

In Pioneers, the task of mobilizing new workers is not left exclusively to someone in the "home office." It is shared by everyone. Team leaders and new missionaries are encouraged to recruit other missionaries to their teams. Often the best time to do this is during the early stages of team formation. Effective recruitment involves a highly relational process. The goal of office and mobilization staff is to help people move forward in their journey with God, toward greater involvement in God's mission. *Does everyone in the organization have a mobilization mindset?*

Global, Decentralized Structure: Over time, Pioneers has developed a worldwide operational framework that relies on high levels of trust. For example, there is a clear division of responsibility between "mobilization bases" and the international field leadership. When a new missionary leaves the home country, that worker comes under the oversight of the international leadership—team leaders, area leaders, etc. Even pastoral care takes place primarily at the grassroots level, supported and reinforced by the sending churches and the agency's home team. This decentralized structure presses the decision making close to the ground and frees the mobilization base to focus almost exclusively on mobilizing, training, and servicing even more missionaries. *Is your structure optimized for impact?*

Teams: A Pioneers hallmark predating popularization of the concept in mission circles, the team approach may be the single greatest "secret" to Pioneers' rapid growth. Teams are the fundamental organizational unit in Pioneers. A team philosophy of ministry can be found at every level. Each "cell" contributes uniquely and works to reproduce and multiply. The mission currently has 320 teams in 104 countries. Many teams are multinational. They normally range in size from six to ten adults. Perhaps more than any other single factor, new candidates mention the "team concept of ministry" as the core value that attracts them to Pioneers. The multiplicity of small teams greatly facilitates recruitment, retention, accountability, versatility, and leadership development. Red tape is minimized, and new teams are launched routinely. *Is there a strong sense of community among your members?*

Excellence: Someone once criticized Ted Fletcher, saying, "You run this place like a business!" Ted took it as a compliment. Fletcher's relative inexperience in the evangelical missionary subculture (though he surrounded himself with experienced board and staff) had its silver lining. Mission organizations and businesses have important differences, but agencies can learn much from other arenas of God's work.

The freedom to question assumptions has helped Pioneers grow. Are these countries really "closed"? Can a young, aspiring leader be entrusted with responsibility for a new team? Can we outsource many aspects of training and care to specialist agencies? Are multicultural teams a worthwhile goal? Can businesspeople and global professionals participate meaningfully on church planting teams? *Does your leadership and staff exemplify a high level of competence, responsiveness, and efficiency?*

High Touch: Mission work is all about people—those who await the gospel and those who proclaim it. When someone applies for service, a pivotal question is, "How can Pioneers help you and your sending church realize your God-given vision?" The organization's goals are clear but broad. If the vision involves impacting least-reached peoples with the gospel of Christ, we are there to help.

Most missionaries want to enjoy wholesome relationships and teamwork as they go to the nations. Research has shown that a "low sense of organizational connectedness" is a primary contributor to missionary attrition.[1] While Pioneers is now a larger organization, many still comment on its relational ethos. Perhaps this is one reason our retention rate is relatively consistent, despite the challenging locations in which we work.[2] *What are the first impressions of a person inquiring about missionary service with this agency?*

Leadership: From the beginning, Ted Fletcher attracted a number of visionary young leaders to his side. A master mentor, he gave these aspiring leaders many opportunities to try their wings. As the network of teams and challenging ministry environments grew, Pioneers evolved into a leadership incubator. "Participatory servant leadership" emerged as yet another hallmark of the globalizing movement. *Does your agency empower and multiply leaders for the next generation of harvest?*

Ultimately, there is no substitute for the leading of the Holy Spirit as you find your way to the nations. Each step should be guided by thoughtful counsel. There is no magic wand or easy shortcut. Effective mobilization will be the outcome of much prayer, thoughtful partnership, and a long-term investment toward a clear objective.

Steve Richardson was a church planter in Southeast Asia and has served as president of Pioneers-USA (www.pioneers.org) since 1999.

Notes

[1] World Evangelical Alliance (WEA) study, 1997.

[2] The annual attrition rate of Pioneers missionaries averages about 6 percent.

CHAPTER 31

The Evangelical Alliance Mission (TEAM)

Four Practices of our Partner Churches

Josh McQuaid

The mission agency is far from a new invention. We've been around for many years; in the case of The Evangelical Alliance Mission (TEAM), 127 years to be exact. Over those years, many things have changed. We think about people groups differently today than we did at the beginning. We've witnessed the end of colonialism (in certain forms), survived several world wars, seen the global political map change constantly, and watched a continual ebb and flow of people from this place to that.

While it is true that the world around us is constantly changing, none of these changes—be they linguistic, economic, cultural, environmental, or custom—fundamentally alters the truths which underpin human life. People are still lost, broken, and in need of a savior. God remains gracious and loving, drawing men and women to himself through Christ and his Spirit. The church is still called by God to engage his lost world as his ambassador. And so, mission retains a consistent focus from generation to generation. While some change is constant, we are anchored by convictions about God, his world, and our place in that world. These things never change.

The million-dollar question, of course, is *how* churches and agencies can continually adapt in such a way as to consistently apply our unchanging beliefs to an ever-changing context. For TEAM, it is our core conviction about the primacy of the local church's role in global mission that serves to ground us as many other changes come. This belief isn't without its challenges, but it helps us maintain our organizational focus, gives us a foundation to stand on, and is one of the ways that we can measure our faithfulness to God's call.

The Challenge

When it comes to sending missionaries, TEAM believes our role is to facilitate missionary sending for those who have the responsibility to send—local churches. Maybe "facilitate" sounds like a clever linguistic turn, but we believe this conviction should manifest itself in a fundamentally different kind of relationship between agency and church. It is our belief that churches and agencies bring complementary gifts, callings, and capacities to the table, and that those resources are best leveraged through collaboration with one another.

Most churches and agencies would affirm some version of this conviction in theory. Even so, the old adage still holds true that agencies often wish for churches to "pray, pay, and stay out of the way." Unfortunately, it is also our experience that many churches are all too eager to relinquish direct engagement in global mission work. There are exceptions to every rule, and we're excited to see many churches and agencies asking hard questions of themselves and one another, and beginning to work together more proactively. But, by and large, there is still a long ways to go.

Why is it that churches are happy to be unengaged with their members who are called to global mission? Why are agencies happy to proceed without deep engagement with local churches? If churches and agencies generally believe that the other provides complementary gifts and resources to the task of global mission, why is it still so hard to work together? As we have wrestled with these questions, three observations have caught our attention.

First, both churches and agencies tend to believe that expertise in global mission resides with the mission agency. This leads to churches feeling largely unempowered when it comes to global mission and manifests itself in, among other things, a perceived inability to assess a church member's suitability for global ministry, a strategic focus that speaks mostly (or entirely) to local outreach and leaves global ministry in its own silo, or a reluctance to speak directly into missionary accountability. From the agency's side, this perception of our own expertise can lead us to pursue an applicant without receiving an adequate endorsement from a sending church, to change a missionary's assignment without consulting the church, or to fail to engage the church when ministry challenges arise.

Second, many individuals view their missional calling as something that is intensely personal; thus they pursue that calling with agencies before coming under appropriate leadership, care, supervision, or authority from their local church. The assumption here seems to be that missionary assessment is best handled by the global mission expert—the agency. Once that assessment has been completed, then the church and the missionary can begin a dialogue about international service. Unfortunately, this approach cuts the church out of a critical step in the process, all but ensures that the agency and the missionary will overlook assessment resources that might have been available in the local church, and often causes the missionary's first substantive conversations with the church to happen concurrently with their "ask" for financial resources.

Third, these and other factors lead to the belief that agencies can serve as outsourcing agents for a church's global mission work. Again, the thinking seems to go something like this: (1) global mission is complex, and (2) local churches don't have the time or the expertise to navigate that complexity, while (3) mission agencies have needed expertise. Therefore, (4) a reasonable approach would be to send people and money to agencies and let them take care of it.

With our convictions and these challenges in mind, TEAM recently made significant changes to our missionary application process in the belief that until we made these changes, our desire for meaningful collaboration with churches would forever remain merely that—a desire.

The Work

For as long as anyone can remember, TEAM has required our missionaries to have the endorsement of a local sending church. But as we all know, there are endorsements, and then there are *endorsements*. Over the years it became harder and harder for us to get substantive engagement from churches during the missionary application process. Some churches naturally understood the importance of engaging with us during this time, but far more treated our request for their involvement as a formality at best or, even worse, as an annoyance. In at least one instance, we were told that the church's policy was not to engage with the agency or the missionary until the agency had made an appointment decision regarding the candidate.

In this climate, with many churches apparently wanting to outsource mission to us, it would have been easy to just play along. Instead, we've gone the other direction, increasing our expectations regarding church engagement during the application process and providing a clear framework to support that engagement, with free resources available along the way.[1]

" Why is it that churches are happy to be unengaged with their members who are called to global mission? Why are agencies happy to proceed without deep engagement with local churches? If churches and agencies generally believe that the other provides complementary gifts and resources to the task of global mission, why is it still so hard to work together?. **"**

Our expectations revolve around four practices that we now ask all churches to observe as their missionary completes their application for service.

1. The church conducts its own missionary assessment, even as we are doing the same. The point here is to remind churches that they have an important role to play in identifying those God is calling to serve overseas. Without visibility into the applicant's ecclesial life and ministry—which only comes from a church's engagement—agencies struggle to make wise appointment decisions.

2. The church provides a mentor for the applicant. If possible, this person should be outside of the "official" decision-making process, and is intended to provide pastoral support, counsel, prayer, and other practical spiritual care for the applicant while they complete the intense process of discerning their missionary call.

3. The church speaks into the applicant's proposed ministry placement, including both location and ministry type. This is intended not only to draw on the church's observation of the applicant's gifting, but also to help the church think about the applicant's assignment in light of the church's own strategic vision. Is there a connection between the two? If not, what does it mean that God is calling this person to a ministry that is out of alignment with the larger church body? Should the applicant consider an assignment that would be more in line with the church's vision?

4. Finally, we ask churches and applicants to honestly share their expectations with one another regarding communication, accountability, financial

support, missionary care, etc. Of the four practices, this is one that we encourage churches and missionaries to regularly revisit, as it is all too easy for tension to arise if expectations are left unexpressed and unmet.

Conclusion

Front-loading these four practices into our missionary application process fundamentally changes the nature of the agency, church, and missionary relationship. These practices create a context in which agency, church, and missionary are free to speak openly with one another, challenges are identified before they become problems, and the assumption of clear communication is created from the beginning. We also believe having churches deeply engaged from day one will make it harder for relational distance to arise later on. Finally, we believe a critical strength of these practices is that they do not require human or financial resources to execute. Any church can engage in these practices with nothing more than love for their missionary and a commitment to pursue God's calling with them.

To be sure, these four practices do create additional work, and they will need continual refinement. But they support our conviction that the local church has a critical role to play in global mission, and they help us remain true to our calling to facilitate that activity. We have included these additional steps in our process as a practical refusal to play the hand we've been dealt and to gently suggest that there might be a better way for churches and agencies to collaborate in God's global mission.

Josh McQuaid is the director of organizational engagement at The Evangelical Alliance Mission (TEAM, www.team.org).

Notes

[1] As we develop and update resources to support this process, we post them for free here: https://team.org/engage/churches/church-resources.

CHAPTER 32
WorldVenture

Church Partnership Is in Our DNA

Harold Britton

WorldVenture (formerly Conservative Baptist Foreign Mission Society) was founded in May 1943 as seventy-five pastors gathered in Chicago, Illinois, to pray about remaining true to the Word of God and focused on reaching the world for Christ. Many of these Baptist congregations saw a need to send their brightest and best to regions beyond (Rom 15:20), planting churches among the least reached. Today, WorldVenture partners with over 2,500 evangelical churches to send short- and long-term workers to the nations. These churches value the complementary services of a comprehensive mission agency. Below are ten steps we take to come alongside each church to mobilize the next generation of missionaries.

1. **Mobilizing the Local Church.** We believe the mission of God is core to the local church. Jesus is building his church around the world, and the gates of hell will not prevail against it. God desires each local congregation to be a sending church. Led by the Holy Spirit, this is both a great privilege and an awesome responsibility.

   Our God is a sending God. He sent his Son, his Spirit, and his church into the world (John 20:21). We are part of his plan to reach the nations! The church is especially suited and called to disciple its own people in community, and to send them out into our world with the love of Christ. The Great Commission is the primary task of the church, to make disciples of all nations, both locally and globally (Matt 28:18–20, Acts 1:8, Acts 11:19–26, 13:1–3).

" Our passion is to help the local church *be* the church by coming alongside local congregations, equipping and mobilizing each church to significantly participate in crossing continents and cultures to transform lives. **"**

Many evangelical churches seek to clarify their specific vision and role in the mission of God. However, international missions can be the last thing on the agenda for many churches. But WorldVenture hopes to change that. Our passion is to help the local church *be* the church by coming alongside local congregations, equipping and mobilizing each church to significantly participate in crossing continents and cultures to transform lives. We recommend three practical leadership actions to help activate each church, cultivating a biblical vision and growing a global awareness:

- **Prayer.** Prayer is critical to all mission work. WorldVenture employs a national director of prayer mobilization. Our headquarters intentionally displays Matthew 9:38 around our office, asking God to send more laborers into the harvest. Each workday our staff takes the time to gather for prayer, focusing on a specific nation and the missionaries connected to that area of the world. We believe prayer is essential to raise up missionaries in every church to reach the poor, the lost, and the least. Jesus told us to pray this way. Prayer is vital for the increased spiritual warfare that accompanies cross-cultural ministry around the world. One excellent resource for mission-focused prayer comes from Operation World (www.operationworld.org). This prayer tool can also enhance a church's specific missionary prayer requests.

- **Education.** Vision and awareness grow with increased understanding. Inspire your leadership team! Attend a local Perspectives on the World Christian Movement class (www.perspectives.org) and encourage your leaders to join you. Perspectives is the number one mission course in the US to learn about "God's mission heart, our part, and unreached peoples." Better yet, be a catalyst and host a course for your entire community of churches.

- **Relationships**. Invest in the current missionaries that your church supports, and respond to their needs on the field. Many churches have formed a "care team"or "outreach team" to get more involved locally and globally. Your current missionaries might be ready to receive a short-term mission team or a few interns. Listening to missionaries, agreeing on field needs, determining the best time to visit, deciding on the ideal group size to send, and getting cultural training can increase, even multiply, the impact. Increasing your missionary exposure can inspire your congregation and challenge the next generation (think video, Skype, or speaking engagements in your church). Encourage your church small groups to adopt a missionary and help with prayer, support, and ongoing care.

2. **Candidate Assessment Coaching**. Although we connect with potential candidates from many US college campuses and seminaries, often the most prepared candidates seem to come from local churches instilled with a God-given vision to reach the nations. Using web inquiries, phone calls, and network connections, we screen and respond to candidates from every sector of society (young leaders, nurses, teachers, engineers, counselors, artists, social workers, businesspeople, and pastors, just to name a few). Most claim to have a call on their lives to serve Christ, his church, and the poor. This initial coaching process is a relational "getting-to-know you" as we hear their story and passion to cross cultures with the gospel.

   The candidate coach begins to look for individuals with a clear call, strong spiritual disciplines, a solid church endorsement, healthy family relationships, self-awareness, marketable skills, and active humility. We contact our global field leaders to determine if we might have an appropriate team where the candidate can visit, serve, and eventually join—applying their gifting, experience, and passion. We try to get a clear picture of each candidate: their character, competence, chemistry, and capacity as a person, couple, or family. This initial screening leads us to connect with the candidate's home church. We ask the candidate to notify their church leadership in advance of our contact, enabling our coach to set up a productive appointment for everyone involved.

3. **Church Connection and Endorsement**. Each candidate hopes for a clear and wholehearted endorsement from their home church

leadership. Our mobilization team connects with the church leadership, preferably a pastor or mission leader, to learn more about the candidate. We ask thorough questions about the candidate's active role in their local church.

Some questions include: Is the candidate known and respected within the church? Does he or she have a clear calling and vision that fits with the local church? Is the candidate able to cross cultures and minister to others? Has this been practically demonstrated in the church community? Are there any growth goals one might suggest for this person? Are there any reservations or concerns WorldVenture should address to move forward? Can the church leadership wholeheartedly endorse this candidate and begin to partner with WorldVenture? Is this candidate the kind of leader the church would seriously get behind for prayer and financial support?

Church partnership is part of WorldVenture's DNA, something we consistently foster to empower and serve each congregation with a growing heart for missions. We regularly visit our sending churches for face-to-face collaboration and to provide additional mission resources. We often gather churches together with a common vision or connect churches that have adopted a particular unreached people group (UPG). When mission agencies and churches work together, we can complement each other as we join God in raising up and sending the next generation of missionaries.

4. **Application and Interview**. If the initial candidate assessment and the church endorsement is positive, the candidate may then apply to WorldVenture. This online application is quite comprehensive; personal history, testimony, doctrinal statement, a resume with education and work experience, psychological testing, background check, and several references are required. The completed application is reviewed by a team of mission experts. When approved, an interview is scheduled with the leadership team at WorldVenture. Often, growth goals are assigned to help the new appointee develop a more holistic overseas ministry. Following the interview and appointment, prefield ministry orientation begins immediately.

5. **Prefield Ministry Orientation.** New appointees are trained within a small group and introduced to WorldVenture leadership and support

systems. Training includes examining one's identity in Christ; embracing a holistic view of our physical, social, mental, and spiritual health; improving our communication; using teamwork in crossing cultures; and cultivating marriage and family relationships. We also train appointees to understand budget and finances, best practices of social media, tips on public speaking, online support services, and the ongoing process of mobilizing your sending church. We encourage each appointee to have a home church mentor from appointment through departure to the field, in addition to online resources that help reinforce learning.

6. **Appointee Partner Development and Communication.** WorldVenture provides every appointee with the training needed to be effective in raising funds for their monthly needs and outgoing expenses, as well as the prayer support that is so essential to successful ministry. We have a dedicated staff whose primary goal is to serve their partner development and on-field needs. A project manager is dedicated to fulfilling related communication needs, producing a publicity package (including digital resources) for appointees and missionaries. WorldVenture helps appointees share their calling and story, inviting partners to participate in God's work. This gives each appointee a good start as they return home and begin preparing for overseas work. A prefield mentor walks alongside each appointee and their home church to encourage appointees and help keep them on track until deployment. Their home church is connected each step of the way, which will continue when they go to the field.

7. **Missionary Account Planning and Personal Development.** WorldVenture works closely with appointees to develop their financial support packages and ensure adequate funding in all areas deemed necessary. We work with the field and global cost of living services combined with the unique needs of each ministry. Our desire is to create a sustainable plan that helps missionaries thrive in another culture. We provide ongoing opportunities for leadership experience and development. Continuing education benefits everyone, and missionaries are encouraged to pursue graduate programs, professional seminars, and conferences to prepare for greater fruitfulness on their fields.

8. **Appointee Launch Fund.** One of the great challenges of appointees is to manage the time and effort needed to discover support partners and transition from work to overseas ministry. WorldVenture has

formed a loan/grant program that can supplement the reduction of work hours and help supply basic living costs for up to six months. Appointees have another option to request a lump sum for final outgoing costs. This fund was established to speed appointees to the field. It helps to remove common barriers for appointees to get to the field. When missionaries return to their field for a second term, the loan is converted to a grant and does not need to be repaid. Churches love when agencies and foundations participate in the costs of sending laborers to the field. Finally, when missionaries get to 100 percent support, we also assist their home churches to offer an inspiring commissioning service.

9. **Missionary Care and Counseling**. A commitment to cross-cultural ministry calls for growing in Christ, developing one's God-given gifts, acquiring additional ministry skills, and sharpening one's interpersonal skills for collaborative relationships. But when challenges arise on the field, WorldVenture is there with both formal and informal services to strengthen members for effective, ongoing ministry. WorldVenture provides a child care and education specialist to help kids make the adjustment to missionary life and meet those challenges successfully. Not all solutions work for all kids, and each child is different. In seeking the best solutions, WorldVenture partners with parents, bringing our expertise to help parents weigh all the options. Counseling, emotional wellness checkups, and crisis intervention are available to help contend with any mental health matters or difficult situations which can result from life on the field. WorldVenture provides support when it is needed in partnership with the sending church.

10. **Supervision and Long-Term Work.** Strong leadership and dynamic teams can help create a thriving community of cross-cultural workers. WorldVenture actively trains local and national leadership to make disciples, prayerfully producing annual strategic plans. WorldVenture has a medical plan that provides worldwide coverage for missionaries. This coverage includes doctor visits, hospitalization, dental, vision, and medical evacuation, if needed. All missionaries are covered with life insurance for both husband and wife. WorldVenture contracts with tax preparers to handle federal and state tax returns. This service is provided

by knowledgeable professionals who understand the implications of living overseas. WorldVenture offers long-term missionaries a retirement savings account with a partner institution. The amount contributed to a retirement account is included in the missionary support package. WorldVenture also provides referral to an investment advisor for answers to retirement planning questions.

WorldVenture believes that the success of international mission work is fortified by missionaries who are effectively prepared and adequately supported to do the work God is calling them to do. Consistent with this vision is our commitment to providing the training, resources, and support necessary for missionaries to thrive, whether for the short or long term. From the founding of the early church, God has used missionaries sent and supported by local churches to take the gospel to unreached people all over the world. WorldVenture exists to help the next generation of missionaries and their sending churches more effectively fulfill that calling.

Harold Britton is director of church-missionary relationships at WorldVenture (www.worldventure.com) in Denver, CO.

CHAPTER 33

Wycliffe Bible Translators

Developing and Launching People into Ministry

Jamie Farr

Wycliffe Bible Translators USA is part of a global movement called the Wycliffe Global Alliance that spans six continents and impacts over 2,200 languages. Wycliffe's workforce needs are diverse and complex, encompassing ministry locations, role types and duration, ethno-linguistic varieties, age, professional experiences, and church experiences. No single approach can effectively connect with and attract all the types of people needed to do this work.

There are over 500 types of roles in Wycliffe today, with opportunities available across a breadth of occupational categories. We recognize that we are part of a much larger work, and our contributions are focused on inviting the US church to participate as part of a global mosaic.

Three values guide our work in recruitment and placement: dependence on God, a spirit of generosity, and a commitment to do the work of the Great Commission together. We apply these values in our day-to-day actions in order to accomplish our goals for this global workforce.

> Three values guide our work in recruitment and placement: dependence on God, a spirit of generosity, and a commitment to do the work of the Great Commission together.

Dependence on God

Dependence on God is lived out in a threefold approach: We look to God for help, we tell others what we see God doing, and we seek out leaders of peace in communities and invest time with them.

Look to God for Help

We look to God for help through a deep commitment to prayer.

> And he said to them, "The harvest is plentiful, but the laborers are few. Therefore pray earnestly to the Lord of the harvest to send out laborers into his harvest." (Luke 10:2)

Prayer involves intentionally listening to God; therefore our recruitment, staffing, and global workforce leaders spend a half day each month in community waiting on God for direction and asking him to touch the lives of those we serve through our recruitment efforts. Recruiters, team leaders, and the executive team pray for future recruits, for the events where we will present Wycliffe, and for the identification of leaders of peace as we enter communities to share the work of Wycliffe. As recruits are identified, we pray with and for them. We seek God's direction for strategies to engage them and their churches in the work.

Tell Others

We tell others what we see God doing as instructed by Christ before his ascension.

> But you will receive power when the Holy Spirit has come upon you, and you will be my witnesses in Jerusalem and in all Judea and Samaria, and to the end of the earth. (Acts 1:8)

We want to position our recruiters and speakers in as many strategic places in the US as possible, so they can be faithful witnesses in their areas of professional experience. This past year our staff shared 1,300 times in college classrooms, chapels, campus ministries at secular universities, and Perspectives on the World Christian Movement courses.

Throughout our history, Wycliffe staff members have had many opportunities to share in partner churches, but today those opportunities in churches are greatly reduced. We intentionally seek out strategic opportunities to share what we see God doing globally.

Seek Out Leaders of Peace

We seek out leaders of peace in communities and invest time with them by intentionally pursuing them and developing relationships of trust. Investing in key campus and ministry leaders enriches relationships and provides doorways for our staff to support local ministry outreaches. It also earns us the opportunity to open their eyes to what God is doing globally. Discovering these key leaders in different communities takes perseverance and commitment to knock on doors. "And if a son of peace is there, your peace will rest upon him. But if not, it will return to you" (Luke 10:6).

For example, we approach professors about discussing with their students the service opportunities we offer that align with their programs of study, such as intern, volunteer, and future vocational positions.

A *spirit of generosity* is demonstrated by giving away what God has generously supplied to us.

> The steps of a man are established by the Lord, when he delights in his way; though he fall, he shall not be cast headlong, for the Lord upholds his hand. I have been young, and now am old, yet I have not seen the righteous forsaken or his children begging for bread. He is ever lending generously, and his children become a blessing. (Ps 37:23–26)

Collaboration is our global context for engagement. We choose to do our work with others and not alone. Our joy is to share the talent, experience, and knowledge that God has invested in our people for his glory. In the US our staff members share their professional experiences and skills—accounting, medicine, aviation, international relations, linguistics, and Bible translation—with others considering service.

The range of experienced people needed in the work of Bible translation represents over 500 different roles. When the church is exposed to this reality, it's frequently eye-opening and helps communities begin to see that their skills are useful across the kingdom context. A distinguishing part of Christian generosity is a recognition that we are responding to a God who has lavished so much on us, so we will be a blessing for others. This is frequently evidenced when we redirect people who may not be a good fit for Wycliffe to other ministries who could use their skills. We pray that God would help people find a good fit for their skills in ministry opportunities.

A *commitment to do the work of the Great Commission together* means an intentional focus both internally (with other Global Alliance organizations) and externally as well, as the willingness to redirect people to other ministries mentioned above exemplifies. We recognize that Wycliffe has a portion of the Great Commission task given to the global church, but we cannot do it all, and God has raised up others to do their parts.

> But as it is, God arranged the members in the body, each one of them, as he chose. If all were a single member, where would the body be? As it is, there are many parts, yet one body. (1 Cor 12:18–20)

Internally, we have begun working more intentionally with our global partners to understand their long-term people needs and how God might resource them. Similarly, we are working closely with "supply" (sending) partners to understand where the resources are coming from for work in certain regions.

We recognize that different organizations are better able to provide different segments of the people resource needs into the Bible translation movement. We are also intentionally working to redirect resources to better-positioned partners to focus on other aspects of ministry work in the global body of Christ. We celebrate partners who have different and complementary skills and find ways to work closely with them rather than attempting to add those functions to our own organization.

Our partnerships with *Faith Comes By Hearing* and *Jesus Film Project* are examples of this intentionality in action. We have seconded people to these and other organizations, or worked intentionally to have Scriptures translated early so that the local church and these partners can create audio or video portions early in the projects.

Our methods have changed over time as our dependence on God and the principles in his Word have grown us. Our desire is that we are more in tune with God and the bride of Christ than at any time since our inception as an organization seventy-five years ago.

Jamie Farr is senior director of people engagement with Wycliffe Bible Translators (www.wycliffe.org).

CHAPTER 34

Camino Global

The Movement of the Global South
David D. Ruiz

In *Mission Under Scrutiny,* Andrew Kirk powerfully describes the major transition of the times in which we are living:

> Until the last two decades of the twentieth century, Western Christianity has been dominant. Mission has been seen largely as emanating from the West and having as its object the rest of the world. However, in a short period of time the situation has changed dramatically. The "Third Church" is making its presence felt, not least in the number of missionaries going to the original sending nations.[1]

This new reality is challenging the North Atlantic sending agencies to adapt and reinvent themselves in order to become relevant in a world that is different than that of their founding.

As a 127-year-old North American mission agency making the shift from regional to global, Camino Global faces this very challenge. We have sought the Lord's direction regarding a number of key transitional questions. What kind of mission does he want for such a time as this? What are the challenges ahead of us? What changes do we need to embrace in order to become full participants in this new era of missions, when the Global South is emerging with a vibrant church and a viable mission movement?

The emergence of COMIBAM (Ibero American Mission Cooperation) in 1984 infuses a dynamic missiological reflection from Latin America and an awareness of the important role the Global South church now plays in the missionary sending process. Since the first COMIBAM congress in Sao Paulo in 1987, thousands of missionaries have been sent from Latin

America to plant churches among the needy and most neglected people groups in more than sixty other countries. COMIBAM serves as a catalytic element connecting missiological reflection to the reality of the Latin American church, and increasingly connecting the Latin American church to the global church. COMIBAM is actively involved in the most important global forums and is working hard to share the contributions and lessons of the Latin American missions movement, especially among the emerging Majority World movements.

COMIBAM statistics show that the number of Ibero American missionaries has grown with the growth of the number of churches (www.comibam.org). "In 1982, 92 organizations sent a total of 1,120 Latin American missionaries to other parts of the world. Figures published in 1997 [during the Second Congress] indicated 3,921 Latin American missionaries."[2] "At the Third Congress [2006] it was revealed that there were almost 9,000 Latin American missionaries on the field sent by more than 400 agencies."[3] As COMIBAM prepares for its fourth Ibero American congress in Bogotá, some have said that the number of Ibero American missionaries serving globally today is more than 12,000.

Camino Global is optimistic about succeeding in this context of great change. Since our founding, we have pioneered neglected areas for the church in the evangelization process. We saw the needs of our Samaria when most of the Western church was looking at the ends of the earth. We confronted the status quo when we saw the need for the gospel in Central America, at a time when the organizers of the 1910 Edinburgh congress defined Latin America as an evangelized continent.[4] And, we challenged the church in North America to send its best disciples to undeveloped places to share the gospel and serve the people of Central America.

Now we have a new challenge ahead of us. We need to pray and seek to understand what kind of missional strategies and structures are needed to serve the growing church and mission movement among Spanish speakers. What do we need to do in order to move from regional to global in our scope? What challenges do our missionaries face in shifting from a pioneer mentality to becoming facilitators and catalysts of change, aligned with all that the Lord is doing among and within the Spanish-speaking church? What is the major challenge for us as a sending agency to become servants of the Spanish-speaking church worldwide?

"
*Serving the Church, Camino Global
will journey with Spanish speakers
everywhere to transform communities,
equip believers, and reach the world.*
"

Camino Global has made major advances in an intentional and transformational process, starting with organizational rebranding which sought not only to change our name but to review and refresh our vision. The process has aligned a new organizational structure and identity to respond to the major challenges and questions in this season of change. Our new vision is exciting and challenging: *Serving the Church, Camino Global will journey with Spanish speakers everywhere to transform communities, equip believers, and reach the world.* We understand that in such a moment as this, the Lord desires to use the Spanish-speaking church to make a deep impact in global evangelization, and we, as Camino Global, want to partner with them.

Camino uses the metaphor of a "cancha"[5] to explain and visualize its vision. The term *cancha* refers to a soccer field, and is a very popular and exciting word in Spanish, with roots in the Quechua culture and language. It is defined by the *Real Academia Española* (RAE) as a "playground for the practice of certain sports or events." The RAE goes beyond this basic description of the word by conceptualizing what it means to "be on the cancha" or "be in the field" with the purpose of being prepared and trained to carry out a particular action.

Cancha is an interesting term in the context of America, because it causes our thoughts to focus on the fun we experience when playing football (real football), whether in a formal or improvised field, and the memories we Latinos create in our childhood. The cancha is a meeting place that provides us with a great deal of fun, but also team building, improvement of skills, and fellowship together.

For Camino Global, our ministry fields now become canchas. These canchas are the playing fields where our diverse teams and missionaries carry out a variety of strategies, activities, and ministries to score goals together (fulfill our mission) and defend our goal (work together to defend our focus of ministry).

Where we must score goals is prescribed by our mission statement. As a team, we work in collaboration to "make disciples of Jesus Christ, serving among and with Spanish speakers globally." All that we are and everything we do focuses on this goal. Reproducing disciples of Jesus Christ, among and with Spanish speakers, is the measure of success of our ministry together.

While a team must score goals, another important aspect of teamwork on the cancha is defense. For Camino, this part of the ministry is defined by all that we do as a team, in collaboration with our partners, to constantly evaluate what we are doing and how we do it. This helps us ensure our first priority of serving the church and, secondly, of executing our vision focused on transforming communities, equipping believers, and reaching the world, serving among and with Spanish speakers everywhere.

If the endlines of our cancha represent mission and vision, the sidelines frame our core values and organizational culture. As on the soccer field, one side belongs to our home team: our coaches, assistants, and all of Camino's structure and services. They help us in every possible way to remain on the cancha, to stay in the game with the right attitude and a clear strategy to score goals. In this metaphor, this home-team side of the field is represented by our organizational core values of Christlikeness, community, collaboration, compassion, and creativity. These values remind us who we are, what our identity is, and our commitment to behave according to those values when we are playing on the cancha.

The other sideline represents the "opposing" team. These are the fans and the public who are watching how we are playing, trying to understand our strategy and how we plan to win the game. This side is represented by the organizational culture which permeates every player on the team. These are the characteristics that we hope the people we serve will see in us. In living this out on the playing field, we seek to serve others as connecters, facilitators, modelers, and catalyzers of disciplemaking ministry.

We understand that these four elements (mission, vision, core values, and permeating culture) frame our cancha, and that in order to be part of the game we must respect these limits. At the same time, we don't see this framework as limiting. On the contrary, the clarity it affords creates a wide-open space for innovation and collaboration in the context of unity and teamwork.

When thinking in terms of Camino's cancha, we recognize that there are rules to observe, the commitments required of each team member, and a responsibility to work effectively as a team during the game. There are no individual players or stars in our teams. Only a united and well-trained team is capable of making goals. The Camino cancha is defined as teams with ministerial clarity, working collaboratively to achieve the goal of making disciples of Jesus Christ among and with Spanish speakers everywhere.

Camino Global's desire, for such a time as this, is to facilitate a *journey with Spanish speakers.* We want to join hands with them *to transform the world.* We understand that this is a time when the Lord wants to use the Spanish-speaking church to make a deep impact in world evangelization. It is a time when the Lord is calling the church in Latin America to do something significant with the great blessings he has poured out among our people.

Camino Global is working hard to partner with the Spanish-speaking church globally, looking for opportunities to serve the Latino church to become missional and effective in transforming not only its own local context, but also to effectively evangelize the world. We want to serve the Latin missions movement to become even more effective and to walk alongside them in their journey to the ends of the earth.

David D. Ruiz is the global consultant for the president of Camino Global (www.caminoglobal.org).

Notes

[1] Andrew J. Kirk, *Mission Under Scrutiny: Confronting Contemporary Challenges.* (London: Fortress, 2006), 157.

[2] Samuel E. Escobar, *Changing Tides: Latin America and World Mission Today* (Maryknoll, NY: Orbis: 2002), 160

[3] Samuel E. Escobar, report on COMIBAM 2006, [unpublished] "En este Tercer Congreso se afirmó que hay casi 9,000 misioneros latinoamericanos en el campo enviados por más de 400 agencias."

[4] Arturo Piedra, *Evangelización Protestante en América Latina* (Quito: CLAI, 2000).

[5] *Cancha* is a Quechua word defined by the *Real Academia Española* as a venue for sport and spectacles, commonly known as the place where soccer contests happen.

CHAPTER 35

Greater Europe Mission (GEM)

Mobilizing TCKs/MKs

Becca Martin

Binders clank open and closed, backpacks zip up and down, and pencils tap repeatedly as students anxiously anticipate a "normal" first day of school. The second generation Filipino-Austrian defends his favorite football team while the Dutch student, son of a businessman, flings his arms around as he describes the latest Lego video he is creating. Across the aisle, the American missionary kid fills a friend in on the different churches her family visited over the summer, and the Pakistani diplomat boy raves about his family vacation.

While at a glance, these sixth grade math students all appear quite different, they all bond quickly and have something in common, even with the new kids. This commonality I discovered was their shared experience of being third-culture kids.

The students in my classroom at the International Christian School of Vienna (ICSV) represented over fifty different countries over the five years I taught secondary mathematics classes. They came from all different religious backgrounds, time frames for being in Austria, and reasons for studying at our school. Yet, the majority of them fit the category of third-culture kids, or TCKs.

David C. Pollock wrote this definition of a TCK:

An individual, who, having spent a significant part of the developmental years in a culture other than the parents' culture, develops a sense of relationship to all of the cultures, while not having full ownership in any. Elements from each culture are incorporated into the life experience, but the sense of belonging is in relationship to others of similar experience. [1]

I began to learn this definition was the common thread of many of my students. While they held such a variety of passports, many of them did not connect with those respective countries as "home," but also did not necessarily totally fit in or feel at home in Austria. They connected with each other over the shared experience of their own mixed third cultures. Most knew what it is like to be the new kid, and, in general, were open and welcoming to other new students, of which we had many throughout the year. I loved getting to know each of them, their stories, how they learned math in their previous schools, and especially their understanding of God. In my training for and teaching at ICSV, I gradually learned general traits about TCKs and ways to encourage them, as well as topics to tread lightly in. At the same time, I continued to recognize that each student had individual needs, personalities, strengths, and weaknesses.

As the church desires to mobilize the next generation, we must wisely consider the TCKs of the world, and specifically those who grew up as missionary kids, or MKs. Growing up as a TCK, specifically an MK, whom we will focus most closely on here, comes with unique traits that equip one to be an excellent missionary, but these traits must be fostered. MKs can suffer under the weight of generalizations, and I want to emphasize the fact that each one of them, even within the same family, is unique. However, as the church seeks to encourage MKs to serve the Lord wherever he may call, let us look at some general characteristics about them that can help us walk with them well.

Benefits and Challenges of the Missionary Kid

Growing up as a missionary kid abounds with benefits. From the Association of Christian School International's prefield orientation for teachers, Dan Egeler listed several of these strengths and benefits: [2]

MKs are often . . .
- Independent
- Confident in change
- Entering relationships at a deeper level
- Exhibiting empathy for others
- Highly skilled cross-culturally
- Motivated to make a difference

MKs can make great future missionaries with these strengths, especially being able to navigate different cultures, often speaking at least one other

> **❝** As the church desires to mobilize the next generation, we must wisely consider the TCKs of the world, and specifically those who grew up as missionary kids, or MKs. **❞**

language, and having seen models of full-time ministry. With these traits, adult MKs often naturally seek opportunities to work/serve where they grew up or in a new international location.

One Greater Europe Mission missionary, Melanie Simmerman, grew up in the Middle East and described her own journey this way:

> As a kid I never had any interest in being in missions. I always knew though that whatever I did with my life, it had to be in the international realm somehow. Part of what it means to be an MK (to me at least and many MK friends of mine) is dissatisfaction with doing what everyone else is doing. I've always felt the need to have my finger on the global pulse, and never wanted to be tucked away somewhere remote, not engaged with the rest of the world and their concerns. In the end though, I accepted this as an admirable life calling because I watched my parents pursue it with perseverance and integrity for over two decades. They loved people, gave generously, and invested themselves entirely in a new people.

With the great benefits of living cross-culturally, MKs experience unique challenges as well. As Melanie alluded to, MKs often have a sense of restlessness. Some long for deep roots, a place that actually could be "home," but most of my students said they would choose moving every three years over being in one place for the majority of their lives.

MKs can come off as arrogant or frustrated with people's supposed ignorance. Surface-level relationships or small talk can annoy or stress many of them, sometimes from lack of knowledge of pop culture or cultural norms or simply a longing for deeper relationships. However, seemingly contradictory, going deep into a relationship can be hard because of all the goodbyes they say. By the time MKs reach adulthood, most have said goodbye to more friends and family than the average person would have in an entire lifetime. As individuals and the church, let us walk alongside them, encouraging and maximizing these benefits, while being sensitive to the challenges they face.

The Church's Role

As the church seeks to serve, disciple, and mobilize MKs, we must remember that relationship is fundamental. Our end goal is not more missionaries, but authentic discipleship and community that will multiply to see God glorified. Here are some helpful tips I have gleaned in seeking to develop such relationships:

Do Not Put Missionaries on Pedestals

Be careful not to elevate MKs or their parents. They want to be part of the congregation and not feel undue pressure to be perfect or extraordinary. There is no need to overemphasize growing up in a foreign country, but generally treat them as you would other kids.

Seek Out People Who Can Be A Personal Connection

Find peers and mentors from within the church who will connect with them, especially when they are back on home assignment or in your area attending university. Offer mentors who can help MKs tap into the gifts God has given them and guide them as they seek where God is leading them. Remind them that other career paths besides full-time ministry are not less important, again removing that pedestal mentality. I believe it is quite strategic to mobilize the next generation of MKs who individually feel called into global missions, but first helping them discern if that is their calling rather than just a default. If there are adult missionary kids or other international workers within the church that can connect with MKs, that would be ideal, but not essential.

I have recognized, as I am now currently working as a regional mobilizer in the United States for Greater Europe Mission, a unique connection with MKs when I am visiting universities. When I recognize the high school name an MK attended or describe ICSV, a sense of understanding grows between us, just like the students in my classroom seemed to have with each other. Internationals are drawn to other internationals even if they are technically living in their passport country. Among these students I have met, some are eager to serve, some want to help mobilize, some just want to blend in as a normal student, and some simply want to share stories with someone who at least somewhat "gets them." If there are not other internationals in the church, another great option is to connect them with someone who has been on a short-term team and served alongside or in the country of their family.

Be Listeners

Whether you have lived abroad or not, showing you care by listening goes a long way. Try to avoid making assumptions or ignorant comments about their life, but do genuinely ask questions to get to know them. Ask what they like to do in their free time, about their school, or fun, random questions, while recognizing a few questions, like "Where are you from?" might require a more complicated answer for MKs than for most.

Create Opportunities for Community and Service

Community is essential for an MK, as it is for all of us. Whether on home assignment or on the field, MKs long for the opportunity to be a part of their own community. One thing that Greater Europe Mission has done well is coined the term *GEMk*. These missionary kids have a community they know they belong to. GEMks have their own retreats in the winter and summer, along with other special chances for connections. Beyond connecting with kids in their own mission, I have personally observed the joys and benefits of MKs serving together on short-term mission trips across Europe. Through serving together, they can connect with peers, see new types of ministry, and have leaders pour into them as they explore more of God's heart for the nations and their role in it. Many missionaries point back to pivotal experiences they had while on short-term mission trips that led them to the field longer term. Short-term trips expose kids, whether in your local church or MKs, to new cultures and provide opportunities for discipleship and leadership development. Better yet, missionaries on the field can be encouraged and impacted by these teams. What if your MKs could join the high school mission team sent from your church, or the team came to their country to serve with them?

These intentional relationships, whether through mentors, short-term teams, or otherwise, will help anchor MKs to their own connections to the local church, rather than just knowing a few "friends of their parents." This personal connection will be helpful no matter where the MK may work or serve in the future, but especially in the case of needing to personally raise support for full-time ministry. They can then go beyond the notion of "You have given to my parents. Can you add more and give to me?" Provide opportunities to equip them to raise their own support and train them for their unique ministry, instead of assuming they learned everything from their parents. Yes, they will have a greater understanding of crossing cultures, but just as everyone needs training in our unique field of work and ministry, they need it as well.

Ultimately, what a joy it is to see more and more globally minded Christians in our churches living out the disciplines of going, sending, welcoming, mobilizing, and praying. Let us encourage those in our church, whether they live in our town or in a foreign country, to find their role in seeing God's kingdom come. Let us raise them up first and foremost to find their identity as a child of God, a citizen of heaven, and one who is unconditionally loved by the Father. Out of that identity, may the church encourage and guide all third culture kids to live for his glory as they use their unique gifts, experiences, and personalities to impact the nations with the hope of the gospel.

Becca Martin is a regional mobilizer for Greater Europe Mission (GEM) (www.gemission.org) in Wheaton, IL.

Notes

[1] David C. Pollock and Ruth E. Van Reken, *Third Culture Kids: Growing Up Among Worlds* (Boston: Nicholas Brealey, 1999, 2001, 2009).

[2] Association of Christian School International's prefield orientation for teachers, Dan Egeler, www.acsi.org.

Connecting to the Pipeline

At a recent mission conference, I was approached by a very bright young missionary candidate. She was interviewing all the different missionary sending agencies and had an incredible list of questions. As soon as we finished our discussion, I asked if I could include a copy of her list in *Pipeline*, to which she agreed. As you meet with your mobilization team to discuss your partnership with a sending agency, these questions should help guide your decisions and interactions with future partners:

- What is your mission statement?
- What is your doctrinal statement / distinctives / foundations?
- How do you go about ministry / What does an ordinary day look like?
- What are your strengths as an organization?
- What are the goals you are working on this year?
- What kind of training do you offer and/or require?
- What is your retention rate / attrition rate?
- Describe your missionary care emphasis?
- Do you have a family support system?
- What are your lifestyle expectations?
- What is your philosophy of support raising?
- What are the administrative fees / percentage?
- What does your retirement savings plan look like?
- How do you partner with the local church here in North America?
- What is your mode of operation concerning women in ministry leadership?
- What is your practice regarding locals taking responsibility of ministry?
- Are you open to different nationalities on your team / staff / membership?
- What is your strategy for contextualization?
- Where do your missionaries live: missionary compound, among the nationals, virtual / commuting?

Part 6

Special Partners: Linking the Church and Agency

Besides the missionary sending agencies, there are other parachurch organizations that exist to help churches, leaders, and missionary candidates be the best they can be. They often stand in the gap that exists between churches and agencies to make sure our missionaries are well equipped, trained, and sent. Some offer in-house training while others offer off-sight coaching, depending on the needs of the organization and individuals.

The book of Proverbs says this many times and in many ways: "Without counsel plans fail, but with many advisers they succeed" (Prov 15:22). These "advisers" you are about to meet have already learned hard lessons over many years, and they are presented here so that you do not have to relearn hard lessons.

CHAPTER 36

Advance Global Coaching

What if Missionaries had a Life Coach?

Sherri Dodd

Advance Global Coaching has been serving missionaries and those who send them for over ten years across more than forty-five countries. We started with an idea and have grown into a full-fledged mission coaching organization. But we didn't start off that way.

After serving twenty-two years as cross-cultural missionaries, my husband and I returned to Georgia to be with our aging parents. During my years in Europe, I saw many missionaries leave early. Most of them were sincere, called, and talented, but there simply was not enough emotional and spiritual support for the challenges of cross-cultural living.

In 2002 I first heard the term "life coach." As a champion of people, I resonated with the concept. I thought, "Wouldn't it be great if missionaries had a life coach?" That is when God planted the seed for Advance Global Coaching in my heart.

I went into sixteen months of private training to become a life coach. I began coaching friends and people I met in my speaking ministry, but my heart was always for missionaries. Knowing what it was like to leave home, family, and friends, to struggle with language learning and cultural adaptation, I felt coaching could make a meaningful difference.

Understanding the loneliness that missionaries face, the challenges of getting along with people of different personalities and ideologies, and the pressure to "perform" in order to be "worth" the financial support, I felt repeatedly compelled to do something. Having felt the upheaval of international moves and the sorrows of loving people and having them leave you, I wanted to put my "care for missionaries" into action.

Feeling a bit like Moses, with a task far bigger than myself, I told God all the reasons he had the wrong person for this job. After wrestling with God for about four years, I surrendered to his will and, in January 2007, started an organization providing professional life coaching for the missions community.

My vision included a team of coaches setting a standard of excellence in coaching and advancing God's kingdom around the globe. In order to do that, I went back to school and started over with professional life coach training and acquired credentials with the International Coach Federation. In addition to that, I completed a two-year master's program for ministry leaders to lay a solid foundation for AGC. First I developed a prayer strategy for the whole organization. Then I created and executed a year-long pro bono research project where I coached four new missionaries, always learning more about what our next steps should be.

Today Advance Global Coaching is over ten years old and growing. We have a team of professionally trained and credentialed coaches. Each one has significant cross-cultural experience and a heart for missionaries and the challenges they face. We passionately provide a safe, objective place for missionaries to continue to grow personally, no matter where they are in their season of service.

We meet with our missionary clients on a regular basis via telephone or internet, utilizing whatever works best in the area where the missionary lives. The missionary sets the goals for the coaching season and brings the topic of their choosing to each of the scheduled calls. So we are always focused on what is relevant for the missionary's life, growth, family, or ministry. We engage the missionary on a deep level. We encourage, challenge, question, and explore to produce a different way of thinking about their current circumstances. At the end of each call, the client comes up with their own action steps to work on in between coaching calls.

To date, AGC has assisted cross-cultural workers serving with many varied organizations in over forty-five different countries. We partner with sending churches and sending agencies, helping them achieve their goals of developing staff and then providing support for those workers they send out. Most organizations give or require some form of training up-front, and many provide counseling if a missionary faces a severe crisis. But in between training and what I call "the ditch," missionaries are basically struggling without much intentional ongoing support of any kind. AGC was formed to help fill this gap.

> We desire that future generations of missionaries will not only be intentional about their personal growth, but will affect others in a healthy way through a coach approach to ministry.

One of our best partnerships to date is with North Point Community Church, where Andy Stanley is the pastor. Since 2010, AGC has been coaching all the new missionaries that North Point's globalX department has sent overseas. We also have done some coaching for missionaries who were already on the field and some returning ones. North Point is a church that truly invests in those they send. "It is the best money we spend on our missionaries," says Jim Erickson, director of equipping at globalX.

We would one day like to have a team of sixty to one hundred life coaches and see coaching become "the norm" in missions. We desire that future generations of missionaries will not only be intentional about their personal growth, but will affect others in a healthy way through a coach approach to ministry. In order to accomplish this goal we will need to find more sending churches and agencies as partners, grow our funding base, and continue to connect with missionaries around the world. We are adding to our coaching staff as the client load increases.

Who Does AGC Serve and What Are Some Common Topics?

Missionary candidates—fundraising, preparation for the field, and healthy deployment

New missionaries—transition, cultural adjustment, language acquisition, and ministry development

Established missionaries—life balance, team dynamics, and ministry effectiveness

Returning missionaries—reentry, renewal, and future direction

Mission pastors and mission board staff—personal growth, life balance, and strategy

College-aged missionary kids—Transition and adjustment to college life

What are some of the benefits missionaries experience having a coach?

1. Hearing positive feedback and encouragement

2. Being challenged to grow

3. Receiving objective input

4. Being held accountable to take action steps toward their goals

5. Having regular contact with someone who cares for their well-being

6. Processing experiences in a safe, confidential environment

7. Learning coaching skills to enhance their ministries

8. Living more intentionally

9. Managing time better

10. Dealing with conflict better

11. Asking more questions that lead to self-discovery

12. Asking more questions of others instead of telling them what to do

13. Understanding personal goals better

14. Defining their God-given purpose

15. Being more effective in evangelism and discipleship

Testimonies from AGC Clients

From New Workers

Coaching has given me better tools and skills to work effectively with my spouse in our new roles together.

Coaching alleviated my sense of "aloneness" and gave me community and fellowship as I transitioned from familiar to unknown. My coach offered strength and encouragement to lean into the call.

Coaching gave me perspective on myself and my roles that allowed me to grow in ways I had never thought possible. I faced significant challenges and overcame them and was able to walk through major life transition with greater confidence and peace.

Our AGC coach helped us deal with the pressures of foreign culture, team relationships, and marriage in a new context. We were much better missionaries and team members because of our coach.

From Established Workers

Coaching has given me an objective sounding board. I haven't really had a "safe" place where I could discuss things openly, so I'm extremely grateful!

Coaching helped me tackle issues in my life that I knew needed to be dealt with, but I continually put off. Dealing with them has made me more confident in my walk with the Lord.

Having a coach was an invaluable resource to help me process through my options. In addition to the personal effect that coaching has had on my life, decisions, and character, it has also helped to prepare me for the future.

Coaching gave me hope when I had run out of hope and provided practical steps to take so that I could move into the future with a positive outlook.

From Returning Workers

Upon entering the mission field, it's easy to have unrealistic expectations. Without the perspective I received from coaching, I would be leaving feeling like a failure.

Meeting with my coach has helped me finish my service in my second homeland well, and work through the process of returning well to my first homeland. What a blessing it was knowing that my coach was walking with me on this challenging journey and praying for me.

Coaching helped normalize the experiences I was having as part of reverse culture shock so I could effectively recognize and deal with them.

Advance Global Coaching exists to help sending churches and mission agencies do a better job providing the support necessary for missionaries to thrive—not just survive—on the field.

Sherri Dodd is founder, chief executive officer, and Christian life coach with Advance Global Coaching (www.AdvanceGlobalCoaching.com), which helps churches build resiliency in their missionaries. You can email her at Sherri@AdvanceGlobalCoaching.com.

CHAPTER 37

Center for Intercultural Training (CIT)

Through the Lens of Partnership

Mark Morgenstern

For almost two years I've been a member of the team at Center for Intercultural Training (CIT). My role is director of CIT Next, our new effort at providing ongoing training and development opportunities to the thousands of CIT alumni who have benefited from our prefield training programs over the last nineteen years. Before filling this role, I enjoyed thirteen years as a church planter in Russia and Ukraine followed by nine years as the training director of a denominational mission. Being a newcomer on the CIT team has given me the opportunity to experience, in word and deed, their deepest beliefs and commitments.

The 1980s and 1990s introduced the North American missions community to the concept and commitment to purposeful prefield training for missionaries. Newer training approaches dispensed with the assumption that all missionaries would receive their primary preparation through formal academic biblical education. Most concluded that topics like culture and contextualization, spiritual warfare, teamwork, and cross-cultural living would be more effectively embraced and enacted through focused and intensive training programs of one to fifteen weeks in length. CIT stands in this tradition and embraces these assumptions. And we've built upon this shared foundation with some commitments of our own.

Partnership

The CIT should, first and foremost, be understood through the lens of *partnership*. We are foundationally committed to ministry in cooperation

It is a beautiful thing when the sending entity and the training organization work together to move an individual toward healthy and fruitful service.

with those who are sending out cross-cultural workers. We view the *senders* as our clients, not just the sent. Our one-week, two-week, and four-week residential training programs provide intense learning opportunities. We explore topics that can become very personal and "rock your world." Missionary appointees are challenged in thought, in heart, and in action. During this process many deeply hidden realities about an individual can surface, and it is a beautiful thing when the sending entity and the training organization work together to move an individual toward healthy and fruitful service. Though messy at times, CIT is committed to that kind of collaboration.

In both philosophy and practice, CIT runs as a partnership. The facilities and facilitation team, the resources to operate, the efforts to get the word out about CIT, and the visionary direction of the ministry are all provided through a cooperative effort of partnering organizations. As of 2017 we currently have fourteen partners. It's possible to be relational and deep with our participants and our partnering organizations because the CIT team models the things we teach and lives them out during our training events both informally and formally. Our team is top of the line "been there, done that" qualified. We are cross-cultural ministry practitioners, not academics and not therapists.

Center for Intercultural Training offers three distinct stand-alone, yet integrated, prefield training programs:

1. Equipping for Cross-cultural Life and Ministry (four weeks)
2. Second-language Acquisition for laying a groundwork of language learning skills and perspectives (two weeks)
3. Engage Retreat for exploring and putting into practice spiritual growth processes (one week)

While these three learning modules are conceptually fully integrated with each other, they are offered at CIT in an à la carte manner with an aim to best meet the needs of the various sending entities and their missionaries.

Integration

That said, integration is the second foundational strength of the ministry of CIT.

Who God is,

who people are,

who I am, and

what God is doing (with me or without me)

are core realities that impact every conversation, every ministry model that is proposed, every lecture about cultural contextualization or language learning methodologies, and every game, simulation, or observation activity that takes place at CIT. Being a healthy missionary and being a fruitful missionary are two inseparable realities. We really believe that! There is no silver bullet strategy or methodology that will guarantee fruitful missionary service. Rather, when one's heart is right before the Lord, knowing and experiencing how these four realities of the universe harmonize with each other, a cross-cultural worker will be on the pathway to growing into and being a productive fisher of men (Matt 4:19).

Specialization, Stability, and Commitment

Specialization, stability, and commitment to the task of missionary preparation is a third reality that is lived out at CIT. Although most of our faculty could still serve on the field ourselves, those on our team have chosen the long-term role of missionary training as an ongoing commitment and embrace this role as a passion. We are constantly learning ourselves and refining how we talk about contextualization and ministry methods in light of the changing world around us. And we do that while maintaining strong roots in classic, unchangeable biblical concepts of missiology.

During 2017 we will be blessed to build into the lives of over 200 adults and over seventy-five children who are being sent out by God and the church into cross-cultural life and ministry. Most of them will come to us by requirement of a missionary sending organization. A few are being sent to the field directly by a local church and some by a denominational entity. On occasion a local church will send an individual to us for training even though the sending agency is not requiring CIT participation. The organizations we work with are willing to "outsource" the prefield training piece of what they provide to their workers. Most do so because they realize that the specialized service provider is a wise option for balancing cost, quality, and timeliness of training. While many organizations we serve are small to medium-sized, a few (United World Mission, SIM, and Greater Europe Mission) are on the larger side and could attempt to provide training themselves, but realize there is an advantage to entrusting this piece to CIT.

While there are a few parts of the missionary preparation process that CIT and other training organization play very well, there are many others that can best be accomplished by the church. The church uniquely brings to the table a relationship with the future missionary of longevity and trust. The church is the place where faith is matured in the context of real life within a multigenerational community of diverse life stories and giftings from God. In the context of church, an individual feeling a call from God to cross-cultural ministry has many opportunities to confirm that call, prepare for fulfilling that call, and be encouraged by a church family to boldly pursue the call. These essentials are not practically possible in the context of the missionary training organization.

The church is the right place for spiritual formation to take place, over time, in the context of an ongoing, loving community. Although CIT can help put some measures into place to help a missionary to continue and accelerate spiritual growth once leaving the "nest" of a comfortable home culture experience, we can't generate that momentum if it is not already there.

Although I've spent the last twenty-five years with "missionary" as the blank that I fill in for occupation on my tax returns, the real work of forming who I am happened long before I filled out an application to join a sending agency. It even happened long before I ever attended my first seminary course or attended a ministry training workshop or conference that I was sent to by my agency. Development took place through ministry successes and often ministry failures. I was blessed to grow up in a church that robustly embraced the concept of every individual being an essential member of the body of Christ. The real foundations of my Matthew 4:19 experience of following Jesus and being on mission with him began with the rich training that was provided me as a child, youth, and young adult through many ministry experiences with my home church.

The biggest challenge that is faced by a training organization like CIT is the disparity between an individual's felt need for cross-cultural ministry training when showing up on the first day of a training program and the more accurate perception of need felt by the same individual when leaving on the last day of the program. Many come to training saying "I'm not sure why I'm here," but nobody ever leaves CIT saying "Wow, that was a real waste of my time and money!" The maxim "you don't know what you don't know" is accurate. And overcoming this challenge is where trusted communities come in. As we build into our up-and-coming missionaries, we earn their trust and they'll take us at our word when we say, "This training's going to be good for you, trust me. You'll understand after you've been there awhile."

Today as I'm writing these words, a familiar sound has reminded me of another email arriving to my inbox. This time the chime heralds a prayer reminder from JR, a recent participant in the language learning program at CIT. She's been in Germany just three months, and each time I read her Facebook posts and send up a short prayer of thanks or petition, I'm reminded of the encouraging example that I see in her life and story. The church, the sending agency, and CIT are working together to build into the life of an individual who is fruitfully, with health and humility, following Jesus into the calling he has for her.

Mark Morgenstern is the senior director of Grow2Serve (www.grow2serve. com), a ministry that aids missionary development through the use of current training technologies and methodologies. Currently Mark is on loan to Center for Intercultural Training, developing new ongoing distance learning programs for CIT Next.

CHAPTER 38

Mission Training International (MTI)

Lovers, Learners, and Servants

Steve Sweatman

Jesus clearly asks all of us who follow him to join him on his mission. We are to be missional. Of these truly missional followers, the Spirit sets aside some to cross cultures to make disciples "to the ends of the earth." If they obey, their assignment is one of the loneliest, most stressful vocations ever endeavored.

Perhaps this lonely, stressful vocational assignment is why our Master Jesus would, in essence, encourage these cross-cultural messengers through Scripture to slow down. Let's plan and see if we have the right material to complete this. Let's face the harsh realities and the vulnerabilities. Let's figure out how not to take our wrong cultural views of God overseas, and stay on target with the most effective tool for My Commission—your love for one another. Please never forget that I will be with you the whole time, so come to me to have life, especially when you are weary.

Could it be that in our attempt to awaken a missionally slumbering church, we are unwittingly neglecting the Master's wisdom of *how to* "equip the saints for the work" (Eph 4:12) and "send them on their journey in a manner worthy of God" (3 John 6)?

Those of us who confirm, send, prepare, or support these cross-cultural messengers would benefit greatly by searching the Scriptures *for how God has "sent" messengers* for centuries. Here are two that should be first considered in order to create an honest exploration of the pipeline of which we are each a part:

Desire without knowledge is not good, and whoever makes haste with his feet misses his way. (Prov 19:2)

The hasty feet is sinning (Philip's Literal Translation)

The one who acts hastily sins (Holman Christian Standard)

The one who moves too hurriedly misses the way (New Revised Standard Version)

Haste makes waste (The Message)

Any worthwhile pipeline review will first shed the frenetic pace endemic to the current culture of missions and return to the *wisdom of slow.*

> Which of you, desiring to build a tower, does not first sit down and count the cost, whether he has enough to complete it? Otherwise, when he has laid a foundation and is not able to finish, all who see it begin to mock him, saying, "This man began to build and was not able to finish." (Luke 14:28–30)

Exploring the pipeline also requires that we *first sit down,* turning our attention to the actual desired "end" and what materials are required to complete that end—*count the cost.* This flies in the face of a marketing missions culture which unintentionally conveys "Get building, go, build . . . It's better to burn out for Jesus than it is to sit there and rust out."

If we truly slow down, sit down, and consider the cost with completion in mind, we can now consider scriptural concepts like these:

- Are we willing to be like the early church, turning people away for a period of maturing, even though they have a clear conversion, a clear calling to cross cultures, and great training, yet are lacking in the area of loving one another? (Acts 9:1–31)
- Are we willing to be like the early church, initiating a time of prayer, asking the Spirit, "Who do you want set apart to send to other cultures?" rather being consumed with ferreting out which self-appointed volunteers should go? (Acts 13:2)
- Are we willing to state the harsh realities head-on like God does, so that people know what they are signing up for? (Matt 10:16–25 and Jer 12:5)
- Are we considering the leadership preoccupation and other cultural values of the US that if we unwittingly exported would make others "twice as much a child of hell"? (Matt 23:15)
- Are we committed to sending relational support along with our financial support and to offering hospitality of the highest caliber? (2 Cor 7:5–7 and 3 John 5–8)

" Any worthwhile pipeline review will first shed the frenetic pace endemic to the current culture of missions and return to the *wisdom of slow.* **"**

Borrowing terms from the business world, Jesus' mission for us could be deemed as a "fully integrated global supply chain"—a "pipeline," if you will, that has both disciples as the precious commodity and the infrastructure to distribute and replicate disciples around the globe.

Each year at Mission Training International (MTI), we have the joy of training and debriefing the 1,200 missional Jesus-followers who are sent to us. Our role in the pipeline is to prepare your cross-cultural messengers before they go, honing their character and equipping them with skills that have been known to make or break cross-cultural messengers of the gospel of Jesus (this program is called Compass). We also receive them back when they visit the US between cross-cultural assignments for a time of confidential debriefing and personal renewal (DAR—Debriefing and Renewal).

MTI was founded in 1954 by an Irish missionary to China who observed that sending agency pipelines had started to wrongly over-focus on issues that were not directly related to cross-cultural effectiveness. MTI continues to play a vital role in the Great Commission pipeline with more than thirty thousand alumni around the globe. Many attribute their cross-cultural effectiveness, endurance, and personal vitality to the things they learned at MTI.

Since our founding, trainers and debriefers have all been veteran cross-cultural messengers who have pioneered highly practical, family-based, community-enhanced, experiential and reflective residential programs where the ratio of staff to trainee is about one to three.

From our vantage point there are so many things that are encouraging about the disciples we encounter in the US—the ones you are putting into Jesus' pipeline of cross-cultural work. Those going are clearly doing so of their free will. They are also action-oriented, willing to sacrifice the comforts of home, and armed with great compassion for those suffering without Christ.

Yet, we have some sobering observations about various US pipelines that might cause us all to pause and revisit some of our pipeline issues.

There is no way to sugarcoat this: as we survey the US based cross-cultural pipelines, it seems to us that there are certain trends in our "industry":

MISSIONS CULTURE: Processes that quickly gloss over the work's lonely, stressful realities

HARSH CONTEXT: Seems different than the others: simple reality with no indictment

THOSE GOING: Naively zealous, less-resilient, gospel-vague, low-Bible-thirsty messengers

THOSE CONFIRMING and SENDING: Never-been-there idealist

THOSE PREPARING: Trained using wasted-effort methodologies and low-priority topics

THOSE SUPPORTING: Few sanctuaries of understanding: caring communities in the relationally lonely desert of missions; those listeners who can help them make sense of the inevitable soul fog in their first assignment

What can be done about these disconcerting trends? I am not sure this is the venue to address each one, yet it may be beneficial for us to succinctly communicate to you, as a local church, those goers whom we find are the most *effective, enduring,* and *full of vitality.*

At MTI, we have a unique vantage point of how it really plays out on the field, as we do just as many confidential personal debriefings as prefield trainings. Although we could recount to you thousands of stories of those who painfully fell out of the pipeline, we are refreshingly asked this question by churches, mission pastors, and sending agencies: "Given all the confidential debriefings with hundreds each year over 63 years, surely you've seen the traits of those who do well in this cross-cultural ministry. Can you tell us what you are seeing?" Our answer:

Those who did well entered the pipeline as clearly experienced *lovers, learners,* and *servants,* who were *already bearing fruit* in the US in the same vocational platform they were targeting overseas.

Lovers

The mark of a true Jesus-following disciple is that they are known by their love for others. This hallmark characteristic, which shines best in the face of differences and conflicts, lets the lost of the target culture learn of God's Son who was sent to rescue them. Lovers of God are known for saying, "search me, Father, and find if there are ways in which I can love better. I know this is what pleases you most and I'm willing to change." Lovers depend daily on receiving

God's love as they convey, "thank you, Father, for your compassionate touch as I live in a fallen world that hurts me, and for your steadfast lovingkindness toward me even when I fall short of loving others as you do."

Learners

True learners have a deep reservoir of fascination, curiosity, and hope for the people group God has assigned them. Learners are known for saying, "Father, teach me how to exit my world and enter someone else's, just like you did when you came to earth. I'm willing to empty myself and sacrificially learn through my mistakes, even if it takes a million of them."

Servants

You don't know if you are a servant until you are treated like one. True servants do not need accolades, authority, or advantage and will be reluctant to accept praise, control over others, or extra benefits. They enjoy serving behind the scenes, knowing they have a Master who sees them and who consistently cares for the well-being of his servants. They seek the applause of heaven and are willing to obey blindly in areas that are countercultural or counterintuitive—like his command for regular times to cease striving, relinquish desired outcomes, and rest. A servant can be heard frequently saying, "Father, help" or "Spirit, I need your guidance" or "I want to know your will: nothing more, nothing less, nothing else, because otherwise my efforts are completely wasted."

Already Bearing Kingdom Fruit Vocationally

Although there are rare exceptions, we notice that those who already bear kingdom fruit in their targeted vocational platform have a much higher success rate for bearing future kingdom fruit, despite the loneliness and stress of crossing cultures. It continues to baffle us why people are allowed to enter a vocation for which they have no experience, let alone fruit, with the expectation that somehow the harshest of environments is the best place to plant the seed of one's new vocation.

For true disciples of Jesus, being missional is our clear mandate. For some disciples, they are given the assignment to cross cultures with the message of Jesus' love. For other disciples, like us who send and train, I trust that in our obedient slowing down, sitting down together as we are doing in this book, and counting the cost, that God will teach us how we can equip these saints for all good works.

Steve Sweatman is president and CEO of Mission Training International (www.mti.org).

CHAPTER 39

TRAIN International

Born out of Prayer

Brian Gibson

Nothing of consequence happens without prayer.—Charles Finney
Unless the Lord builds the house, those who build it labor in vain. Psalm 127:1

The story of how the ministry of TRAIN International came to be would certainly reinforce both the declarations above, for it has truly and literally been born out of gatherings of prayer. If you will indulge me, I will paint the picture, hopefully with that ideal combination of fullness and brevity that I can provide and you can enjoy.

Beginnings

Over the course of seven decades, the intertwining legacies of leaders of faith and institutions of learning would converge in a most unexpected place and in a quite unforeseeable way.

In the town of Joplin, Missouri, where just over fifty thousand souls lie down each night to rest, a stream separates my office at TRAIN International from the college campus next door. Ozark Christian College graduates fewer than a hundred students each year, but in the Lord's strange economy where the weak are strong, last are first, and less is often more, an astonishing number of earthshaking women and men have emerged from those halls to serve Christ powerfully among the nations and scattered across our own.

And so throughout the past seven and a half decades, many well-trained and loftily intentioned graduates have been flung afar, though in the course of time some have also taken leadership at churches right here in Joplin. They have instilled a vision of the world viewed through the eyes and heart of our global God. A number of these churches became instrumental in sending out hordes of missionaries to impact nations, and leaders in these churches quickly recognized the need and value of extensive prefield training for those they sent to cross cultures as gospel-bearers.

So off these missionaries went to some of the few places to find such quality preparation, to the heroes and pioneers in the art and science of missionary training. Over time, as such missionaries returned to the US and faced unique difficulties in reentry and in reintegrating in the States, off they went again for reentry debriefing experiences to equip them with tools for navigating what Jeff Manion has aptly named "The Land Between."[1]

Before long, other churches expressed interest in learning from the successes and failures experienced as local churches embrace the role of strategically sending out global workers. What does it require to both send well and sustain well? How can a church allocate resources and personnel in such a way that neither the sending nor the sustaining become neglected?

These experiences and encounters in prefield missionary training, reentry debriefing, and church coaching would become the foundation for the eventual formation of the ministry of TRAIN International.

It is often said that experience is the best teacher. Less often quoted is the adage that rings truer, that *evaluated* experience is in fact the best teacher, as there is no shortage of people with a litany of experiences but who have failed to integrate those experiences into their knowledge and practice. And so after reflection upon much of what had been learned to that point, ideas began to form and dreams began to take shape. Some important realizations began to crystallize.

- Much of the "low-hanging fruit" has been harvested and brought in, and more attention must be and is being given to sending workers to some of the hardest places on earth.
- The need for prefield training is strong and only likely to rise, while sources for such training remain limited. In other words, there exists a high demand with a low supply. (How many training waitlists have you or your people been put on over the years?)
- As we send people to these harder places, the need increases for reentry debriefing to help them process their experiences, their victories, traumas, and losses. As the rate of change in US culture continues to accelerate, the need to orient returnees to the rapidly shifting landscape of our culture will only increase as well.

- Many of those in need of training in the process of going or returning have bypassed training due to the costs involved and their need to raise the financial support for it. In other words, essential training can become cost prohibitive.
- As more churches seek to become sending churches and more effective at sustaining their global workers, the desire for and pursuit of coaching in the processes of sending and sustaining well is also likely to rise.

And so began the local gatherings to pray, to ask what if, and to seek God's leading and direction. Nearly a year passed before the Lord gave the green light, and in the summer of 2008, TRAIN International was formed. Drawing on the experience of the stunning array of missionaries current and former, preachers, mission ministers, college professors, and TCKs who reside in and around Joplin, and learning from the experience of friends serving at centers of training for cross-cultural skills, a dedicated group came together asking the Lord to breathe life into this creation he had called into being. TRAIN held its first trainings that year, and elements of a unique DNA were etched into our commitment to equipping individuals, families, and churches for cross-cultural effectiveness.

We train whole families, with age-appropriate prefield and debriefing opportunities for children and youth of any age. We solicit substantial donations and raise support to maintain low overhead and reasonable training costs so as to enable full participation from those who might otherwise bypass training altogether. We offer ongoing interaction and coaching as needed to those who attend our prefield trainings and subsequently arrive on their fields of service; strike while the iron *is* hot when possible, strike when the iron *gets* hot when circumstances dictate. We provide resources and follow-up after the fact to those who debrief with us and who continue to unpack what it means to come "home" to a place that may feel as foreign as the field to which they went. We combine highly experiential and immersive training with the more traditional classroom-based training to better equip missionary candidates for self-discovery and field effectiveness. We offer biblical, facilitative, and principle-centered coaching that enables participants and churches to contextualize and scale the application of those principles to their environment and resource base.

We gladly serve alongside giants of the faith and of the practice of training cross-cultural servants, and I am thankful for the collaborative and partnering work that has helped us become established, serving dozens of sending agencies, coaching dozens of churches, and training hundreds of missionaries in both their outbound and inbound journeys of going and returning.

> **"** What does it require to both send well
> and sustain well? How can a church
> allocate resources and personnel
> in such a way that neither the sending
> nor the sustaining become neglected? **"**

We are indebted to our friends at Mission Training International (MTI), the Center for Intercultural Training (CIT), and those veterans of the craft of cross-cultural training and care who together host the annual gathering of Pastoral Training in Member Care.

Continually Learning

Charles Spurgeon is famously quoted as having said, "He who will not use the thoughts of other men's brains proves that he has no brains of his own." This has bearing in the ways we continue to learn with and from our older siblings in missionary training, from churches pursuing excellence in strategies for sending and sustaining, and from the very people we train in prefield and in reentry.

We are constantly learning as we continue to offer missionary trainings and coach churches toward strategically sending and holistically caring for missionaries. In debriefing returning workers, gems are unearthed in their stories. The facets of those gems each uniquely refract light and bring out a variety of gleanings, both positive and negative. Among other things, the facets of those gems reveal points at which we as the family of God fall short in sustaining those missionaries we send out. Part of every missionary's story involves the broken expectations of self, of God, and of the sending and supporting churches. What we learn through these stories helps us better align our own church coaching with realities that missionaries face, needs that slip through the cracks, expectations that must be clarified, made healthy and realistic, and must then be well communicated.

Every missionary family, couple, and single who pursues prefield training and goes on to reach the mission field also becomes a source of ongoing learning. Each generation is brought up with its unique distinctives, strengths, and giftings, along with its vulnerabilities and blind spots. We learn the topography of the hearts of each generation as they individually and collectively embark upon such adventures as cross-cultural life and ministry. In which areas and by which means are we best preparing them? What needful content has gone unaddressed, which proverbial stones left unturned in the process of their preparation? Though our trainings are most substantively principle-based, we must ask these questions so our efforts do not become static, based on the benefits of training content from yesteryear.

Building the Team

I have been asked what pool I draw upon as I seek to build our training teams. University professors? Successful career missionaries? Those who have endured and come back from burnout? Recovered from disillusionment and broken expectations? Floundered through reentry? My answer is yes, all of the above.

Have you noticed what Jesus, our perfect high priest, does with his knowledge, insight, and experience of having lived a perfect human life? In Hebrews 5, the high priest is described as one who is able to "deal gently" with those he served, because both parties understood what it is to be subject to weakness. So how now does Christ, having tasted the experience of humanity—of temptation and the costliness of obedience, of the reality of tiredness, pain, and death—deal with us? Is he now described as declaring definitively? As speaking authoritatively? No, as dealing gently. And how strengthening and comforting are those words, for one who deals gently with us can certainly call upon us greatly.

It is such people we pursue for our training teams. We don't seek to assemble panels of experts to declare from on high the missiological principles by which missionary candidates will achieve greatness on the field. Nor do we seek out master missionaries with flawless track records of ever-increasing success. We pursue wounded healers, those who in service to and with the Father, walking alongside our Good Shepherd, have endured trials and costly sacrifices, seen glories and many answered prayers, and who also bear the scars befitting of those who walk in the way of the suffering servant.

A Story Still in Process

Our story, of course, is still at this very moment being written, and is one of an ongoing pursuit of learning, honing, building the team, and growing into what the Lord has for the ministry and what he desires to pour out through it to the community of those who send as well as those who go, to those who sustain and those who return. It is a story I am humbly and gratefully part of.

Brian Gibson is executive director of TRAIN International (www.traininternational.org) in Joplin, MO.

Note
[1] Jeff Manion, *The Land Between: Finding God in Difficult Transitions* (Zondervan, 2010).

CHAPTER 40

Sixteen:Fifteen

Five Marks of a Mobilized Church

Matthew Ellison

Since 1995, I have had the amazing privilege of mobilizing local churches to be central players and full partners in global missions. After many years of evaluating and observing the most effective churches, I began noticing many of them had certain commonalities. I believe these commonalities reveal some of the key marks of a church that has been mobilized to reach the nations. You might say that the marks answer the question, "What does a church that has been unleashed for global missions look like?" Understand, these marks are not a mobilization formula, because it is the supernatural work of our sovereign God; therefore, mobilizing local churches for missions must take into account the unique gifts, talents, and passions he has given to each church. Still, churches that desire to engage the world effectively would do well to consider these marks.

Mark #1—God-Centered

Leaders have a holy ambition to see the nations glorify God for his mercy. John Piper says it best, "Worship is the fuel and the goal of missions. Missions begins and ends in worship. Where zeal for worship is weak,

 What does a church that has been unleashed for global missions look like? . . . Mobilizing local churches for missions must take into account the unique gifts, talents, and passions God has given to each church.

zeal for missions will be weak."[1] In order for churches to effectively engage in missions, they need solid methodologies, sound strategies that are in touch with global realities, the ability to partner effectively, and an understanding of the complexities of planting churches among the world's remaining unreached and least reached peoples; in short, churches need an abundance of mission skill and knowledge . . . and make no mistake, the absence of these things will hinder our global work. But if churches do not know, love, and worship God, mustering the zeal needed to reach the nations, especially the unreached ones, will be nearly impossible.

 Is our passion for God strong enough to sustain enduring commitment to reaching the nations?

Mark #2—Activated Leaders

Leaders are committed to missions. They affirm and participate in the church's global vision. In my experience, members of a church with a passion to reach the nations can begin the missions conversation, but without the participation and engagement of church leaders, mobilizing a church is tough sledding.

One missiologist, now serving in Central Asia, absolutely nails how critical it is for church leaders to participate in their church's mission vision:

> Members of a congregation can be a catalyst for missions envisioning . . . but until senior leadership has embraced the vision . . . we are not yet dealing with the process of a church. An important milestone is for the church, as a WHOLE, to reach a place where it can fully embrace the idea of focusing its resources, giftings, energies, financial resources . . . to reach the world.

When I first began offering missions coaching to local churches, I was happy to meet with anyone from a church that asked for help. Usually, these were marginalized groups of big-hearted, mission-minded people who desired change but lacked the necessary influence to initiate it. I realized that without the input and affirmation of church leaders, missions would likely remain in the margins. When we started requiring church leaders to participate in our missions coaching process and they began to shed the spiritual blood that forging a world-changing vision requires, they became champions of that vision.

 Do our leaders share a unified passion to reach the nations?

Mark #3—A Biblical Definition of Missions

The church has a missions definition that aligns with the biblical mandate to make disciples of all nations. Today there is great confusion about the meaning and goal of the Great Commission, and the consequences are unimaginable.

One of the most important questions a church needs to consider is, *What is missions and why does it matter?* This is especially critical today because a massive number of churches in the West have come to adopt a philosophy that says every good, altruistic, or evangelistic work is a mission work and that every follower of Christ is a missionary. But are these biblical concepts? Are they helpful? Do they lead to more missions work being accomplished or less? Without a biblical definition of missions informing and shaping a church's missions decisions and actions, they may find that much of what is considered missions work is not that at all. Moreover, having a biblical definition of missions will help with not only missions methodology but also with missions motivation.

If you were to do a quick survey of church leaders and mission-minded, missions-active people in your church, asking them just a couple of basic questions about the Great Commission, I am convinced that you would get many different and often conflicting answers. Sometimes the differences would just be semantic, but in other cases they would be fundamental. In my missions coaching and consulting work I repeatedly encounter serious confusion and stifling disagreement among church and mission leaders about the purpose and goal of the Great Commission.

Following are some questions that I continue to ask church leaders:

- What is the Great Commission purpose Christ gave to his church?
- What exactly are we supposed to be doing?
- What has he called us to accomplish?
- What is the goal of the Great Commission?
- What is it that we work toward?
- What does the fulfillment of the Great Commission require of us?

Responses often reflect a seriously hazy understanding of the Great Commission. And if churches are unable to state clearly and concisely their Great Commission purpose, I believe it will be nearly impossible for them to serve that purpose well.

One of the approaches that I often use to help clear the fog is to simply ask some more fundamental questions like these:

- If a church defines missions simply as "serving those in need" or "reaching lost people"—does that align with God's heartbeat for the Great Commission? Does it fully represent his heart for the whole world?

- Has Jesus left the interpretation of the Great Commission open to individual churches?

- When Jesus gave the Great Commission, did he give definite, clear, and distinct instructions? If so, what are those instructions? If so, why all the confusion?

In an article on "involving all of God's people in all of God's mission," Ed Stetzer explains the importance of God's people defining his mission:

> It will help all of God's people to be involved in all of God's mission if we will do the work of both defining the mission and choosing an appropriate cultural articulation of the mission. As Stephen Neill has said, "When everything is mission, nothing is mission." The mission of God cannot be the catch-all that includes everything from folding bulletins, to picking up trash on the highway, to coaching a ball team, to the gospel infiltrating a previously unreached people.[2]

Perhaps one of the most important questions that we should be asking when reading about the Great Commission in Scripture is this: Does God expect us to pool our good ideas and pursue the things we care about, or did Jesus intend to convey objective meaning and purpose when he gave his final marching orders?

In essence, the question we should be concerned with is whether or not Jesus cares about definitions. If he doesn't care, then it does seem that the meaning and goal of the Great Commission are up for grabs. If he does care about words and their meaning, we would do well to think seriously about what he really meant when he commissioned us to make disciples of all the nations.

 Have we allowed the Bible to shape our definition of missions and do we have a relative global purpose that flows from that understanding?

Mark #4—Churchwide Engagement

George Miley, in his book, *Loving the Church, Blessing the Nations,* writes about body-wide sacrificial commitment of resources, time, and prayer:

During the reformation of the Church, the reformers wanted to make the word of God accessible to every believer. Now we live in a time when God's leaders recognize that we must make the work of God accessible to every believer. [3]

Reaching all people groups calls forth the gifts and contributions of *every believer*. Visualize an overall process of initiation, strategy development, implementation, management, pastoral support, and funding, and you will begin to see a wide range of roles, each of which is a channel for the involvement of *every believer*. Most folks will not leave home permanently to minister on the mission field. If they are to participate in world missions, they must be released where they are, in the context of their local church.

Are we prepared to enlist the sacrificial commitment of our entire congregation and will we create broad sets of opportunities that will give everyone the opportunity to participate?

Mark #5—Partnership

The church joins forces with other like-minded ministries, creating synergies through extended capabilities and expanded resource pools to further the Great Commission. I have discovered that when we talk about the Great Commission we often talk about going *for* Jesus, but when we rightly understand the mandate given to us in the Gospel of Matthew, we discover that we do not go *for* Jesus, we go *with* Jesus, for he says, "I am with you always" (Matt 28:20).

"I am with you . . ." These are some of the most solemn words that can be spoken in a relationship. These words echo the promise of covenant and they evoke the hope of fellowship and partnership. Now when God calls us to be on mission with him, he calls us not only to partner *with* him, he calls us to partner with his people, his bride.

Daniel Rickett, in his book *Making Your Partnership Work*, defines partnership like this: "A complementary relationship driven by a common purpose and sustained by a willingness to learn and grow together in obedience to God." [4]

Let me list just a few of the reasons why churches should *not* pursue the Great Commission's fulfillment in isolation:

• Partnership is biblical
• Partnership *can* increase effectiveness

- Partnership *can* leverage resources, abilities, opportunities, etc.
- Partnership *can* lead to greater impact
- Partnership *can* decrease the time frame of fulfilling a mission

Of course partnering with others to proclaim the gospel around the world won't be without its challenges. But even the challenges, if faced with humility, can serve to strengthen the bonds of fellowship. Partnership is messy; it can be risky, but the end result will be well worth the effort.

 Are we prepared to work with others in order to reach the nations?

Certainly, effective global engagement consists of more than these marks, but hopefully they will be a starting point for your church to begin thinking through and then doing our all-important work of making disciples of all nations, all tribes, and all tongues.

To learn more about how missions coaching can help churches realize their potential to reach the nations, visit www.1615.org or contact Sixteen:Fifteen at info@1615.org.

Matthew Ellison is currently the president and cofounder of Sixteen:Fifteen, where he coaches with churches in strategically focused missions, helping them to discover and use their unique gifts in partnership with others to make Christ known among all nations.

Notes

[1] John Piper, *Let the Nations Be Glad! The Supremacy of God in Missions* (Grand Rapids, MI: Baker, 1993/2003), 17.

[2] Ed Stetzer, "Involving All of God's People in All of God's Mission," June 4, 2010, The Christian Post, www.christianpost.com/news/involving-all-of-gods-people-in-all-of-gods-mission-part-2-45427/

[3] George Miley, *Loving the Church, Blessing the Nations* (IVP, 2005).

[4] Daniel Rickett, *Making Your Partnership Work* (S.l.: Daniel Rickett, 2015).

Connecting to the Pipeline

1. As your team has been discussing a variety of topics, from your church's theology of calling to where in the world the Lord is sending your people, you probably have more questions than answers. Write down a "Top ten list" of questions for which you would like to seek counsel.

2. What are the major concerns and/or obstacles for your church in developing a unified vision for your part of the Great Commission?

3. What are the opportunities that keep coming up in your discussions that get your team / church leaders / congregation excited?

4. If you reach an impasse in your dialogue as a team, or you just need some helpful encouragement, plan a video conference call with one of these Special Partner "Advisors" with the whole team. They are eager to help.

For an up-to-date list of consultants, training organizations, coaches, and other Special Partners, go to www.MissionaryPipeline. org and click on "Resources."

Part 7

Preparing the Sending Church
for the Next Generation

Our current understanding of the world mission movement may be, in large part, a hindrance to what needs to happen with the next generation of missionaries and our future understanding of what they will be doing. In this section, we are highlighting a few key innovations that are taking place. While it is difficult to predict what the future holds, the three innovative forecasts highlighted here are most certainly emerging trends that church leaders need to be aware of: business as mission (BAM), church-based teams (CBT), and the missionary sending capacity of fields of service that were formerly missionary receivers.

CHAPTER 41

Business as Mission

Real Business, Real Mission

Larry W. Sharp

Dan and Jodi loved Jesus and wanted to serve him, so after graduating from university they headed off to Asia for two years as missionaries. They had a good experience, learned a fair degree of the national language, and returned to the US, praying that God would clearly lead them on to the next steps. But God had touched their heart for the people, so he led them back to a large city in a more unreached area of the country. By this time Dan was realizing that God had gifted him with entrepreneurial skills, so they started a business: one of the hardest ones—manufacturing.

God led them to investors in their country and in the US, and the business grew to nearly thirty employees as relationships developed in the community. Dan joined the chamber of commerce as the only American member, and he gained a vision for extending his kingdom business beyond his city to more unreached areas.

Real Business

The business was clearly for real. With nearly $500,000 a year in sales, they had created jobs for twenty-eight employees, and their product was being sold internationally. But Dan knew enough to know he needed help. Although he was trained in evangelism and missions, he had no background in business. He had experienced his first bad account, he needed to modernize his financial record keeping with modern software, and he needed capital to expand. Thankfully, God's people serving as consultants provided necessary training and support, so the business continued to grow.

Dan and Jodi have found their niche in the making of disciples among the unreached. They seek to hire people in need, and they contribute time and funds to a local orphanage.

Real Mission

Making disciples of Jesus has been an integral part of the project from the beginning. They live out kingdom values in the business and community. They pay fair wages; they pay their bills and taxes; and they produce a quality product (a variety of textiles and sports equipment). They are respected as "different" in a positive way in their city. They live out the gospel.

They also seek opportunities to give spoken testimony of the hope that is within them. They share that they are "Jesus-followers," and how he makes a personal difference as well as helps the business be different and respected. This has led to several coming to faith in Christ, being discipled by Jodi and Dan, and joining house churches in the area.

What Is Business as Mission?

Many business professionals and church leaders today are hearing of the term "business as mission" (BAM). While there are many variances of a perfect definition, I like the expression of J. D. Greear of the Summit Church in Raleigh-Durham, North Carolina: "Christians in the marketplace today are able to gain access more easily to strategic, unreached places. Globalization, great advancements in technology, and urbanization have given the business community nearly universal access."

Greear reminds us that God has placed in his church the skills necessary to penetrate the most unreached parts of our world—and those skills are business skills. Businesspeople, says Greear, should focus on a twofold vision: "Whatever you are good at, a) do it well for the glory of God; b) and do it somewhere strategic for the mission of God."[1]

> "Christians in the marketplace today are able to gain access more easily to strategic, unreached places. Globalization, great advancements in technology, and urbanization have given the business community nearly universal access."

Mats Tunehag, one of the leaders of the global BAM movement, suggests that Business as Mission (BAM) is simply "a legitimate economic activity (business) by a workplace professional which serves as a vehicle for sharing the love of Christ."

Many Christians mistakenly see their work life as distinct and separate from their spiritual life. This is an old error, a remnant of first-century dualism that separated the spiritual from the secular and the clergy from the laity. Bonnie Wurzbacher, vice president of Coca-Cola, noted that "What we need is to understand the biblical worldview that says that there is no secular-sacred split and God wants us to understand that what we do should fulfill and advance God's purposes in the world."

BAM could, should, and does take place in every workplace in the world where God's people in business are faithfully living like Jesus and looking for ways to bring people to know him. Christians in business see their work as a testimony and a mission. Michael Cardone, CEO of Cardone Industries, says that "Service and excellence create a platform to talk about who God is and Jesus Christ . . . I am not called to be a pastor or missionary; I'm called to be a businessman, and I see no difference."

Similarly, David Green, CEO of Hobby Lobby, notes that "We try in all decisions to ask what God would have us do. . . . We don't put our Christian faith on the shelf when we come to work."

Three propositions developed by John Warton may help to justify and explain the business as mission movement:

1. **The Sanctity of Work.** It is important that we all have clarity on the biblical divine understanding that God is a God of work, and he intends his people to be workers (Gen 1). We should not feel guilty or feel like second-class Christians when we succeed in business. God expects us to drive for excellence, to be ambitious, and to do "all for the glory of God" (1 Cor 10:31, NIV). While business and work can tempt us to sin, work and business are fundamentally good and provide many opportunities to glorify God.[2]

2. **The Christian at Work.** This proposition suggests that Christians should engage in work like anyone else, but live differently from everyone else. Christians work ethically, view their customers differently, love and serve others, seek justice, and use their work to serve their communities. In so doing, believers become a testimony and draw others to become followers of our Savior.

3. **Work and the kingdom of God**. The Gospel of Matthew suggests that the kingdom of God is "not yet" (heaven) but also "here and now." As we create jobs and wealth, we are advancing the kingdom of God, which essentially is obedience to the Second Commandment (i.e., to love our neighbors). The Great Commission enjoins us to make disciples of "all peoples." So the Christian businesses that we develop here in our home neighborhoods represent a transferable model. We can participate in business start-ups, franchises, or multinational business efforts abroad in the developing world and all the while live like Jesus. That is business as mission.

A recent memo from a friend who is a kingdom business entrepreneur in an Asian country demonstrates this:

> Upon entering a local office where local authorities facilitate some aspects of our company, I saw my national friend who manages the office. Amidst the hubbub we greeted one another and caught up on personal news. Suddenly my friend asked, "Do you have a divine connection? I'm sensing a positive energy emanating from you and I don't know what it is." Stunned, I replied, "Well as a matter of fact, I do have a divine connection to Jesus!" I then went on to explain who Jesus is and his presence in my life. He listened intently. Something is going on in this man's heart.

Business as mission is not "business as normal." Neither is it "missions as normal." It is living out the commands of Jesus in the workplace: to love our neighbor and make disciples so individuals and communities are transformed—spiritually, economically, and socially—for the greater glory of God and the establishment of his church.

A BAM Business Will Be Profitable and Sustainable

Tunehag and the Lausanne committee on BAM insist that BAM activities must be 1) profitable and sustainable, 2) create jobs and local wealth, and 3) produce spiritual capital (disciples of Jesus). This triple bottom line is a guiding force for the BAM movement. The first is the importance of a business which is profitable and sustainable.

For most of the twentieth century, businesses and MBA programs would answer the question "What is the goal of your business?" with a simple response: "To maximize shareholder value" or "To make a profit." However, the real goal of business is more importantly to serve others and bring glory to God. The original purposes of God are evidenced in the creation mandate which reveals that he is a God of enterprise, creativity, and production—for his glory. From the first human couple until now, God intended creation to grow and expand as mankind began to produce food, distribute food, build, manufacture, and trade goods.

The fundamental function of creating wealth is that it is intended to be a "high and holy calling." Van Duzer expresses the purpose of business as twofold: "1) to provide the community with goods and services that will enable it to flourish and 2) to provide opportunities for meaningful work that will allow employees to express their God-given creativity."[3]

Clearly the nobleman's command in the parable of the ten minas to "engage in business until I come" (Luke 19:13) carried with it the expectation of a profit. Business is the only human institution which actually creates wealth. Education, the church, and government all consume wealth. Business creates it! "You shall remember the Lord your God, for it is he who gives you power to get wealth . . ." (Deut 8:18).

While it is true that profit can be abused as with any good thing, profit is a necessary and important component in adding value, providing good stewardship, and multiplying resources as a way of helping people. Profit is that which results from a business which generates value and expands the total economic pie. "Profit is a sign that others are being served effectively, not that advantage is being taken of them."[4] Profit is a necessary condition if we are able to continue to provide value to customers. Profit, however, is not the goal.

In recent years, many businesspeople have come to the conclusion that there is a wider purpose of business. John Mackey, CEO of Whole Foods Market, puts it this way: "The purpose of business is to create sustainable value for all stakeholders."[5] Mackey and others are focusing on the dignity of all their stakeholders, not just the shareholders. They want to make a difference, seek a common good, and make the world a better place. This idea is incorporated in the modern trend toward CSR—corporate social responsibility.

Traditionally, development agencies, churches, and governments have focused on providing aid to poor countries. While there is a place for aid and disaster relief, aid will never alleviate poverty, and these are rarely self-sustaining projects. When funding dries up or interest declines, the "false market" which created dependency is exposed and more problems often develop than were solved. Only investing in sustainable profitable businesses creates employment and true economic development for poor countries.

Theologian Wayne Grudem states,

> I believe the only long-term solution to world poverty is business. That is because businesses produce goods, and businesses produce jobs. And businesses continue producing goods year after year, and continue providing jobs and paying wages year after year . . . If we are ever going to see long-term solutions to world poverty, I believe it will come through starting and maintaining productive, profitable businesses.[6]

A BAM Business Creates Jobs

The second bottom line is the creation of value, particularly jobs. Since the kingdom of God is also "here and now," kingdom living is about living out the principles of Jesus in every sector of life, including the workplace. It demonstrates the integration of our faith with our work.

We bring the kingdom of God ". . . on earth as it is in heaven" (Matt 6:10) via business transactions because business creates value, and we have the opportunity to create holistic value based on the fruit of the Spirit—love, joy, peace, patience, kindness, goodness, faithfulness, gentleness, self-control (Gal 5:22,23). A business owner in Asia, Pete, says it succinctly, "Every day on the factory floor is an opportunity for discipleship."

One of the key values created by business is jobs. When we think of Jesus being very aware of the social condition of his day and doing something about physical realities such as hunger, danger, illness, and death, we can easily transpose his practical concerns to the concerns of today. Martin Luther stated, "The gospel that does not deal with the issues of the day is no gospel at all."

The Gallup Company surveyed over 150 nations in their renowned World Poll of major issues of life. They wanted to "discover the single most dominant thought on most people's minds," says CEO Jim Clifton. "Six years into our global data collection effort, we may have already found the single most searing, clarifying, helpful, world-altering fact. What the whole world wants is a good job."[7]

Consider the world conditions of today—extreme poverty (30 percent of the world living on less than $2 a day), unemployment in some countries over 50 percent, victimization and exploitation, disease, wars on several fronts, and persecution. Job creation will not heal all of this, but growing economies creating good jobs brings dignity, opportunity for positive relationships, and is vital in the ultimate transformation of individuals and communities.

God created humans to work and be productive (Gen 1:28), to work heartily "as for the Lord and not for men" (Col 3:23), and ". . . shine before others, so that they may see your good works and give glory to your Father . . ." (Matt 5:16). This all takes place in the marketplace of work.

Note a few affirmations from the 2004 "Business as Mission Issue Group."

- We believe in following in the footsteps of Jesus, who constantly and consistently met the needs of the people he encountered, thus demonstrating the love of God and the rule of his kingdom.
- We believe the Holy Spirit empowers all members of the body of Christ to serve, to meet the real spiritual and physical needs of others, demonstrating the kingdom of God.
- We believe that God has called and equipped businesspeople to make a kingdom difference in and through their businesses.
- We believe the gospel has the power to transform individuals, communities, and societies. Christians in business should therefore be a part of this holistic transformation through business.
- We recognize both the dire need for and the importance of business development. However, it is more than just business per se. Business as mission is about business with a kingdom of God perspective, purpose, and impact.
- We recognize that there is a need for job creation and for multiplication of businesses all over the world.
- The real bottom line of business as mission is—"for the greater glory of God."

A BAM Business Makes Disciples of Jesus

The third bottom line is the development of spiritual capital—making followers of Jesus. Most writers and practitioners of kingdom businesses recognize that the spiritual (or mission) bottom line is the raison d'être for any activity and certainly a BAM company. This bottom line requires that there be an intentional living of kingdom values in every element of the company, and a continual striving to honor God in every aspect of corporate life. A kingdom company is specific, conscious, clear, and intentional in establishing Jesus' kingdom in the world.[8]

Ken Eldred describes this as spiritual capital which includes a corporate culture of integrity, accountability, honesty, hope, loyalty, trust, servanthood, fairness, and love. Incarnational living is observed every day in a kingdom business and becomes the basis for proclamation of faith. BAM businesses have a vision, mission, and strategy evidenced in their policies, procedures, and culture that encourages godly values.[9] They do what is right from God's perspective.

The end of such integration of faith and work, a truly biblical concept, creates an optimum climate for people to decide to follow Jesus. The business provides the context for discipleship. One such Asian business that benefited from IBEC consultants is noted by Dale Losch:

> For Andrew, the answer laid in living out the gospel every day by being fair with employees, paying his taxes, paying a fair wage, placing verses from the book of Proverbs on the office door and starting the day in prayer for everyone (all employees were non-Jesus followers). It involved building relationships, caring for families, and even weekend camping trips with employees. It meant talking about the real issues of life and showing them who Jesus is and how a follower really lives. Some call it discipling people into the kingdom. [10]

Reconciling and integrating all the bottom lines is a key issue for a BAM business. It is not an easy task and involves more than just a business plan. It necessitates an integrated plan which brings together all three bottom lines.

In summary, the triple bottom line includes *profit* because it is biblical and is what sustains an authentic economic life; it includes *job creation* because that helps fulfill the Great Commandment to love our neighbor (Mark 12:31); and it includes the *making of disciples of Jesus* and in so doing we obey the Great Commission (Matt 28:18,19).

Larry W. Sharp is the vice president emeritus at Crossworld (www.crossworld.org) and founder and director of training at IBEC Ventures (www.ibecventures.com).

Notes

[1] J. D. Greear, *The Next Wave of Missions* devotional, December 2, 2011, https://jdgreear.com/blog/the-next-wave-of-missions/.

[2] Wayne A. Grudem, *Business for the Glory of God: The Bible's Teaching on the Moral Goodness of Business* (Wheaton IL: Crossway, 2003).

[3] Jeff Van Duzer, *Why Business Matters to God: and What Still Needs to be Fixed* (Downers Grove, IL: IVP, 2010), 46.

[4] Ken Eldred, *The Integrated Life: Experience the Powerful Advantage of Integrating Your Faith and Work* (Montrose, CO: Manna Ventures, 2010) 45.

[5] John Mackey and Rajendra Sisodia, *Conscious Capitalism: Liberating the Heroic Spirit of Business* (Boston MA: Harvard Business Review, 2014).

[6] Wayne A. Grudem, *Business for the Glory of God: The Bible's Teaching on the Moral Goodness of Business* (Wheaton IL: Crossway, 2003).

[7] Jim Clifton, *The Coming Jobs War* (Washington, DC: Gallup, 2013), 10.

[8] Mike Baer, *Business as Mission* (YWAM Publishing, 2006).

[9] John Mulford and Ken Eldred, "Kingdom Entrepreneurs Transforming Nations," article, 2008.

[10] Dale Losch, *A Better Way: Make Disciples Wherever Life Happens* (Kansas City MO: Crossworld, 2012).

CHAPTER 42

Church-based Teams

Joint Venture, Serving Together

Dave Hansen

In the mid-2000s, an Avant missionary, Dr. Doug Wilson, did a large research project on 1,200 megachurches in the United States. The focus was on their present and future "missions" outreach. By "megachurch" we are talking about a church of 1,000 or more attendees. While many churches have both domestic and international outreach ministries, Dr. Wilson's focus was on foreign mission work. Some of these churches had a long history of international work, while others were newer megachurches that had grown rapidly and were just starting to think about reaching the nations for Christ.

From this research a couple of things were very clear and impacted how Avant approached "church-based teams." First, if a megachurch was already involved in missions at some level, *planting churches* was very important to them. Secondly, the megachurch wanted more ownership in selecting missionary personnel and the location of ministry. They were not interested in just sending people and money to a mission agency. It needed to fit into their total church strategy.

Keep in mind these were trends. Some churches had well-developed missions programs: good missions structures, missionary preparation and care programs, and good resources to support their missionaries. But many of the newer, fast-growing megachurches didn't have such programs developed. But they did express a desire for these programs if and when the time came to focus on foreign missions.

So with this in mind, in 2008 Avant branded its renewed focus on church-based teams as Joint Venture. An article published by Avant, "A

Seat at the Table," indicated their willingness to partner more closely with the local church. As an agency, they realized that changes were necessary if they were going to work with megachurches. This was easy to say, but not so easy to do. Avant is over one hundred years old and had its own system of selecting, training, overseeing field ministries, and providing member care and administrative services to its missionaries. These were things that historically churches were happy for agencies to do as long as they did them well. So what would Avant be willing to change? How much control were they willing to relinquish? Did they know what it meant to have a true partnership? Did they even want to do this or were they content to stay as they had been for the last hundred-plus years?

Avant had changed significantly just a few years earlier by narrowing its focus to short-cycle church planting. Avant has always been a church planting mission, but over the years many good ministries such as camps, Bible schools, and media ministries were added. By implementing short-cycle church planting, Avant dedicated itself to sending teams to plant nationally led churches as rapidly as possible. These teams would concentrate on those things that led to establishing a church. They would demonstrate high trust by not doing things that the young church could do themselves. Metrics to measure church progress would indicate when that short-cycle team should move to phase two in which part of the team would move on to plant yet another church.

Previously, short-cycle teams were formed by putting together a group of five to eight missionaries coming from varied areas of the country, with different backgrounds, worship practices, etc. Due to the support-raising process, many teams struggled to arrive on the field together. What if a team could be formed where the team members came from the same city, could work weekly on team building before they even left for the field, raised their support together, arrived in country and did language study together . . . ? What if a church assembled a team from their own church body and caught the vision of planting a church overseas?

Would a megachurch be willing to send a church-based team using short-cycle church planting principles to plant a church among unreached people?

In 2008 Avant held a Joint Venture summit at a megachurch in Nebraska. It convened at Lincoln Berean Church rather than at Avant, intentionally trying to communicate the value the agency placed on the local church. Pastors and mission leaders from several megachurches attended. The agenda was to communicate that the leadership of Avant wanted to listen to what they had to say. Avant wanted them to know it recognized there were tensions between mission agencies and churches, mostly because of lack of communication. It was an opportunity to share the short-cycle church planting philosophy, and explain how they could become part of Joint Venture.

These churches loved the concept. One of the churches later sent a church-based team with another mission organization. One church has sent two Joint Venture teams with Avant. Some churches indicated they weren't ready for this yet. One church didn't want to take on such a focused approach to missions. And one church did not commit to a Joint Venture team but contacts Avant regularly for names of missionaries to support in countries where they are focused. The fact that megachurches came and dialogued with the mission was considered a success.

The first Joint Venture team was sent by Lincoln Berean Church to Gdansk, Poland. Here is their story. Because it is a partnership, both the role of the church and the agency will be covered.

First Joint Venture–Lincoln Berean

Lincoln Berean is a church with a strong history of sending homegrown missionaries. Every two to three years the church commissioned someone to the field (pilot, school teacher, traditional church planter, someone involved in media ministry or camping). These missionaries went out under many different mission agencies. The church's mission pastor, Jeff Petersen, was passionate about missions and willing to work hard at sending out a Joint Venture team. But how would the church find five to eight people called by God to form this team? Lincoln Berean's strong missions history and established mission policies seemed to indicate this might not be all that difficult, but it was! Resources were not the roadblock. Church size does not indicate how well prepared people in the church are to discern the missionary call. Churches whose people have been well grounded in the Word, have a passion for the lost, and have experience in evangelism and discipleship are better equipped to find qualified team members.

Determining a location to send the team came about as the church and agency talked about needs. Lincoln Berean did not want to send its first team to a difficult, remote part of the world (as if winter in Poland was easy!). It was agreed that Gdansk, Poland, would be the location.

Poland was also where Avant had sent its first short-cycle team made up of selected veteran missionaries.

Now the question was "Who would go?" A woman who had grown up in the church returned to Lincoln from out of state with her new husband whom she met in college. They had both earned degrees that prepared them for cross-cultural service and were ready to go! God had provided team leaders . . . now who else would become part of the team?

To acquaint the church body with this new Joint Venture and give interested people a chance to explore short-cycle church planting, Pastor Jeff launched the "ultimate spring break." Those taking the trip would see an Avant short-cycle team in action. Part of the group would visit a team in Italy; the others would visit a team in the Czech Republic. They would all end up in Gdansk, Poland, where the proposed Joint Venture team would live and minister.

In the spirit of partnership, Avant provided training to those going on the "ultimate spring break" and Avant leaders accompanied each of the two teams. This provided mission leadership with the opportunity to sense the heart of those going on this ten-day vision trip. The goal was to see who God might be leading to become part of the team. Two weeks after the trip, they all came together to talk about the trip and answer the question, "Is it I, Lord?" As a result of that "ultimate spring break," two more people joined the Joint Venture Poland team. The last member to join the team was a missionary already serving in Poland with another mission agency. She had observed Avant's first short-cycle team in Poznan, Poland, and wanted to be part of such a team.

On September 9, 2009, a team of five people boarded a plane and moved to Gdansk, Poland. The megachurch had processed the applications and selected its team. The team attended Avant's candidate orientation program and team training, just like any other Avant missionaries. The church committed to providing 50 percent of the team's financial support, and each team member raised the rest of their support and enlisted prayer supporters. During the process, the team met regularly for prayer, team building, and learning about Polish culture. Lincoln Berean Church commissioned the team, with participation from Avant leadership at the service.

This was the model Lincoln Berean would use for its next Joint Venture team going to Spain a year later. Little did Lincoln Berean or Avant know what would happen over the next six years.

The team members found apartments in the same part of the city. The winter was hard—even for Nebraskans! Language school was difficult. They all tried different methods of language acquisition (formal language school, tutors, etc.). A small Polish Baptist church welcomed them. The church people gave the team good exposure to the Polish culture. The Joint Venture team brought new excitement for evangelism to the church. Just as with Avant's first Polish team, southern gospel music became an avenue for several on the team to connect with Poles. Slowly friendships were being formed and spiritual contacts made.

After a year and a half, one of the team members chose to return to the States. No one saw this coming, as she was one who was doing well in the language and had built good friendships. Over the next few years, one by one everyone but the team leader couple left the team, all for different reasons. It was disheartening to Avant and especially to Lincoln Berean, who had invested so much into training, financial support, member care, and coaching.

Despite the disappointment, that wasn't the end of the story. In Matthew 16:18b Jesus said, "I will build my church, and the gates of hell shall not prevail against it." And he did! Today, through the power of God and the perseverance of the team leader couple, a group of fifty to seventy people are meeting regularly in Gdansk. A leadership team is in place, and as a church they are focused on planting another Polish church in the future. The Joint Venture team leaders continue coaching the original church as well as the new church plant.

How a church selects a location and members of the team is different in every case. But it must be bathed in prayer. Avant doesn't want to tell a church where they should send a team. They need to know for sure it is where God has directed them to ministry. It is interesting that on many of our Joint Venture teams, someone from the church staff is "called" to join that team. Having that leadership is a big plus for the team, but the sending church may need to be ready to fill a staff position as a result of forming a Joint Venture team.

One of the advantages of a Joint Venture team is having its members as part of the same church. They get to know each other and function as a team before moving overseas. One of the Avant Joint Venture teams was formed using two megachurches to build a team. One couple was from a church in Colorado and two couples were from another church in

> **"** One of the advantages of a Joint Venture team is having its members as part of the same church. They get to know each other and function as a team before moving overseas. **"**

Washington. The leadership of both churches agreed on the focus of the country. One church brought much stronger member care to the team. Just as the team was about to embark for the field, the mission pastor from one of the churches resigned. Unfortunately, Avant then discovered that a Joint Venture team had really been only the mission pastor's passion—not that of the entire church. From then on, Avant began advising all potential Joint Venture churches to go through coaching with Matthew Ellison (Sixteen:Fifteen ministry, www.1615.org). This ensures the entire church leadership team is committed to a church-based team.

Whether a church forms a Joint Venture team or not, that coaching process is beneficial for any church. Is it possible for two churches to go together to form a Joint Venture team? Yes, but it is much better if they are in the same city or very near each other. A powerful advantage to a Joint Venture team is what the team experiences each week during the preparation before leaving for the field.

More Joint Ventures—RockPointe and Liberty Christian

The next two Joint Venture teams to deploy both went through the Sixteen:Fifteen church coaching. RockPointe is a church located in Sterling Heights, Michigan, an area suffering from a serious economic downturn. Out of cash and with a budget in the red, they still felt led of God to send a Joint Venture team to West Africa. Three couples (two from the church staff) agreed to go. After their step of faith and obedience, church finances turned around. The Joint Venture team was sent out and the church even raised enough funds to provide a vehicle for each family. RockPointe lights a candle every Sunday to remind the church body of its team in West Africa. Often the team joins in for Communion services via Skype. Besides the impact this church has in West Africa, the local church has now reached out to a West African community in its own backyard. To date, this team is faithfully sharing the love of Christ with the hopes of seeing the church established in West Africa.

Liberty Christian Fellowship in Missouri went through the Sixteen:Fifteen coaching. A future preaching pastor became the leader of their Joint Venture team to the Middle East. Three couples and two singles from the church body made up the team. As of this writing, the team has completed a year of language study and is engaged in ministry. As a result of this journey, another member of the church felt called to become a regional director for Perspectives on the World Christian Movement. His goal is to see even more people get involved in mission work. While often we focus on the impact of a team on the mission field, it can also have a lasting impact on those at home.

Joint Venture Impact

How does Joint Venture impact the mission program in a local church?

- It can give a more concentrated focus on a particular country or people group. That is what some churches want and need.
- It provides the church an opportunity to work in true partnership with a mission agency. Since some churches might not have much experience in selecting missionaries, the agency can assist them in the process.
- Churches that have a number of career missionaries with other agencies may find that those missionaries feel slighted as the Joint Venture team takes so much focus (time, energy, finances). Churches need to work hard at valuing all missionaries supported by the church.
- The younger generation especially wants to be part of a team. Joint Venture provides this opportunity.
- The Joint Venture team will receive better member care from their church. Often the pastor and mission pastor will visit them. Short-term teams may come to catch the vision and help out on projects/events. With more exposure in the church, the team will have a greater number of people praying for them.

In summary, church-based teams bring together churches passionate about planting churches internationally and agencies with years of cross-cultural experience. The two parts coming together provide a beautiful picture of the body of Christ. If you are an agency reading this, go for it! If you are a church, start growing and training future missionaries today.

Dave Hansen served for eleven years as a missionary in Italy. He was the VP of the international division for Back to the Bible for twenty-three years before working with Avant Ministries for ten years. He and his wife, Judy, retired in 2017 and currently reside in Arkansas.

CHAPTER 43

Missionary Recipients Becoming Senders

The Global South on the Move

Larry Janzen

In its humble beginnings, Gospel Missionary Union (GMU), which is now Avant Ministries, first landed in Latin America in 1892. For over 125 years, hundreds of missionaries have left their homes to live and serve there. Some were martyrs. Most were, and still remain, persistent champions.

My parents, Don and Beth Janzen, started out in Bolivia in 1964 with the Evangelical Union of South America, which later merged with GMU. Over the next forty-five years they faithfully served there and in Argentina, Colombia, Ecuador, Spain, and several other countries. As you may have guessed, I grew up more "Latin American" than the culture of my birth country of Canada, with a firsthand look at what missionaries were doing from the metropoles to the jungles. In 1993, my wife, Marbella (Marbi), and I joined GMU and headed to Belize, Central America. That also happens to be where Marbi was born and where she was raised in a church that was planted by GMU (Avant) missionaries. It is because of this, and for God's glory, that she also brings a unique and important perspective to what I will share in this chapter.

What has been the result of 125 years of faithful service by so many missionaries? It has been the goal from the start that each mission field eventually have multiple nationally led churches, seminaries to excellently train workers and leaders, camps, mature and capable leaders, organized associations, autonomy in governance and finances, new horizons, and new strategies for future ministry.

In most Latin American countries this is now happening without the presence of foreign missionaries, as Avant has chosen to withdraw their personnel and redeploy them elsewhere. This is a beautiful testament to God's incredible power to produce good fruit through his willing workers.

So what is next for Avant in Latin America? What is left for us to do? Furthermore, if our mission statement clearly delineates a purpose to start the church where it did not previously exist, then what does that mean for countries into which we are no longer sending church planters? Perhaps we can answer those questions with another question. Where will the next major wave of called, mature, motivated, effective, adaptable missionaries come from? My humble opinion . . . no, my emphatic conviction, is Latin America!

If that is the case, then what seems to logically and naturally follow our withdrawal from such countries where autonomous national church associations are flourishing and growing without dependency on the missionaries, is for us to reapproach them intentionally as promoters and facilitators of that potentially world-changing movement. Is there interest? Yes. Is there already some movement in that direction? Yes again. Is there a need for help? There most definitely is! However, I believe it is not an "on our shoulders" type of help, but rather "shoulder to shoulder" guidance, encouragement, training, and mentoring. This implies that I don't see this as a replacement of our missionary vision and active sending from North America, but rather an addition to the same. I also suggest that it is no longer financial facilitation, but rather provision of tools and practical experience, that will tangibly prove that the Great Commission is impartial to location or culture, and that God's necessary provision is not dependent on demography or economy.

Why Latin Americans? Here are a few practical reasons:

1. **They are adaptable.**
   - In many cases, having come from humble origins may facilitate adjustment and contentment in a third-world missionary context.
   - Culturally, the Latin American is by nature quite loving, accepting, and loyal in friendship.
2. **They are passionate.**
   - Many live their faith with passion, due in part to the difficulties they have faced.

- They are intelligent. Today more than ever, with increasing opportunities, more and more individuals are reaching high levels of education.
- They are passionate about family and friendship.

3. **The national church in most Latin American countries has, by God's power and grace, grown to large numbers.**
   - There is a large pool of mature Christians, many who may sense God's call to become missionaries, from which to draw.
   - I believe that the fact that it is a large and active church will also allow the missionary movement from within these churches to be financially independent and personally "owned" by the national churches. I also believe that this is necessary to further development and growth in the body of Christ, much like in the lives of our children as they reach adulthood and become independent. They may not have many financial resources as we do in North America, but they do have strength in numbers.

4. **They have the potential to be more easily accepted in the countries they go to.**
   - Appearance, cultural norms, and even geographical origins can greatly help them to "blend in" more easily than most North Americans.
   - This is already very evident among Arab Muslims, Turks, Indians, and other people groups, with those Latin Americans who are working among them.

They are already expressing a desire and are capturing the vision. Yet they need to overcome the mindset that "Missionaries are foreigners who come from outside our borders," or "We do not have sufficient funds to do this." In a recent conference, I listened to missionary representatives from various countries affirm that this is one of the areas of prime focus in our

> Where will the next major wave
> of called, mature, motivated, effective,
> adaptable missionaries come from?
> My humble opinion . . . no,
> my emphatic conviction, is Latin America!

work as a mission in Latin American countries where we no longer feel the need to send our own church planters.

There is already a platform in place for all of this.

- There is an extensive and strong church body infrastructure, both in ministry training and leadership.
- There exists, in most contexts, mature national leadership with vision.
- There are seasoned, proven training grounds, such as seminaries, training conferences, mentorship, workshops, etc. At this point almost all of these are independently administrated by nationals.

The truth is, since the inception of the very concept of foreign mission, at least for those who took the Great Commission of Jesus as the motive and basis, it has always been about the missionary "only doing what only the missionary can do," to quote our Avant missionary training notes. In other words, as soon as a national is capable, prepared, and willing, the missionary should be willing to step back and let them shine. The same thing applies here. The "receivers" of missionaries must at some point become "senders" as well. It is far more than just the act of "evangelism" or verbal expression of the gospel truth. Jesus stated emphatically that beyond the salvation of one's soul, there is an essential, committed follow-up teaching "to obey everything I have commanded you" (Matt 28:20a, NIV). The very concept cries multiplicity, since it comes right on the heels of the command to "go and make disciples *of all nations*"!

I must emphasize that this has been taught in as many ways as possible by his faithful disciplemakers over the years. Yet, in God's impeccable timing and methodology, it seems that it was necessary to reach this point where independent leadership, ministry, and outreach are now being carried out, apart from the somewhat "parent-like" dependency that so naturally existed while the missionary was present. Although it was appropriate in the early stages of disciplemaking, it was always the intention of the missionary to work diligently in such a way as to eventually no longer be needed. It is the experience of most, if not all, that some key components of maturity and well-functioning independence come only after this point is reached. This is precisely why we encourage our young adult children to step out of our nest and go on to independent, capable maturity as we watch, cheer, encourage, and remain available. I love the story of the relationship between Paul and John Mark in the New Testament.

Some time later Paul said to Barnabas, "Let us go back and visit the believers in all the towns where we preached the word of the Lord and see how they are doing." Barnabas wanted to take John, also called Mark, with them, but Paul did not think it wise to take him, because he had deserted them in Pamphylia and had not continued with them in the work. They had such a sharp disagreement that they parted company. (Acts 15:36–39, NIV)

Paul later writes the following about the very same young disciple: "Only Luke is with me. Get Mark and bring him with you, because he is helpful to me in my ministry." (2 Tim 4:11, NIV)

Paul seems to recognize here that although he was hesitant about John Mark at the beginning, even to the point of a lack of confidence in him, he later comes to see John Mark's true value and potential. He also shows the same confidence in others, such as Timothy, Aquila, and Pricilla, as he willingly entrusted ministry to them when he was led by God to new mission fields. We have seen a similar transition in Latin America in terms of local ministry and leadership. Now is the time to join hands in reaching the unreached people groups of the earth together as equal partners in mission.

There is one final question. What can the church in North America do to be a part of all this? At this stage, the most vital answer is . . . PRAY! Pray for the leaders, pastors, and called missionaries in the Latin American churches. Pray for them "specifically." Whatever specific challenges we and our missionaries from North America face, they will also face. Pray for them "realistically." They are humans just like us, with the same fears, weaknesses, financial needs, health needs, and difficulties with a new language and culture. Also, pray for them "militaristically." The enemy is relentless, full of hatred, and completely opposed to everything mentioned in these paragraphs (Eph 6:10–20). Let us not forget that we still have our missionaries on the ground and on the front lines, and they depend on our prayers and support, both relational and financial, as they work hard to see this come to life. This is ultimately God's work now, yet as a team with our missionaries we are, and always have been, instruments in his hands. That implies also that we should stand behind the missionaries on the front lines who are dedicated to the development and motivation of this missionary vision in Latin America. They seek ways to be effective in their teaching and training without getting in the way of the development of their "disciples" and their ownership of what they are being taught. This requires resources, wisdom, and encouragement. That is why regular communication with them is vital in accomplishing this. As we move forward, it will be those missionaries, and especially the national church leaders, who will identify the best ways that we can be involved.

We are not alone. Vital organizations are already on the move, such as COMIBAM (www.comibam.org). I have met and spoken to missionaries from various agencies who share the same vision. These are very exciting times for global mission, yet there are many logistics to delineate and define. There are over 6,000 people groups still unreached by the Light that will end their darkness and spiritual death. In my lifetime I might be able to assist in reaching a few by going to them. However, there is another alternative to add to the mix. We could be a part of sparking and facilitating an unexpectedly large movement of missionaries from Latin America that would come alongside our existing and future Avant church planting teams, to effectively reach far more than we can do alone in the short time we have left!

Larry Janzen and his wife, Marbi, joined Avant Ministries in 1993 and served in Belize (1994–2004), Guadalajara, Mexico (2005–12), and Uruguay (2015–17). They currently live in Canada and are developing a strategy and action plan with the goal of seeing Latin America become an independent, vital participant in global mission to the unreached people groups of the world.

Connecting to the Pipeline

1. Make a list of business leaders and entrepreneurs in your church who may be open to missions engagement; include any and all professions, such as medicine, education, law, business, nonprofit, etc. Discuss ways your team can engage these people: from first steps, next steps, stepping up, and stepping out.

2. Has your church identified a people group or a place in the world where it would make sense for you to invest deeply with a church-based team? Maybe there is an ethnic minority in your community that could influence your church's global focus. Do you already pray for a certain place in the world? Do you have a special relationship with a mission agency that sends CBTs?

3. Your church may have sent missionaries to places in the world that are ready to make the switch from being missionary recipients to being missionary senders. If so, how can you start a conversation with them about getting your church involved with equipping and empowering this movement? Does your church have the savvy it takes to get involved in helping to mobilize those in the developing world without imposing on them our North America methods and paternalism?

4. Begin a season of prayer for what the Lord may want to do in and through your church in the future. There are so many things that you *can* do, but what is the one thing that no other church *could* or *would* do?

5. As the years go by, there will be new and emerging trends. Go to www.MissionaryPipeline.org for an ongoing blog from special contributors and strategic thinkers who will be addressing the future of the church's engagement in the Great Commission.

Conclusion

When we first began this journey to discover best practices in church-based missionary mobilization, we conducted interviews with missionary sending practitioners, visited globally engaged churches, and listened to the stories of actual missionaries who were very successful on the field. The original design for this book was to collect this information and then write about the research from our perspective. However, we quickly realized that would be a very shallow treatment of this vast and complicated endeavor of mobilizing God's chosen servants to reach the nations for Christ. Because of our connections with mission leaders over the years, the Lord has blessed us with an incredible network of significant Great Commission servants who graciously agreed to write the preceding chapters that make up this remarkable collaborative effort.

The best part of this book is that you are given firsthand information in the field of missionary mobilization straight from specialists who not only know what they are doing, but are doing what they know. We hope that this resource will serve as a virtual mission conference exhibit hall where you can meet people who are ready and willing to help your church on its journey to accomplish the Great Commission.

As we conclude our research, here are the big-picture takeaways for mission leaders in the local church to glean from and help establish desired outcomes on your mobilization journey. The most important chapter of this book is where we began—prayer for the harvest. Luke 10:2 and Matthew 9:38 describe Jesus' missionary mobilization strategy. We can build the pipeline, but he is the one who causes the flow of missionaries. And if we pray with eager anticipation, our pipeline needs to be equipped to handle an abundant flow. Wouldn't it be great if everyone in your church set their personal alarms to go off at either 9:38 or 10:02 every day, just to "pray earnestly to the Lord of the harvest to send out laborers into his harvest"?

The primary point to remember from part 1 is that God is still calling out people who hear his voice, instructing them to go to the nations with his message of hope and salvation. Within our churches, we need to cultivate a sensitivity to the Spirit of God and learn to, as Neal Pirolo would say, "Dial into his frequency." As these servants start hearing that "still, small voice," we need to help them learn how to overcome the obstacles and hindrances that are inevitable in the life and calling of every child of God, as revealed in part 2.

Throughout this emphasis of God's missionary pipeline, we continually referred to the church as the key to effective mobilization, which either locks or unlocks the fountainhead, wellspring, source, and flow. Please let the words *intentional* and *proactive* be the repetition and refrain as you develop a mobilization team in your church. The churches that were highlighted in part 3 are all faithful representations of these concepts and ideals for making mobilization of missionaries a reality. They have given you a behind-the-scenes look into what it takes to make the Great Commission come alive in a church.

Part 4 provided some important things to consider as you lead your church in the preparation phase of developing a mobilization strategy. There are many more issues to study, but hopefully these contributors gave some perspective that goes beyond the glamorous side of missions. There are some harsh realities to consider when it comes to sending "sheep in the midst of wolves," so it would only be sensible as a church to establish discipleship that teaches missionary candidates to be "wise as serpents and innocent as doves."

In part 5, you were introduced to mission partners who want to serve alongside you as you send the brightest and the best from among your congregation. These missionary sending agencies are eager to form strategic, effective, and long-lasting relationships with sending churches and partner with you to reach the nations for Christ. There are many more organizations in North America, but these are representative of the kinds of organizations which you should consider, since they have a very high view of the role of the sending church. In addition, there are other types of organizations, as highlighted in part 6, which stand in the gap that sometimes exist between the church and agency. These training organizations and coaches have a wealth of experience in both realms (church and agency) and can provide guidance along your journey.

Lastly, in part 7, we provided just a glimpse into the future of this great gospel enterprise of sending missionaries around the world. We may not know what the future will look like, but if we look at the trends that are beginning to emerge, we will notice that business as mission, church-based teams, and mobilization from Latin America are among the most exciting things in the mission world today. We eagerly await what will happen next, but in this we can rest assured: Jesus said, ". . . I will build my church, and the gates of hell shall not prevail against it" (Matt 16:18).

There are 7.6 billion people on earth right now, according to the United Nations. There is an estimated 4.7 billion people who are living without Christ. And of that number, 2 billion have never heard the name of Jesus.

We are striving to change these statistics, and we all know that we are stronger when we work together. The pipeline is all about making connections and joining forces, since the Great Commission was not intended to be accomplished alone. As we build this pipeline together as churches, agencies, and missionaries united by the goal of global evangelization, we acknowledge that the Lord is our provider. Our job as mobilizers is to pray and be ready for those whom the Lord sends our way.

As we close, we lean on the wisdom from the Teacher in Ecclesiastes about the value of partnerships:

Though one may be overpowered, two can defend themselves. A cord of three strands is not quickly broken. (Eccl 4:12, NIV)

Bibliography

Addison, Steve. *Movements that Change the World.* Smyrna: Missional, 2009.

Ahrend, Todd. *In This Generation: Looking to the Past to Reach the Present.* Colorado Springs: Dawson Media, 2010.

Alcorn, Randy. *The Treasure Principal: Unlocking the Secret of Joyful Giving.* Colorado Springs: Multnomah, 2005.

Baer, Mike. *Business as Mission.* YWAM Publishing, 2006.

Barnett, Betty. *Friend Raising: Building a Missionary Support Team That Lasts.* YWAM Publishing, 2002.

Beirn, Steve. *Well Sent: Reimagining the Church's Missionary Sending Process.* Fort Washington: CLC, 2015.

Brewster, Tom, and Betty Brewster. *Language Learning IS Communication— IS Ministry!* Lingua, 1982.

Borthwick, Paul. *Missions: God's Heart for the World.* Downers Grove, IL: IVP, 2000.

Bradley, Zach. *The Sending Church Defined.* Knoxville: The Upstream Collective, 2015.

Bryant, David. *In the Gap: What it Means to be a World Christian.* Regal, 1984.

Buford, Bob. *Half Time: Moving from Success to Significance.* Grand Rapids, MI: Zondervan, 2007.

Carnes, Patrick. *In the Shadows of the Net: Breaking Free of Compulsive Online Sexual Behavior.* Center City, MN: Hazelden, 2007.

Carter, Greg. *Skills, Knowledge, Character: A Church-Based Approach to Missionary Candidate Preparation.* Valparaiso, IN: Turtle River, 2010.

Chambers, Oswald. *So Send I You: A Series of Missionary Studies.* London: Simpkin Marshall, 1930.

Clifton, Jim. *The Coming Jobs War.* Washington, DC: Gallup, 2013.

Corbett, Steve, and Brian Fikkert. *When Helping Hurts: How to Alleviate Poverty without Hurting the Poor and Yourself.* Chicago: Moody, 2009.

Dennis, Jay. *Christians & Pornography; Pastor & Church Leadership Resource Guide.* Pink Elephant Resources, 2015.

Dillon, William P. *People Raising: A Practical Guide to Raising Funds.* Chicago: Moody, 2012.

Duewel, Wesley. *Touch the World through Prayer.* Grand Rapids, MI: Zondervan, 1986.

Elred, Ken. *The Integrated Life: Experience the Powerful Advantage of Integrating Your Faith and Work*. Montrose, CO: Manna Ventures, 2010.

Erickson, Dan. *Grandfathering, Live to Leave a Legacy*. Grand Rapids, MI: Credo, 2014.

Erickson, Millard. *Christian Theology*. Grand Rapids, MI: Baker, 1993 and 1998.

Escobar, Samuel E. *Changing Tides: Latin America and World Mission Today*. Maryknoll, NY: Orbis, 2002.

Feire, Paulo. *Pedagogy of the Oppressed*. New York: Continuum, 1990.

Finzel, Hans, and Rick Hicks. *Launch your Encore: Finding Adventure & Purpose Later in Life*. Grand Rapids, MI: Baker, 2015.

Foster, Richard. *Celebration of Discipline: The Path to Spiritual Growth*. Harper San Francisco, 1998.

Frazier, David. *MissionSmart: 15 Critical Questions to Ask before Launching Overseas*. Memphis: Equipping Servants International, 2014.

Friesen, Garry, and J. Robin Maxson. *Decision Making and the Will of God*. Sisters, OR: Multnomah, 2004.

Georges, Jayson. *The 3-D Gospel: Ministry in Guilt, Shame, and Fear Cultures*. Time Press, 2016.

Graybill, Ruth Ann. *The Emotional Needs of Women on the Mission Field*. Biola Counseling Center, La Mirada, CA.

Greear, J. D. *Gaining by Losing: Why the Future Belongs to Churches that Send*. Grand Rapids, MI: Zondervan, 2015.

Griffiths, Michael. *Get Your Church Involved in Missions!* Singapore: OMF Books, 1987.

Grudem, Wayne. *Systematic Theology*. Grand Rapids, MI: Zondervan, 1994.

———. *Business for the Glory of God: The Bible's Teaching on the Moral Goodness of Business*. Wheaton IL: Crossway, 2003.

Guinness, Os. *The Call*. Nashville, TN: Thomas Nelson, 2003.

Hagberg, Janet O., and Robert A. Guelich. *The Critical Journey—Stages in the Life of Faith,* Second Edition. Salem, WI: Sheffield, 2005.

Hale, Thomas. *On Being a Missionary*. Pasadena, CA: William Carey Library. 1995.

Hay, Rob. *Worth Keeping: Global Perspectives on Best Practice in Missionary Retention*. Pasadena, CA: William Carey Library, 2007.

Hicks, Kathy. *Scaling the Wall: Overcoming Obstacles to Missions Involvement*. Waynesboro: Gabriel, 2003.

Hoke, Steve, and Bill Taylor. *Global Mission Handbook: A Guide for Crosscultural Service*. Downers Grove, IL: IVP, 2009.

———. *Send Me: Your Journey to the Nations*. Pasadena, CA: William Carey Library, 1999.

Hopkins, C. Howard. *History of the YMCA in North America*. New York: Association Press, 1951.

Hulbert, Terry. *Discipling Leaders with a Vision for the World: The Role of the Local Church in Missionary Preparation.* Columbia International University: Worldteam, 1984.

Jethani, Skye. *Futureville.* Nashville: Thomas Nelson, 2014.

Jethani, Skye. *With.* Nashville: Thomas Nelson, 2011.

Johnstone, Patrick. *The Future of the Global Church: History, Trends and Possibilities.* Downers Grove, IL: IVP, 2011 and 2014.

Julien, Tom. *Antioch Revisited: Reuniting the Church with Her Mission.* Winona Lake: BMH, 2006.

Kirk, Andrew J. *Mission Under Scrutiny: Confronting Contemporary Challenges.* London: Fortress, 2006.

Knowles, Malcolm. *Andragogy in Action: Applying Modern Principles of Adult Learning.* San Francisco: Jossey Bass, 1984.

Lane, Timothy S., and Paul David Tripp. *How People Change.* Greensboro, NC: New Growth, 2008.

Lewin, Kurt. *Field Theories in Social Science.* New York: Harper Collins, 1951.

Lewis, Jeff. *God's Heart for the Nations.* Orlando: Pioneers. 2011.

Losch, Dale. *A Better Way: Make Disciples Wherever Life Happens.* Kansas City, MO: Crossworld, 2012.

Lowry, Eugene L. *The Homiletical Plot: The Sermon as Narrative Art Form.* Atlanta: John Knox, 1980.

Mackey, John, and Rajendra Sisodia. *Conscious Capitalism: Liberating the Heroic Spirit of Business.* Boston, MA: Harvard Business Review, 2014.

Manion, Jeff. *The Land Between: Finding God in Difficult Transitions.* Grand Rapids, MI: Zondervan, 2010.

Mason, James. *The Church Unleashed.* Core 4 Research. Perspectives.org.

Mays, David. *Building Global Vision: 6 Steps to Discovering God's Mission Vision for Your Church.* ACMC, 2005.

Mays, David. *The Mission Leadership Team: Mobilizing Your Church to Touch the World.* Stone Mountain: The Mission Exchange, 2010.

———. *Stuff You Need to Know about Doing Missions in Your Church* vol. 3. Brownsburg, IN: David Mays, 2008.

Meade, David. *Here to There: Getting from CROSS to the Mission Field.* Newnan: Propempo International, 2013.

Metcalf, Sam. *Beyond the Local Church: How Apostolic Movements Can Change the World.* Downers Grove, IL: IVP, 2015.

Miley, George. *Loving the Church, Blessing the Nations.* Downers Grove, IL: IVP, 2005.

Morton, Scott. *BlindSpots: Leading Your Team/Ministry to Full Funding.* Fayetteville, AR: CMM Press.

———. *Funding Your Ministry Whether You're Gifted or Not.* Colorado Springs; Dawson Media, 1999.

Munroe, Myles. *Understanding The Purpose And Power Of Prayer: Earthly License for Heavenly Interference.* New Kensington, PA: Whitaker House, 2002.

Newell, Marvin J. *Commissioned: What Jesus Wants You to Know as You Go.* St. Charles IL: ChurchSmart Resources, 2010.

Newell, Peggy. *North American Mission Handbook: US and Canadian Protestant Ministries Overseas.* Pasadena, CA: William Carey Library, 2017.

Nouwen, Henri J.M. *Creative Ministry.* New York: Image Books, 1971.

Ott, Craig, et al. *Encountering Theology of Mission: Biblical Foundations, Historical Developments, and Contemporary Issues.* Grand Rapids, MI: Baker, 2010.

Parker, Michael. *The Kingdom of Character: The Student Volunteer Movement for Foreign Missions 1886–1926* 2nd ed. Pasadena, CA: William Carey Library, 2008.

Palmer, Parker. *To Know as We Are Known: Education as a Spiritual Journey.* San Francisco: HarperCollins, 1993.

———. *The Courage to Teach: Exploring an Inner Landscape of a Teacher's Life.* San Francisco: John Wiley & Sons, 2007.

Pearson, Dick. *Missionary Education Helps for the Local Church.* Palo Alto: Overseas Crusades, Inc. 1966.

Pederson, Wayne. *Reach Beyond: Comfort, Courage and the Cause of Christ.* Colorado Springs: World Radio Missionary Fellowship, Inc., 2014.

Piedra, Arturo. *Evangelización Protestante en América Latina.* Quito: CLAI, 2000.

Piper, John. *Let the Nations be Glad.* Grand Rapids, MI: Baker, 2010.

Pirolo, Neal, and Yvonne Pirolo. *Prepare for Battle: Basic Training in Spiritual Warfare.* San Diego: Emmaus Road International, 1997.

Pirolo, Neal. *Serving as Senders: How to Care for Your Missionaries.* San Diego: Emmaus Road Int'l, 1991.

Pirolo, Neal. *Serving as Senders, Today.* San Diego: Emmaus Road International, 2012.

———. *I Think God Wants Me to be a Missionary.* San Diego: Emmaus Road International, 2005.

Platt, David. *Follow Me: A Call to Die. A Call to Live.* Carol Stream, IL: Tyndale, 2013.

Pollock, David C., and Ruth E. Van Reken. *Third Culture Kids: Growing Up Among Worlds.* Boston MA: Nicholas Brealey, 1999, 2001, 2009.

Rainer, Thom, and Eric Geiger. *Simple Church: Returning to God's Process for Making Disciples.* Nashville: B&H, 2011.

Rankin, Jerry. *To the Ends of the Earth: Churches Fulfilling the Great Commission.* Nashville: B&H, 2006.

Rickett, Daniel. *Making Your Partnership Work.* S.1.: Daniel Rickett, 2015.

Seger, Paul. *Senders: How Your Church Can Identify, Train & Deploy Missionaries.* 2015.

Shadrach, Steve. *The God Ask: A Fresh, Biblical Approach to Personal Support Raising.* Fayetteville AR: CMM, 2013.

Shedd, Clarence P. *Two Centuries of Student Christian Movements: Their Origin and Intercollegiate Life.* New York: Association, 1934.

Sills, M. David. *The Missionary Call: Find Your Place in God's Plan for the World.* Chicago: Moody, 2008.

Sommer, Pete. *Getting Sent: A Relational Approach to Support Raising.* Downers Grove, IL: IVP, 1999.

Spitters, Denny, and Matthew Ellison. *When Everything is Missions.* Orlando, FL: Pioneers-USA & Sixteen:Fifteen, 2017.

Sutton, Joel. *Whom Shall We Send?: Understanding the Essentials of Sending Missionaries.* International Mission Board of the Southern Baptist Convention, 2016.

Taylor, William D. *Too Valuable to Lose: Exploring the Causes and Cures of Missionary Attrition.* Pasadena, CA: William Carey Library, 1997.

Van Duzer, Jeff. *Why Business Matters to God: And What Still Needs to be Fixed.* Downers Grove, IL: IVP Academic, 2010.

Vella, Jane Vella. *Learning To Listen, Learning To Teach: The Power of Dialogue in Educating Adults.* San Francisco: Jossey Bass, 2002.

——. *Taking Learning to Task: Creative Strategies for Teaching Adults.* San Francisco: Jossey Bass, 2001.

——. *On Teaching and Learning: Putting the Principles and Practices of Dialogue Education into Action.* San Francisco: Jossey Bass, 2008.

Willard, Dallas. *Hearing God: Developing a Conversational Relationship with God.* Downers Grove, IL: IVP, 1999.

Willis, Avery. *The Biblical Basis of Missions: Your Mission as a Christian.* Nashville: Convention, 1992.

Wilson, Brady G., and Alex Somos, *Juice: The Power of Conversation.* Toronto: BPS, 2009.

Wilson, David. *Mind the Gaps: Engaging the Church in Missionary Care.* Redlands, CA: Believers Press, 2015.

Winter, Ralph, and Steven Hawthorne. *Perspectives on the World Christian Movement,* A Reader. Pasadena, CA: William Carey Library, 2009.

Mission Organizations

SERVICES/MINISTRIES

Advance Global Coaching	www.advanceglobalcoaching.com
Brigada	www.brigada.org
Center for Mission Mobilization	www.mobilization.org
Emmaus Road International	www.eri.org
Future Missionaries	www.futuremissionaries.org
IBEC ventures	www.ibecventures.com
Michèle Phoenix TCK Advocate	www.michelephoenix.com
Perspectives	www.perspectives.org
Sixteen:Fifteen	www.1615.org
Support Raising Solutions	www.supportraisingsolutions.org
The Traveling Team	www.thetravelingteam.org
Three Strand Partners	www.threestrandpartners.org
Thrive	www.thriveministry.org

TRAINING

Center for Intercultural Training	www.cit-online.org
Mission Training International	www.mti.org
Train International	www.traininternational.org

MISSION SENDING AGENCIES

Avant Ministries	www.avantministries.org
Camino Global	www.caminoglobal.org
Crossworld	www.crossworld.org
Frontiers	www.frontiersusa.org
Greater Europe Mission	www.gemission.org
Pioneers	www.pioneers.org
SIM	www.sim.org
TEAM	www.team.org
Team Expansion	www.teamexpansion.org
The Navigators	www.navmissions.org
World Venture	www.worldventure.com
Wycliffe	www.wycliffe.org

CHURCHES

Bethlehem Baptist Church, Minneapolis, MN
www.bethlehem.church

Calvary Church, Lancaster, PA
www.calvarychurch.org

Liberty Bible Church, Chesterton, IN
www.findliberty.net

Lincoln Berean, Lincoln, NE
www.lincolnberean.org

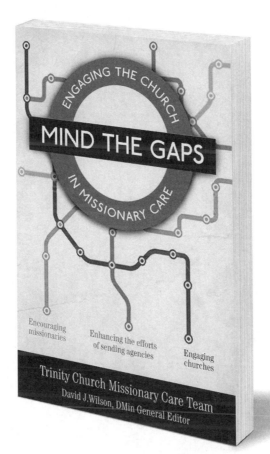

Perspectives™
www.perspectives.org

sixteen:fifteen®
Church Missions Coaching

Mobilizing churches to become central players in the global mission of God.

P.O. Box 3851 Albuquerque, NM 87190
www.1615.org | info@1615.org | 505.248.1615

Help your aspiring missionaries
overcome the fear of fundraising.

Connect them to SRS
for biblical training and
resources to fully fund
their mission and calling.

 Support Raising
Solutions™ | *Visit us at* SupportRaisingSolutions.org